Two Spheres

Explaining the connection between physical and strategic dimensions, this book proposes an aesthetic connection between two equal aspects of architectural design: the ideal and the real. Addressing architectural thinkers from the broad realms of academia and practice, it is suitable either as a seminar text, a guide to contemporary design issues or as a theoretical proposition.

Beginning with a historical perspective, the book looks at some of the key transformations in architectural thought that were brought about by post-industrial change. The discussion shifts to clearly describe the forms of complexity, how these have interacted with architecture and the possibilities of a full embrace with complexity in architectural practice.

Although there are many books focusing on complexity science, there are few that focus on the relationship between complexity and design, and none that take such a comprehensive approach.

Leonard R. Bachman is Associate Professor at the Gerald D. Hines School of Architecture, University of Houston, USA. He has served as President for the Society of Building Science Educators and as Secretary for the Architectural Research Centers Consortium.

Two Spheres

Physical and Strategic Design in Architecture

Leonard R. Bachman

Routledge
Taylor & Francis Group

LONDON AND NEW YORK

First published 2012
by Routledge
2 Park Square, Milton Park, Abingdon, Oxon OX14 4RN

Simultaneously published in the USA and Canada
by Routledge
711 Third Avenue, New York, NY 10017

Routledge is an imprint of the Taylor & Francis Group, an informa business

British Library Cataloguing in Publication Data
A catalogue record for this book is available from the British Library

Library of Congress Cataloging in Publication Data
Bachman, Leonard R.
Two spheres: physical and strategic design in architecture/Leonard R. Bachman.
  p. cm.
  Includes index.
  1. Architectural design.   2. Complexity (philosophy)   I. Title.   II. Title: Physical and strategic design in architecture.
  NA2750.B28 2012
  720.1—dc23
                                                                    2011044520

ISBN: 978–0–415–78246–3 (hbk)
ISBN: 978–0–415–78247–0 (pbk)
ISBN: 978–0–203–12010–1 (ebk)

Typeset in Univers
by RefineCatch Limited, Bungay, Suffolk

MIX
Paper from
responsible sources
FSC® C004839
www.fsc.org

Printed and bound in Great Britain by
TJ International Ltd, Padstow, Cornwall

100624091X

Contents

List of Illustrations

Boxes

Tables

Introduction and Acknowledgments

The most fortunate of authors find that their book takes on a life of its own and unfolds in the writing as a story unto itself. I have been very lucky indeed in this regard with the *Two Spheres* and the encounters along the way have been numerous and widespread. The story of how this book came to be thus includes a cast of many characters, and I will try to acknowledge each of the actors by narrating the sequence of events.

In 2004, Kurt Neubek was the Director of Strategic Services at PageSoutherlandPage and a frequent guest lecturer for my technology courses at the University of Houston. Kurt had previously worked with Willie Peña at CRS and became a compelling advocate for Peña's thinking on architectural programming as *Problem Seeking*. He has since added many of his own new ideas to this vein of architecture and gained deserved notoriety in the field. From this academic relationship, Kurt and I devised our first notions that strategic services were actually strategic design and should be considered tantamount to physical design. We set out to see if that topic was not itself deserving of a book, and initially we modeled the idea as a second generation of *Problem Seeking*. We kept this idea going together for a few years, but Kurt's growing professional responsibilities and the increasing demand for his services prevented us from completing the task together. He has nonetheless remained a steady contributor to the project and remains foundational to the overall thinking.

Another pivotal set of contributions were made by my companion, friend, cohort, and spouse, Christine Bachman. Christine is a social psychologist with extensive additional background in exercise science. This combination of pursuits led her to many insights about the mind–body connections and cognitive coherence. As early as 2003, she and I were co-publishing empirical studies of architectural education, a field that to this day consists primarily of anecdotal observation and well-reasoned argument—but is still supported by a meager amount of measured observation. Eventually, our mutual interests turned to complexity and systems theory as a way of explaining the indeterminate behavior of the situations we were studying across the realms of mind–body, teaching–learning, and building–architecture dynamics. It was in that vein that Christine introduced me to the work of neuroscientist Scott Kelso and his brain–mind distinction as one of body organ versus emergent animation. *Two Spheres* represents these tandem paired dynamics in many dimensions, but the most central notion is that architecture is different from good buildings in the same way that the animated mind is different from the brain organ. The difference is bound up in the tenets of dynamic complexity, self-organizing behavior, and emergent order. The underlying principles are teleology, autopoiesis, and complex systems. Christine has been part of all the work since then. I am thankful for her enthusiastic support, constant involvement, and perceptive critiques. Her insights on human cognition are embedded throughout the book.

The early years of the *Two Spheres* also included ongoing conversation with Ralph Knowles, Professor Emeritus at the University of Southern California, American Institute of Architects Gold Medalist, accomplished educator, and well-known author of books on environmental architecture published across the last forty years. Somewhere before his latest book, *Ritual House*, Ralph and I began talking about the aesthetics of sustainable design. We also managed to draw Mark Childs at the University of New Mexico into the ongoing discussion. This spirited conversation had a cumulative impact on my own thinking that is now part of the Two Spheres idea on sustainability and aesthetics. My paper on eco-aesthetics at the 2007 American Solar Energy Society Conference was a stepping stone that owes much to Ralph and Mark.

So, by 2006 I had decided to continue developing the notion of strategic design and complex animation as a series of papers. The first was an overview paper for the International Conference on Architectural Research in Philadelphia, an event co-sponsored by the Architectural Research Centers Consortium (ARCC) and the European Association of Architectural Educators (EAAE). My paper proposed the original Neubek–Bachman idea of strategic design as tantamount to physical design, and argued for complexity and indeterminism as the unifying Knowles–Childs–Bachman aesthetic of the Two Spheres. Kelso's brain–mind distinction was the operational model for how this operated in architecture. The paper started with a title about "Strategic Design" but migrated to something like "Embracing Complexity." Brooke Harrington was the president of ARCC at the time and a great person to be around as he hosted the event on his home turf at Temple University. In the years since, I have enjoyed both ARCC and EAAE as forums for publication, discourse, mutual support, and a common belief in the positive role of research and systems thinking in architecture. Brooke is also the editor-in-chief of the *ARCC Journal*. He and managing editor Kate Wingert were thus instrumental in the 2009 theme issue co-guest edited by Christine and me on "Affecting Change in Architectural Education."

Serious adventure then started to stir things up. A few weeks after the Philadelphia conference, I received an email from CIB, the Council for Research and Innovation in Building and Construction, with specific reference to their Embracing Complexity Working Group. My first thoughts were that I had unknowingly plagiarized their "Embracing Complexity" name and was in for some embarrassing apologies. Fortunately, the letter was an invitation to give a keynote talk to the group in Liverpool, UK. So in April 2007, at the gracious invitation of Halim Boussabaine at the University of Liverpool, I went to meet this CIB Working Group. It was there that I also met Theodore Zamenopoulos, Katerina Alexiou, and Jeffrey Johnson, all with the Open University's Design Group. One direct outcome of this event was an invitation to contribute a chapter to a 2010 Routledge book, *Embracing Complexity* as edited by those three individuals. Thereafter, Halim invited me to contribute a paper to his July 2008 guest-edited and special-themed issue of *Architectural and Engineering Design Management* (AEDM), also on the topic of embracing complexity. Those two CIB-related publications actually make up a large portion of Chapters 4 and 5 in the *Two Spheres*. I have certainly fed on the collective energy, wisdom, and intellectual spirit of this group. Hopefully they will see this book as a continuation and friendly supplement to their parallel efforts. I am deeply indebted to them for the opportunities and support they offered. Thanks again to all of them for their hospitality, discourse, and collegiality. It always seemed that every door was opening up to two more opportunities.

Coincidentally, I later met Jose Solis from the faculty of Texas A&M University. Jose was also a contributor to Halim Boussabaine's theme issue of AEDM. With that in common, Jose and I have developed a lasting friendship and comradery. His research on systems thinking in construction is another of the key inspirations that are woven into this book. I always look forward to my next chat with Jose. Other constants along the way include my close colleague Rives Taylor. Rives teaches at the University of Houston with me and is equally dedicated to his role as a firmwide sustainability coordinator and principle at Gensler. Rives' candor gives much credence to the proverb that the best mirror is an old friend. I get to try out and swap ideas with him all the time, and that is such a treasure to me.

My dear cohort Robert Morris not only executed the cover art for this book, he has also been a friend and mentor for more than twenty years. I always benefit from his extensive and diverse experience and I always enjoy his wry brand of wisdom. His breadth and depth as an artist, architect, and constructor are an inspiration to me. Robert has always taken a special interest in this *Two Spheres* project, and his ideas always provoke my writing. Aside from that, Robert is just one of those friends that "get it" when you are talking with them.

More recently I have had the pleasure of interacting with Ken Hall, the Director of Sustainable Design Systems at Gensler. I highly value Ken's Foreword to this book because he has placed it in the context of his own work, introduced the concepts without outlining the content, and given the book a voice without imitating mine. Ken has also been a questioning and politely skeptical reader of the work and that too is precious, especially considering the demands on his time in a worldwide firm. Along the way, Ken and I have been sharing hopes and concerns for the future of this profession. I can tell you that we need more people like Ken Hall to help us along the way.

Another continuous weave in the cloth of this story is the Society of Building Science Educators (SBSE). I doubt that there is a more supportive, affable, collegial, and collectively intelligent societal organization anywhere. I intentionally solicited photographs for this book on the SBSE email list serve, just to have another reason to mention the group here. I have been an active SBSE member for more than twenty years and still remember myself years ago as a beginning educator walking into a meeting at the ACSA Summer Energy Institute in Seattle, and finding myself with Murray Milne, Don Prowler, Fuller Moore, John Reynolds, Ed Allen, Jeffrey Cook, and a dazzling host of my other heroes. I am amazed to this day how generously and genuinely I was taken into the fold. The pages of this book are far too short to list all the important and meaningful friendships I have found in SBSE since then.

Special thanks to a cadre of my University of Houston students who willingly directed their studies towards aspects of the *Two Spheres* project: Kiza Forge, Sara Carter, Carrie Gonzales, Jenifer Andreas, Sean Garrison, Eric

Arnold, Ian Spencer, and Joseph Little. I wish I could clone them all. A special hat tip to Ian Spencer for his well-considered and in-depth reactions; and to Joseph "Mac" Little for the Magney House model illustration.

A deep gratitude goes out to Francesca Ford, the Commissioning Editor at Routledge/Taylor & Francis, for her trust, guidance, enthusiasm, and constant encouragement over the last year. I had to work very hard to keep my matching end of the bargain with her. It was absolutely worth it.

Finally, but not least in any regard, I am grateful for the unwavering support and faithful encouragement of all my family, friends, and colleagues. They not only kept me going throughout this project, they put up with my constant babbling about the book and suffered the time I spent favoring the project over other obligations and opportunities. My mother, Dorothy, and my wife, Christine, are especially heroic figures in that part of the story. Special wishes, too, to my ever faithful friend and confidant Richard "Bux" Buxbaum and his wife Jenny as they welcome their first child, Sadie Madison Buxbaum, into their lives.

In closing, I have to include the confession and caveat that much of what is right and clear about this book comes from the ideas and work of the people I acknowledge here, but also that I alone take full blame for any parts that may be cloudy or incorrect. That is why the collective intelligence is always greater than any individual's efforts. And that is why I owe so much to so many.

As mentioned, portions of this book originally appeared in other publications, and are evident here either as excerpts or as material that is partly derived from these previous works. I wish to recognize the contributions of the individuals and organizations that made these prior writings possible. I am grateful for the opportunity to advance that work in the *Two Spheres*:

> "Embracing complexity in building design," Chapter 2 in J. Johnson, K. Alexiou, and T. Zamenopoulos (eds.) *Embracing complexity in design*, New York: Routledge, 2010
>
> "The teaching of research and the research on teaching: Two frameworks and their overlay in architectural education," ARCC/EAAE International Conference on Architectural Research, Washington, DC, June 2009
>
> "Designing student learning outcomes in undergraduate architecture education: Frameworks for assessment," with Christine Bachman, *ARCC Journal*, 6(1) (2009): 49–67
>
> Editorial, "Affecting change in architectural education," *ARCC Journal*, 6(1) (2009): 4–5
>
> "Thoughts toward a clinical database in architecture: Evidence, complexity and impact," ARCC National Conference on Architectural Research, San Antonio, Texas, May 2009
>
> "Architecture and the four encounters with complexity," *Architecture Engineering and Design Management*, July 2008
>
> "Post-industrial society, dynamic complexity and the emerging principles of strategic design," *ARCC Journal*, May 2007
>
> "Post-industrial society, dynamic complexity and the emerging principles of strategic design," ARCC/EAAE International Conference on Architectural Research, Philadelphia, May 2006.

Foreword

Ken Hall

All people, organizations and nations are faced with a dizzying array of challenges that are accelerating and increasing in magnitude and complexity. We are not prepared. Our ancestral heritage has prepared us for many challenges—but not what we face today. We are wired to make instantaneous decisions to fight or flight—but we are not wired to understand slow-moving variables that interact in complex systems over time. Historically, this did not matter to our survival. It does now.

I am part of a multi-minded global organization that is working 24x7 around the world to deliver design solutions for the built environment. We are facing fundamental challenges that are changing the nature of who we are and how we work. We are facing the limits of finite supplies of energy, water and materials. Climate change, species loss and toxicity result in precarious environments. Excessive consumption of energy, water and materials is pressing us against the natural resiliency of ecosystems. These factors are creating global stresses in the financial markets, increasing migrations and failed states. These are simplifications of a complex messy world that require we master a continuous, systemic and intensifying effort to become a learning work organization in partnership with other organizations.

But what should we set about learning to enable ourselves, organizations and nations to adapt to the times and create a better future for those who will follow us and carry on human civilization to its highest potential—and what might we dare imagine that might be?

Leonard Bachman has taken that question to heart and mind, and surveyed the landscape of modern and ancient thought to shine a light on how we can face the dizzying array of complex challenges we face. I warn you, the journey is not easy. Have your dictionary and a web browser ready. But if you are willing to follow the path, you will be rewarded with a rich landscape of thought that you can mine for understanding.

Leonard insists that we embrace complexity—not reduce it to simpler parts. He uses the metaphor of "Two Spheres" to dig into our human nature as symmetrical beings with two brain hemispheres, embodied in a world of left–right, up–down, front–back, present–future. But the magic of his "Two Spheres" framework is that we can be present to both spheres. We are human, each of us with a corpus callosum melding both hemispheres into one whole emergent mind.

This is the great chasm that we must cross in our time. We must unite the masculine and feminine perspective, likewise the challenges of red and blue states, and mono-theism and poly-theism. Our corporations must embrace ecology, and our environmentalists must embrace business. The western Abrahamic religions and eastern Taoist–Buddhist cosmologies must be united in a new story of who we are and how we will live together for the benefit of all life on earth today and tomorrow.

The "Two Spheres" is a learning framework that all people designing solutions for a complex world can benefit from; however, it is especially relevant to designers creating built environments. The Two Spheres is a timely critique of the history and processes of the design profession. It exposes the myth of the "Starchitect" that continues to live in the minds of most designers and educators today.

Leonard tells us powerful stories of the collaborations between the "Two Spheres" that result in the emergence of great Architecture. Like emergent consciousness, he explains how Architecture emerges from the collaboration of the physical (immeasurable) and strategic (measurable) aspects of Architecture. History tells us of the great architectural minds of many individuals, but Leonard argues that historical biography reveals that each was actually a team of at least two people of complementary skills. The challenge we face today is complexity itself.

Think of the Two Spheres as a guide through the landscape of complexity. Depending on where you need to go, you can read this landscape in a variety of ways. More importantly, this is a map you will return to time and again as you grow in your understanding of complexity and your needs change. Heavily annotated, this map will enable you to reach deeper into the landscape with a wide variety of source material. It is literally a tool to help us learn how to learn about complexity. The Two Spheres is a launch point into learning about complexity for the rest of our lives.

For me personally, what I find most salient about the Two Spheres is not just the embrace of complexity, but what it means to me as a professional deeply engaged in the challenges of designing for a sustainable civilization. The process of designing buildings is inherently complex, using complex design and construction technologies to deliver complex products to complex markets. Today, our design professions are on the edge of massive disruptive change as we embrace ever more complicated green building rating systems (Leadership in Energy and Environmental Design—LEED, Building Research Establishment Environmental Assessment Method—BREEAM, Living Building Challenge, etc.) and building science simulation and systems technologies in order to radically improve the resilience and performance of our built environment. As if that were not enough, the Two Spheres points to the next layer of this challenge, the embrace of the complexity of nature and ecological design.

Designers are already deeply skilled at solving messy problems, but the imperative of achieving sustainability adds a new dimension and demands that we move beyond reductionist efforts to tame complexity, and rather fully embrace it with a new art and science of design. Our deeply honed skills of designing space for significant human experience are not enough. Nor is a simple embrace of performance metrics and systems thinking going to patch over our dilemma. Today, we are challenged to extend our understanding of immediate and local scale problems into the realm of complex systemic relationships at the global scale spanning long periods of time.

The *Two Spheres* reveals how to think about a new eco-aesthetic, a bridge between traditional formalism which places high value on affect and experience, and ecological design, which places high value on effect—the performance results embodied in a specific design and place. Formalist architecture advocates for human intention and art, whereas ecological design advocates for science and nature. As Leonard demonstrates, this eco-aesthetic "requires attaching it at one end to our sublime appreciation of immediate physical experience, and at the other end to intelligent understanding of ecological foresight." And from this emerges a new deeply embodied sense of beauty.

If your soul hungers for deeper understanding of, and means to address the complex challenges we face, the *Two Spheres* offers a healthy diet of food for thought that will satisfy your hunger and provide new tools to act in this world.

Prologue

In 1985, writing in the same college library from which this book comes, Alberto Pérez-Gómez declared the predicament of *Architecture and the Crisis of Modern Science*. Now, some twenty-five years later in our emerging age of globalization, human capital, cybernetic intelligence, sustainable design, and dynamic interrelation, there comes a hopeful postindustrial transition. This book explains how the architectural convergence of those evolutionary events is not only historically transitional, but epically transformative. Science, humanities, and design can now make a mindful whole. Society, culture, technology, and nature can be aligned. Mechanistic fragmentation can become complex animation. The full human spirit can find expression. It is time now to put the crisis behind us and repair the rifts that have so divided the pursuits of architecture.

Industrial age divisions in the discipline of architecture were probably a necessary, and even a progressive, transition between preindustrial and postindustrial eras; but the journey was as tumultuous for architects as it has been for society at large. Industrial successes were indeed many, but the costs have proven deleterious, systemic, long term, and unfairly distributed. For society, the expense has come as degradation of our environmental ecology, natural resources, and our social equity. For architects, the fees have been levied against professional identity, disciplinary coherence, and social standing. Architecture and society have accomplished much in the last 200 years, and much of that progress has deeply enriched the lives and cultural standing of the masses; but the constant erosion under our steel-toed boots threatens the integrity of the foundations. It is time to bridge the chasm. It is time we declare an end to the crisis.

Industrial age progress still rings all around us; but this may well be the first generation of children in all history whose lifespan expectation is shorter than that of their parents. We may well build more architecture in the next fifty years than in the past 30,000; but first we must take a closer look at whom we are building it for—and at how we will assert the full value of what architecture provides.

If the crisis is indeed over, there is much to be optimistic about—and so the discussion begins.

Leonard R. Bachman
Houston, Texas
August 2011

Part One

Scoping Complexity

Chapter 1

Postindustrial Emergence

This chapter covers four precepts that are fundamental to the emerging traits of postindustrial architecture. The backgrounds may be familiar in various degrees to some readers, but the connections among these precepts will situate Two Spheres as the affective and effective aspects of architecture; referred to here respectively as physical and strategic design elements.

The first precept describes three epochs of history as a developmental trace of industrialization, technical progress, and social good. This historical perspective is then tied to some of the key conflicts in architectural thought that were brought about by postindustrial change. Louis Kahn's aphorism on the measurable and immeasurable aspects of great buildings illustrates this as a conflict symptomized by two spheres: physical and strategic elements of design. From there, discussion shifts to assertions about wholeness and complexity and their vital role in architecture. Finally, the physical and strategic spheres are detailed as two equal components of designerly thinking. Distinguishing characteristics of the two spheres are laid out; not as simplistic and conflicting definitions, but rather as a systemic and generative dialectic. In sum, Chapter 1 overviews a framework for understanding how physical and strategic elements of architecture operate in tandem, and then lays explanatory groundwork for how their dynamic interplay constitutes whole-minded architecture. Particular details on each of the four precepts are developed throughout.

Precept One: Three Epochs

From 1915 to 1932, Scottish ecologist Patrick Geddes and American historian Lewis Mumford collaboratively framed the story of human civilization as a co-evolving history of technical progress, industrialization, and social good.[1] They classified this story into three sequential eras as the eotechnic, paleotechnic, and neotechnic; indicating progressive, overlapping, and interpenetrating evolutions. These eras spanned from a long age of primary production of raw materials by farming and mining, then to a shorter intermediary period of industrial goods production and consumption, and finally to our emerging cybernetic era of innovation and scientific progress. Our current transition from localized myopic and mechanistic industrial age perspectives to more globally holistic and systemic postindustrial attitudes of the neotechnic is especially important in this sequence. As Paleotects, Geddes wrote,

> we make it our prime endeavour to dig up coals, to run machinery, to produce cheap cotton, to clothe cheap people, to get up more coals, to run more machinery, and so on, and all this essentially towards "extending markets."
>
> (Geddes 1915: 74; cited in Renwick & Gunn 2008: 67)[2]

While Geddes saw the paleotechnic and neotechnic epochs as subdivisions of the industrial era of his own time, he did delineate the paleotechnic from the neotechnic in ways that foresaw the advent of postindustrial society and the ethic of sustainability:

> the first [paleotechnic epoch] turning on dissipating energies towards individual money gains, the other [neotechnic] on conserving energies and organising environment towards the maintenance and evolution of life, social and individual, civic and eugenic.
>
> (Geddes 1915: 60)[3]

Several decades after Geddes and Mumford, the Harvard sociologist Daniel Bell placed the American transition from an industrial goods basis of production to a primarily postindustrial information society as occurring in the 1950s.[4] This passage supposedly marks a point in time when the service economy became larger than the goods economy. The actual economic trends may not quite agree with Bell's contentions, but it is quite accurate to see postindustrial change as an aspect of the post-World War II emerging information society, and most sociologists now place the transition as occurring in the late 1950s (Table 1.1). More specifically relevant to architecture, this postindustrial transition also signaled a move from linear mechanistic bottom-line thinking to a more human-centered perspective of global networks, complex interdependence, and long-term value.

Parallels of Bell's work with the techno-social timeline by Geddes and Mumford are illustrated in Table 1.2. More in-depth discussion on this historical framework is offered in Novak (1995), Lyle (1994), and Renwick and Gunn (2008).[5] Lyle's Regenerative Architecture is particularly valuable in depicting the sustainable design ethic of the neotechnic era.

The decade of the 1960s then witnessed an inevitable surge of postindustrial thought and social transition. Beyond the highly visual impacts of rustbelt decay and urban blight, these influences were manifested in architecture as a whole new range of influential notions such as design programming, systems theory, ecology, and the influence of postmodern philosophy. As Thomas Kuhn's theory on The Structure of Scientific Revolutions (1962) suggests would happen, the existing paradigms of architectural design thinking then eroded to the point where they no longer satisfactorily explained architectural events occurring within the new circumstances of postindustrial transformation.[6] Consequently, when architects working in the early 1960s were faced with having less robust approaches to their work and less relevant theories to explain their intentions, a separation formed between the modernist paradigm and the pluralistic approaches that emerged in promise of new normative explanations for the neotechnic role of design.

Postindustrial society continues to take form and to reshape architectural practice and design thinking on into the twenty-first century. As

Table 1.1 Postindustrial society

Factor	Preindustrial	Industrial	Postindustrial
Profit Yield	Extraction	Fabrication	Analysis
Economic Sector	Agriculture and mining	Manufacture	Services
1900 Sector	U.S.: 110 million in agricultural workforce	U.S.: 9 million in industrial workforce	U.S.: 9 million in services workforce
2000 Sector	World: 6% agricultural GDP	World: 31% industrial GDP	World: 63% services GDP
Transformative Resource	Wind, water, animals	Coal, petroleum, electricity, and nuclear energy	Information
Driving Resource	Raw materials	Goods and finance	Understanding
Operation	Trial-and-error, experience	Expertise	Theory and principle
Skill	Craft	Know-how	Science and design
Time Orientation	Tradition	Current tends	Forecasting, backcasting, and scenario planning
Organizations	Private companies	Corporations	Global networks
Efficiency	Hard work	Fordism and Taylorism	Operations research, industrial organizational psychology
Nature	Nature as the context	Nature as resource	Nature as solution
Interaction	People to nature	People to machines	People to people
Cosmology	Natural explanations	Mechanistic cause and effect	Complex dynamic systems
Ecology	Abundant nature	Pollution, depletion	Sustainable
Morbidity	Diseases of nature, tooth infection, childbirth, accidents, infection	Diseases of industry, cancer, coronary, respiratory, obesity, stress	Old age

Sources: Some portions adapted from D. Bell, 'Welcome to the postindustrial society', *Physics Today*, Feb. 1976: 46–49.

Table 1.2 Techne: Ideals and means of production as a story about civilization

Geddes 1915	Mumford 1934	Bell 1973
EOTECHNIC (life in balance): Geddes apparently did not use this term, but Mumford credits him for its use and meaning	EOTECHNIC, AD 1000 to 1700: Village life, coal and steel, the clock as a model of capitalism and the laudable search for an intensification of life	PREINDUSTRIAL: Agriculture and mining for raw materials as the basis of production
PALEOTECHNIC (life threatened): Private dispensation of resources for individual gain	PALEOTECHNIC, 1700 to 1900: Industrial cities and the megalopolis, problem solving for profit rather than a search for general principles	INDUSTRIAL: Conversion of raw materials to goods and the continual consumption of those goods, practical know-how dominates, productive labor is primary
NEOTECHNIC or EUTECHNIC (life resurgent): Public conservation of resources toward future evolution of the public good	NEOTECHNIC, 1900 to about 1934 and forward: Organic human-scale living, electricity and automation free up labor, innovation, science, communication, and information are primary concerns	POSTINDUSTRIAL: Information as currency, data as empirical reality, knowledge as decision making, stochastic forecasting, codification of theoretical knowledge, primacy of human capital, growth of intellectual technology

context, the 2009 world economy was distributed at about 6 percent farming, 30 percent manufacturing and industrial, and 60 percent service based. A brief statistical overview of world employment distribution and the corresponding gross domestic product (GDP) will illustrate the sweeping and dramatic shifts that are transforming not just the global economy, but also society, culture, and fundamental world perspectives. The numerical references however are only included to illustrate that postindustrial evolution is our core agent of real progress and essential inspiration toward a better world future. This societal context is the systemic, first order, rock-splashes-in-the-water change, after which other issues are symptomatic ripples and secondary after-effects. To be a real and relevant part of this, architecture must become a primary instrument of this transformation and manifest the societal, cultural, and technological mutations within which design operates. Postindustrial architecture is thus presented with one of the most momentous opportunities in the history of human civilization. Figures 1.1 to 1.4 portray some of the social and economic circumstances.

Postindustrial shifts have clearly led us away from goods production and toward information-based production by knowledge workers. As a representative change in thinking, consider the analogy of cooking dinner, which depends both on what is in the pantry, and on how good the recipe is. Industrial age thinking focused primarily on the pantry whereas postindustrial thinking focuses more on the recipe. Recipes of course are just information we can access, select, refine, tailor, and interpret freely, but the better the recipe, the better the dinner, and a really good recipe can apply innovative ideas to readily available and inexpensive ingredients so as to create valuable results. That added value is the basis of postindustrial production and the intelligence coded into the recipe is the strategic design component of how that value is conceptualized, produced, and realized (see Romer, *The Concise*

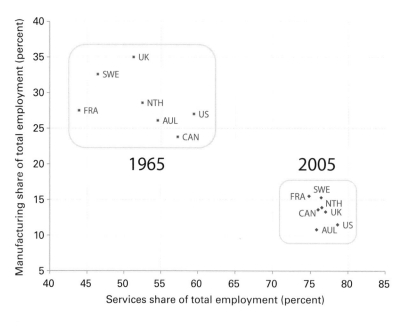

Figure 1.1 Change in the share of total employment for manufacturing and service sectors in selected countries. Notes: AUL: Australia, CAN: Canada, FRA: France, NTH: Netherlands, SWE: Sweden, UK: United Kingdom, US: United States. Source: Data from the World Bank.

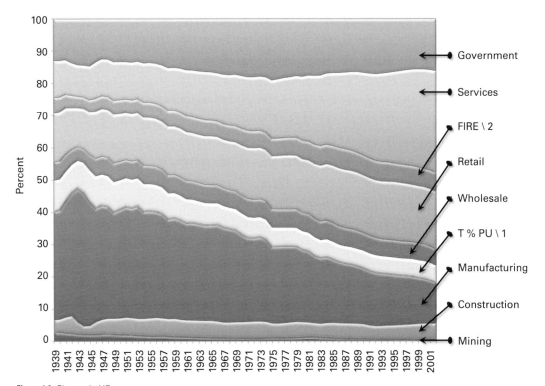

Figure 1.2 Change in US employment by percentage share of each sector. Notes: 1 T&PU: transportation and public utilities; 2 FIRE: finance, insurance, and real estate.

Encyclopedia of Economics).[7] In architecture, that process is observable in the act of design.

Building on the portrayal of three epochs in Tables 1.1 and 1.2, some dimensions of how the strategic sphere of intelligent recipes is pushing architectural design are set out in Table 1.3. The primary thrust is that of holistic, large-scale, inclusive thinking that treats everything and everywhere as an interrelated whole. Left behind are the industrial age failings of fragmentation, isolation, and mechanistic faith in treating the symptom of any problem that might arise rather than dealing with systemic cause and relation.

To use another visual analogy: mechanistic industrial age efforts are like a tree farm, a machine for making trees. Postindustrial age pursuits are like a forest, a set of robust natural processes.

Consider that the tree farm is artificial. It will require ever more fertilizer, insecticide, and maintenance; yet it will produce a continually declining yield of lumber. If struck by lightning it will burn down and disappear. The forest on the other hand will replenish itself indefinitely as long as its system and cycles of nutrient flow are left intact. So robust is the forest that should it be struck by lightning and burn down, it will gradually grow back without human intervention into a similar kind of forest.

The tree farm is a machine. The forest is a system. Postindustrial society is far less concerned with the machine and the lumber it produces than at any time before in history. We have learned that most of the long-term success models in the universe are systems, and we have learned that using those systemic solutions in our own means of production are the most viable.

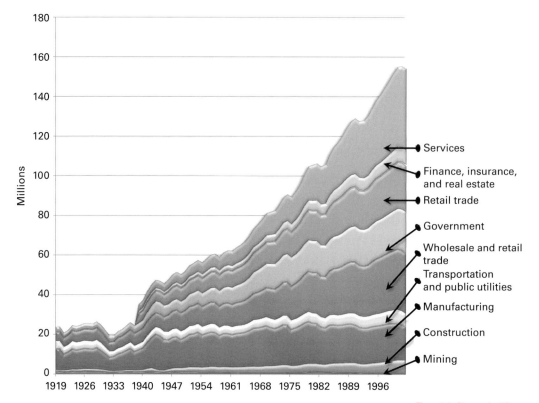

Figure 1.3 Change in US employment for each sector by headcount.

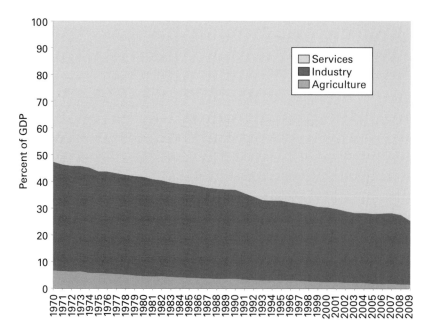

Figure 1.4 The European Union countries: Combined GDP for each sector of the economy from 1970 to 2009. Source: Data from the World Bank.

In doing so we have also moved from a linear "laundry list" issues-based approach to problem solving and progressed toward a more opportune mode of feedback loops and complex dynamics. Harkening back to the 1960s again:

> The aim of science we now see, is to find the relations which give order to the raw material, the shapes and structures into which the measurements fit . . . the relations which the facts have with one another—the whole they form and fill, not with their parts. In place of the arithmetic of nature, we now look for her geometry: the architecture of nature.
>
> (Bronowski 1965: 56)[8]

Or, from the time of Bell's *The Coming of Post-industrial Society*:

> A look behind the footlights reveals that nature has no choice in the assignment of roles to players. Her productions are shoestring operations, encumbered by the constraints of three-dimensional space, the necessary relations among the sizes of things, and an eccentric sense of frugality.
>
> (Stevens 1974: 4)[9]

Note that this progress toward complexity incorporates both postpositive scientific and postmodern attitudes, and does so without forsaking any of the central ideals or ultimate ends of modernist architecture. If science in the postindustrial era is probabilistic, non-linear, emergent, complex, and dynamic; then the ethical corresponding notions of contingency, specificity, construction, and uniqueness apply equally to contemporary society. In either case, it is clear that bottom-line, deterministic, mechanistic, and reductionist attitudes are obsolete; privileged culture is out and the greater common good is in. Now everything can be connected again, and not just in the spiritual, superstitious, and mythical ways of preindustrial eotechnic civilization. Now, in postindustrial neotechnic terms we can begin to see past the eotechnic mystery as well as the technic era mechanical, and we can finally find true appreciation for the underlying complex wonders that unite them. See Tables 1.1, 1.3, and 1.4.

If architecture is to respond, then a substantial reconsideration of its mission and motivations is in order, and current confusion about the role of architecture in society lends some urgency to this mandate. This is not to proclaim the utter loss of timeless design traditions as something to be retired and grieved over; it is merely an inevitable consequence of societal change and the unrelenting march of culture, society, science, and civilization. Just as Mumford's three epochs of Technics and Civilization overlap and interpenetrate each other because agriculture and manufacturing are still necessary in a society where information has become the primary means of value production, so also will current and traditional forms of architectural thought coexist with postindustrial forms. Just as in times past, this evolution is best taken as an essential opportunity for architects to express the new essence of their evolving epoch and to employ their powers in noble response to emerging circumstances, evolving needs, and blossoming aspirations of the society they serve. And, like a host of other diverse pursuits undergoing postindustrial

Table 1.3 Design in the postindustrial era

	Preindustrial	Industrial	Postindustrial
	Before about 1700	About 1700 to the present	The evolving present
	The Eotechnic	The Paleotechnic	The Neotechnic
Design	Craft and design are synonymous	Design as a specialty and a profession	Design as a discipline and universal occupation in age of knowledge professionals
Materials	Raw materials directly from nature	Processed material and mass standardization	Mass customization of components and materials
Knowledge base	Static	Incremental shifts	Continuous change
Cosmology	Mythical explanations	Anthropocentric	Biocentric
Order	Holistic	Hierarchical	Holistic
Development	Refine the prototype	Test unique artifact	Simulate possible artifacts
Change	Conformity	Novelty	Evolutionary
Instrument	Nature as the model	Drawings	Virtual simulations
Method	Normative rules and traditions	Policies and procedures	Cybernetic knowledge and systems integration
Perspective	Holistic	Components in isolation	Integrated systems
Dynamics	Innocent naivety	Self-referential	Intelligent
Lifecycle	Degrade	Use and dispose	Reprocess as nutrient
Solutions	Transient	Fragile and fragmentary	Robust
Effort	Communal	Individual	Team
Educate	Trade apprentice	University: liberal pupilage	Explicit and synthetic
Collaboration	Mono-disciplinary guilds	Multidisciplinary	Transdisciplinary
Application	Need	Art for the elite	Sustain societal goals

transition such as particle physics, complexity theory, holistic medicine, organic farming, global economics, organizational psychology, systems engineering, and learning organizations, just to mention a few, architecture as a discipline must participate in the larger response to shifting context and historic progress (see Table 1.5). To find our way forward, the task will be to recognize this change for what it is; then to embrace that change in its full and unique character.

Precept Two: The Chasm

Like all such sweeping and disruptive forces of history and progress, postindustrial impacts are both technical and ideological. Further, postindustrial change is also both societal and cultural: social because it alters our shared infrastructure and institutions; cultural because it influences our shared values and experiences.

One obvious consequence of postindustrial progress on architecture concerns the ongoing philosophical fragmentation of modernism, postmodernism, and all else that has followed since industrial era modes of explanation eroded. More specifically, a decidedly schizophrenic chasm has formed; a

Table 1.4 The overlay of industrial and postindustrial society in the context of architecture

	Industrial Establishment	Postindustrial Emergence
Planning	Survival sustenance from nature	Ecological sustainability with nature
	Anthropocentric cosmology	Biocentric cosmology
	Linear production	Cyclical flows
	Tactical objectives	Strategic goals
	Short-term plan	Long-term plan
	Incremental shifts	Continuous change
Practice	Product and tradition oriented	Process and discipline oriented
	Local effects of action	Global effects of interaction
	Mechanistic relationships	Systemic relationships
	Machine as the icon	Nature as the icon
	Heuristic procedures	Cybernetic integration
	Physical prototype modeling	Analog simulation modeling
	Mass standardization	Mass customization
Design	Hierarchical and linear	Holistic and non-linear
	Embrace deterministic simplicity	Embrace teleological complexity
	Intuitive heuristics of form	Self-emergent, intelligent form
	Anticipate the inevitable future	Devise future scenarios
	Innovative individuals	Transdisciplinary teams
	Pioneer-as-hero model	Designer-as-collaborator model
	Design for elite status	Design for social justice
	Manual and automatic control	Intelligent automation
	Transient static solutions	Robust dynamic solutions

Table 1.5 Postindustrial professions

Physics	Quantum mechanics and the Unified Field Theory (Bohr, Heisenberg, Hawking)
Engineering	Non-linear and chaotic systems
Psychology	Self-actualization and psychosynthesis (Maslow, Graf)
Sociology	Knowledge-based culture (Kuhn)
Business	Industrial Organization Psychology
Medicine	Holistic health and mind/body healing (Chopra)
Agriculture	Organic gardening and beneficial insects (Rodale)
Economics	Life-cycle costs and externalized accounting (Henderson)

Source: After Bachman (2003).

chasm that is often manifested as a struggle roughly between issues of beauty versus those of accountability. On a broader basis this struggle concerns primacy in the design of affective versus effective outcomes: on one side is the affective aspect of design related to the direct immediate experience of architecture, and on the other side is the effective sphere of design aspirations related to how intelligent foresight is embodied in the built environment. Like

C.P. Snow's vastly influential treatise on the breakdown in shared perspectives between the sciences and the humanities (*The Two Cultures and the Scientific Revolution*, 1959), architectural thinking has, to a great extent, split into two camps.[10] The corresponding two separate cultures of architecture were thus divided and clearly remain mired in this rift between emotive/affective and rational/effective motivations to built form. Furthermore, and within the same 1960s framework that frequently recurs in this theme of postindustrial metamorphosis, architectural discourse also began to embody the split between industrial mechanistic-style, bottom-line, linear thinking versus emerging postindustrial interest with the use of knowledge to create value and invent a better future. Both the affect/effect and the enlightenment/naturalist separations are still present in design considerations today, but rather than construe them as negative contradictions, it is far more accurate, meaningful, and authentically postindustrial to consider them as a constructive tandem and a generative dynamic. Again, the way forward is paved by an embrace of what both elements have to offer and propelled by an open-minded search for what E. O. Wilson terms *Consilience: The Unity of Knowledge* (1998) (see also Gould, *The Hedgehog, the Fox and the Magister's Pox*).[11]

To ground discussion on this rift in design thinking, consider Louis Kahn, writing in 1960: "A great building, in my opinion, must begin with the unmeasurable, go through measurable means when it is being designed, and in the end must be unmeasurable"[12] (quoted in Twombly 2003: 69). Kahn's measurable and immeasurable phases of architecture distinguish a pair of design operations and begin to delineate an under-appreciated dynamic. As such, it is useful to take the "measurable and immeasurable" as a means of exploring what can correspondingly be termed "the strategic and the physical" dynamics of architecture. The intent of this comparison is not so much to build on Kahn's philosophy (after Schopenhauer) of will-existence, but rather to articulate further meanings in a new and divergent story. The analogy of immeasurable physicality and measurable strategy, however, is nonetheless a real and practical division that fully applies to this discussion on how the two aspects have been split so cleanly apart.[13] And though this distinction has been an issue of architectural discourse for centuries, the dynamic interaction of the two became part of the postindustrial transformation of architecture at about the same time as Kahn's 1960 aphorism.

The Immeasurable calls on our direct and immediate experience of architecture as a sublime and meaningful encounter. The immeasurable quality is affective, transformative, and transcendent, and it works through significant human experience in the encounter of a "great building." Immeasurable operations form the physically present and sensually revealed element of architecture. Physicality, in turn, is grounded in our ideal aspirations as to what we find most essential about architecture. These physical characteristics are thus normally and conventionally seen as the center of the architect's work and thinking. For the patron of architecture, as for the society and civilization it serves, this physicality enables our sensual interaction with the built environment. Physical experience of architecture is also what inspires students to study architecture and sustains practitioners in their lifetime pursuits; it is what ultimately informs our imagination of architectural possibilities. Direct, immediate experience of architecture is what manifests this affective mode of architecture: the physical sphere of design.

The Measurable, on the other hand, is the strategic sphere of design. The measurable involves a large and diverse set of architectural essentials vested in strategic modes of thinking: what Kahn termed "the making of things" as well as the subsequent accountability for in-place performance. As such, the measurable factors of architecture include programming and planning, constructability and serviceability, and a host of other "-abilities" such as sustainability, flexibility, adaptability, affordability, and so forth that go into the realization of great buildings. If the physical sphere is "ideal," the strategic sphere is "real."

In common parlance, and from outside the shroud of professional architectural practice looking in, these strategically measured elements of architecture are commonly and conventionally seen as a constellation of minor moons in orbit around that great celestial planet of idealized physical design.[14] In balance however, the conventional attitude about the assumed superior role of the immeasurable element over that of the measurable is in question. In the postindustrial context, this hierarchical view is an important point of departure toward new and more expansive consideration as equal parts of design. Postindustrial evolution insinuates itself into the architectural conversation here with the contention that immeasurable and measurable elements are but two complementary and generative aspects of one whole thing.

This assertion of equally ranked elements and postindustrial relevance can be understood as a vital yet under-appreciated dynamic between physical and strategic spheres of architecture and their true equal roles in the complex whole of architectural design. Oddly enough, it is Kahn's ephemeral and immeasurable quality of great buildings that is manifested in the tangible material physical element of direct experience, while the concretely measurable strategic element is vested in an abstract construct comprised of tangible but immaterial variables such as performance, foresight, intelligence, and sustainability. In the end this seeming reversal of terms is not at all contradictory, as the immeasurable affect of direct immediate experience requires a physical medium to produce effect, and correspondingly, all measurable effect must be produced by strategic configuration and relation rather than by bare material presence. So this is the genesis of the two spheres: one immeasurable and affective, but physical; the other measurable, effect driven, and strategic, yet always abstract and immaterial.

Now given this pairing of the Immeasurable to the material physical sphere of design and of the Measurable with the immaterial strategic sphere: How do we make them into one whole thing that can be called architecture?

Precept Three: The Complex Whole

The whole is different from the sum of its parts.

(Aristotle, *Metaphysics*, 1037)

Complexity is the way in which a whole is different from the composition of its parts.

(M.H. van Emden 1971)[15]

1 + 1 = 3 (for sufficiently large values of one).

(Anon.)

Aristotle's maxim suggests that design must embrace the unity and harmony that emerges when parts are combined in beneficial synergy. On that basis, we should proceed to ask how qualities of wholeness are intentionally targeted by architects and how those benefits of the whole are achieved in the act of design: How do the overarching ideas and the individual design features come together cohesively? How does a conceptual intention become a guiding principle of the details? How do the parts act in unison to make something greater than their simple sum?

As a defining distinction between the complex resulting whole and the simple sum of its constituent parts, this vital power of design is vigorously and continuously explored in all pursuits and across the history of architecture: the greater whole is a fundamental assumption. Consideration of any building as a whole entity is thus a critically identifiable outcome of architectural design, especially if we see design as a process of unifying physical components in a matrix of intellectual decisions toward some great and ambitious end result. Consequently, the synergy of the whole has been frequently involved in architectural theory as to how we generally contemplate design—as well as in architectural critique as to what we have done in any one specific practice application.

We can readily translate these opening ideas about the complex whole into the concept of holism, a term which merely repeats by definition that the whole cannot be reduced to its parts without losing something along the way. A friendly synonym for holism might be the idea of harmony, by which we again mean that some special thought is necessary for parts to be selected and combined together in special ways for a balanced whole to result. The opposite of holism is the architecturally denounced notion of reductionism, which would posit that the whole is merely the total of the parts. The mere existence of these words is a fundamental indication of the vital relation of the parts to the whole in any discussion of design. In architecture then, as in Systems Theory, and as in any creative human endeavor, we like to believe that 1 + 1 = 3.

Precept Four: The Physical and Strategic Spheres of Design

One particularly relevant principle of Systems Theory and cybernetics posits that there are feedback loops in some operations that can steer situations and environmental conditions to the purpose of a set of organized flows. Natural organisms are the ultimate example of such systems in that they all respond dynamically to feedback from their environment and do so in adaptive ways to promote their own survival. It happens that most of the world around us is composed of such systemic behavior; even though our limited perceptions and shortcut heuristics are usually sufficient for dealing with daily circumstances on a much simplified mechanistic level. The stability of the earth's orbit, the ebb and tide of financial markets, the patterns of seasonal climate, the colony of fungi that make a mushroom, and the patterns of convection in boiling water are all examples of complex dynamic systems. Systems are the rule, not the exception.

Within the steering feedback loops that the world of systems exhibits, there is always a balance of differing forces between which the system chooses and prioritizes so that its learned adaptation will be successful. Such behavior is emergent from the complexity of the system; furthermore it is spontaneous, self-organizing, and self-regulating. There is no ghost in the machine that directs this behavior; rather, it is simply the essential nature of the system that its agent components align themselves in this way. This is how holism is defined in terms of a system and its harmony with its environment. The whole is the behavior of the system and is distinct from the characteristics of the pieces that make it up. And, as we are continually learning from advances in all fields of scientific and disciplinary thinking, this systemic behavior is far more ubiquitous and generally characteristic of our world than the old industrial age cause-and-effect point of view.

In architecture these differing and balanced forces of holistic behavior are constituted by the two distinct spheres of design thinking classified here as strategic and physical elements. Much like the way in which the human brain is separated into differing left and right hemispheres of corresponding rational and emotive thinking, architectural design is fundamentally divisible into what is termed here as its physical and the strategic components. And just as the human mind is a complex interaction of the two spheres of the brain organ, architecture emerges from the complex interaction of the physical and strategic aspects of design.

We are more familiar with physical design as the affective or emotive aspect of architecture; it is the direct human experience we have of the built environment in all the ways that lend sublime and transcendent impacts on our psyche through our first order physical senses and personal responses, most especially as conveyed by the visual experience of the building: Kahn's immeasurable quality. Physical design is familiar as the dominant "big idea" most students come to architectural school with and is also the notion most prevalent in popular characterizations of the hero architect such as Ayn Rand's 1943 *Fountainhead* novel character, Howard Roark.[16] Physical design is popularly and conventionally seen in this representation of architecture as the ultimate goal and most critical achievement of the architect. We can visually depict this conventional model of thought with immeasurable physical design being the large central star of architectural design, surrounded by the minor planets of measurable planning, programming, constructability, serviceability, sustainability, and so on (Figure 1.5).

In the postindustrial paradigm, a more cogent and operationally systematic depiction of architectural design would instead show two equal and complementary forces as physical design and strategic design, where the latter is a grouping of all the items conventionally pictured as the minor planets of programming, planning, and so on. This is the Two Spheres model. The strategic activities have a common purpose just as the activities of the physical sphere do. Namely, for the strategic aspect take the many modes of how human intelligence is intentionally embodied in architecture through design. In the systems model of design thought, physical design and strategic design are a paired set of forces (see Figure 1.6). Design, it turns out, is not nested in either of these two spheres. We will see that, in a holistic sense, design is actually what connects the physical and strategic aspects of design (see Figure 1.7) but neither sphere alone can claim dominion.

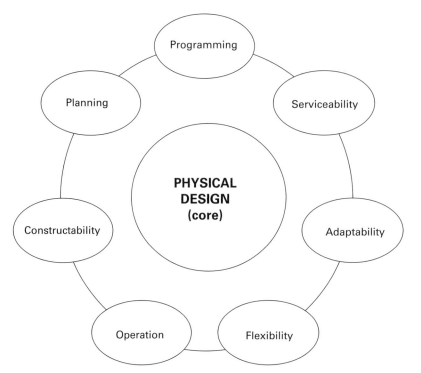

Figure 1.5 Conventional model of architecture.

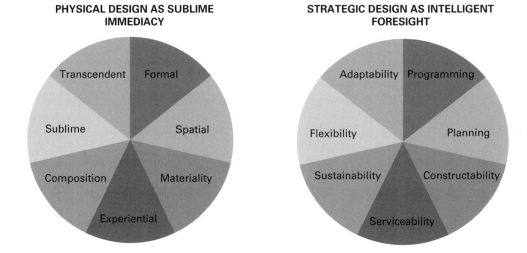

Figure 1.6 Two Spheres model of architecture.

To consider how such a pair of forces operates in architecture we can compare them to dialectics in other systems operations that achieve dynamic holism. As cosmologist John Barrow describes in his 1995 book, *The Artful Universe*, for example, the perfect organism is somewhere between a couch potato and a cliff climber.[17] The couch potato aspect seldom takes risks, but consequently never ventures out to find the resources needed to survive and prosper. The cliff climber, on the other hand, discovers lots of resources, but takes too many risks to survive and prosper for very long. A perfect organism must therefore behave adaptively in harmony with its environment: collecting resources when needed and available, avoiding unnecessary risk, and oscillating between states of behavior in dynamic and balanced ways.

The neuroscientist Scott Kelso provides a more directly relevant example: the human mind. The mind serves as an explanatory and even literal model for the dynamic of physical and strategic design. In his 1995 book, *Dynamic Patterns: The Self-Organization of Brain and Behavior*, Kelso reminds us that the brain is a body organ just like the heart or the stomach is.[18] The brain itself has no metaphysical or transformative qualities that imbue human spirit or that contain animated mindfulness. The human mind is thus something quite different from the brain, emerging out of complex interaction between the brain parts and between the brain and its stimulating environment. For the sake of illustration and relevance to our architectural model of physical and strategic design spheres, we can simplify the brain to its left and right hemispheres (LH and RH) with the integrating corpus callosum and its 250 million connecting nerve fibers interposed between the two halves. Correspondence between the model of the brain hemispheres and the two spheres of design is literal: lateralization of brain functions is known to be divided between the LH as the rational, strategic, effective aspect of design thinking and the RH as the emotive, physical, affective aspect of design. Figure 1.7 depicting the two spheres of design and their aesthetic connection could just as easily be used to represent the left and right brain hemispheres along with the integrating corpus callosum bridging between them.

Although almost every thought process is to some degree impacted by lateralized brain function, it also happens that design thinking and creativity in general requires a whole-minded bridging both within and between the two hemispheres: creativity requires confluence, convergence, and consilience of different brain centers and all its functions. There is now considerable agreement on this condition among neurologists using brain imaging research tools that visually map thinking activity, such as functional magnetic resonance imaging (fMRI). Similar studies have developed a strong and common position in the increasingly numerous meta-studies that cover the past four decades of creativity research: it turns out that creativity is not a lateralized brain function to any extent approaching that of LH versus RH tandems of verbal versus spatial thinking are, for example, or that analytical versus figural reasoning are. For us to be creative, we now understand, both spheres must be engaged

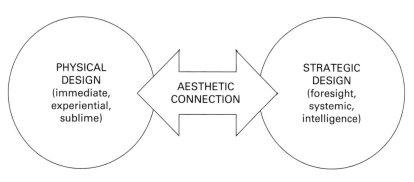

Figure 1.7 Design as an aesthetic bridge.

together. Creativity is a convergent function of the whole mind, not a half-brained act of eccentricity.

There is also a preponderance of agreement in the psychological and neurological literature that creative intelligence as a trait is not discipline bound. So, contrary to the myth that artistic creativity is normally associated with deviant genius RH brain affect while scientific creativity is the realm of eccentric genius LH brain thinking they are in fact both the same basic neurophysiology wiring. It is also held to be true that creative individuals in both artistic and scientific realms have a high tendency toward strong individualistic personalities, but that is probably another discussion entirely. What distinguishes artistic creativity from scientific creativity then is merely some lifelong series of personal choices that each individual makes (see especially Sternberg 1988).[19]

Beyond raw creative intelligence however, operative creativity does demand disciplinary knowledge: one cannot be effectively creative in a domain without a broad working knowledge of that specific field (see Csikszentmihalyi 1997).[20] This broad knowledge must clearly involve both rational LH and emotive RH ways of knowing and thinking. Creativity in action comes from some confluence of the two brain hemispheres working in full-minded harmony, not from extra-special super-ordinary favor of one side over the other.

Likewise for architects, the holistic human mind that emerges from complex LH + RH hemisphere brain interactions corresponds to how whole-minded architecture can emerge from complex and dynamic interactions of physical and strategic design spheres. As a working model, the LH + RH = mindful animation of the brain is parallel to physical + strategic = mindful animation of architecture. With the brain of course, the animated mind does not reside in either hemisphere. In fact, the mind is not even really "in" the brain organ in a technical sense, any more than human love is contained in the heart organ or uneasiness is contained in the stomach organ. In the Two Spheres model then, whole-minded architecture cannot lie separately, hierarchically, or predominately in either the physical or the strategic design sphere: architectural animation to the stage beyond merely good building is achieved by something different from and greater than the simple sum of its LH strategic and RH physical parts. Furthermore, as in all animated organisms, architecture is driven by purposeful interaction of dynamic forces: the physical and the strategic.

So that is the two hemisphere brain model of Two Sphere architecture. Note that the model gains traction by its parallel application: the mind as a creative force and architecture as the artifact of that mindfulness. In other words, both architecture and the mind are complex wholes and each is a manifestation of the other. The model of left and right brain hemispheres in correspondence with strategic (SD) and physical (PD) architectural spheres of design is thus useful and meaningful because it explains both how we can conceive of something as complex as architecture, and also how that mental construct of architecture develops in our thoughts from the same root complexity. The conclusion offered here is that human conceptions and appreciations of architecture are necessarily acquired by fully cognitive and complex human minds; just as artifacts of architecture are made whole by insinuation of the same complexity: LH + RH = mind; PD + SD = architecture.

Finally, and to perhaps close a link or two in the argument; Kelso's model of the mind can be linked back to the postindustrial foci of information and cybernetic intelligence.[21] There is an increasing reliance in contemporary society on such knowledge and evidence-based action. Increasingly as well, this knowledge and evidence is bound up in representations that are abstract and inferential. In the case of LH–RH Brain Lateralization versus the Animated Mind then, the notion of fMRI imaging of brain activity is emblematic of postindustrial insight. Such advanced perspectives focus on our newfound abilities to see beyond what human senses can detect at the first order level of immediate experience. We can now see beyond that local and direct scale of physical experience. We can actually probe and contemplate the microscopic, genetic, quantum, cosmic, relational, and abstract realities of our world.

In architecture the same increased scope of insight now binds physical design aspects with strategic ones. In the place of fMRI, architects are turning to simulation, virtual reality, building forensics, life-cycle value, ecological context, biological interactions, and a host of other tools that give us insights to the invisible relations and complex animation of successful building designs. There is no closing the door on these new insights; there is only the neotechnic and cybernetic intelligence that must be incorporated into our processes and designs.

The Shape of Sections to Come

Part One: Scoping Complexity: this opening chapter makes several assertions that set up Part One to portray the relevance of systems thinking in architectural design, particularly in regards to complex dynamic systems. This perspective distinguishes definitively between the physical and strategic aspects of architecture; then describes how the dynamic between them is itself a complex and systemic relation. Further discussion in Chapter 2 explores the epistemological basis of design itself as a wicked, messy, indeterminate, dynamic, and complex problem. The foundation of this viewpoint is reflected in the works of several influential thinkers who appeared at the early dawn of postindustrial thought. Finally, Chapter 3 closes Part One with a discussion on the essence of architectural problems of emergent order and self-organizing form versus that of human intention and artistic authorship. Emergent order is likened to Aristotelian teleological "final cause" and autopoiesis as components of the strategic sphere of design. Human intention, aspiration, and intervention, meanwhile, are the realm of the physical sphere. The underlying theme of Part One is thus that of complex dynamic systems as a framework toward new intra-disciplinary thinking about architecture in the postindustrial context.

Part Two: Embracing Complexity: the second part of this book traces historical forays of architecture into the dual realms of dynamic complexity and postindustrial thought. Chapter 4 covers wicked, messy, ordered, and natural ordering principles of those encounters. Chapter 5 then illustrates some postindustrial era convergences of design and complexity. Finally, Chapter 6 lays out strategies for embracing the rich ambiguity of wicked complexity. Rather than the Systems Theory basis that dominates Part One from an external view, these chapters work more directly within architecture from an introspective point of view more clearly within the actual history of design. As previously indicated, much of this history dates to that 1960s influence of postindustrial thought on notions of architectural design.

Part Three: Mapping Complexity onto the Realm: four final chapters map the overlay of an aesthetic theory of complexity-in-architecture onto the four domains of the realm:[22] the profession of architecture as an ethical entity, occupational practice, education and the academy, and disciplinary research. Each of these domains is treated as an essay toward a Two Spheres perspective of whole-minded architecture. The concluding scheme suggests a new network of discourses and interactions within and among the four domains.

Chapter 2

Scoping Complexity

Chapter 1 proposed that architecture is made holistic and whole-minded by the confluence of two spheres: namely the strategic and physical aspects of design. Kelso's work on *Dynamic Patterns: The Self-Organization of Brain and Behavior (Complex Adaptive Systems)* offered both an analogous model and a literal mechanism from neuroscience that explains the two-sphere proposition: wherein the animation of the human mind is made whole through the complex amalgamation of our more emotive left brain with our more rational right brain hemispheres.[1] An echo of those left- plus right-side cognitions was also illustrated by Louis Kahn's aphorism on the measurable and immeasurable components of design process.[2] In all cases, the whole is presented as something different and more than just the sum of the two halves. In all cases as well, the whole is predicated on complexity. This chapter will scope the nature of that complexity from different perspectives and examine its basis in dynamic systems, especially in the relation of this complexity to architecture.

Complexity: Tandems, Tangles, and Tapestries

> The finger pointing to the moon is not the moon.
> The map is not the territory.
>
> (Traditional wisdoms)

To frame some introductory thoughts on what does and does not constitute complexity, consider George Rzevski's distinction between merely complicated situations and the more truly complex.[3] Making reference to the Latin roots of the two terms, Rzevski ties complication to the Latin "plic," meaning "to fold." Complexity, on the other hand, stems from the Latin root "plex," or "to weave." In a more poetic sense the difference is that of a complicated tangle as compared to a complex tapestry. Rzevski concludes that "a complex structure uses interwoven components that introduce mutual dependencies and produce more than a sum of the parts. . . . This means that complex is the opposite of independent, while complicated is the opposite of simple." Similar contrasts are made by Peter Senge of the MIT Sloan School of Management who discusses complication as the piling up of combinations and possibilities of factors, or "needle in the haystack" detail complexity as distinct from the

Table 2.1 Characteristics of detail complexity versus dynamic complexity

Detailed Complexity Problems	Dynamic Complexity Problems
Find best combination of many possibilities	Interventions lead to counterintuitive results
Complicated array of details	There is a lag between action and reaction
Combinatorial selection of optimum choices	Different effects at different scales
Factors respond mechanistically	Factors are deeply interactive
Deals with static and predictable flows	Deals with organized and interrelated flows
	Involves self-correcting cyclical feedback loops
	Outcomes are probabilistic rather than certain

Source: After Senge (1990).

"How did that happen?" dynamic complexity (Table 2.1). For more on that discussion see Senge, *The Fifth Discipline* (1990) and Sterman, *Business Dynamics* (2000).[4]

The same contrast of meanings also applies to the often conflated concepts of chaos and disorder; wherein the former is a special kind of spontaneous order exhibited in nature and the latter is just confusion, turmoil, or mayhem. Chaos is not anarchy when taken in the strict terms of natural behavior and systems science; rather, it is a special kind of order, one that is drastically different from the visibly smooth form and regular mathematic geometry humans give to their artifacts and to the world of human perception in general. Instead, chaos is the stuff of rough fractal geometry and indeterminate iterative mathematics of natural forms.[5] The meanings of complexity and chaos are thus intertwined by that distinctive order which nature demonstrates in the technically deterministic but seemingly spontaneous patterns of regular convection currents in boiling water, the organized flocking of birds in flight, or the fractal shapes of everything from a snowflake to a coastline that self-replicate at any scale of magnification.

In Rzevski's terms then, complication, confusion, and anarchy will always result in meaningless tangles, but chaotic and complex systems always exhibit the patterned characteristics of a woven tapestry.[6] It is in this distinction that the indeterminate nature of architectural problems and the quest for synergetic wholeness can be fruitfully pursued. Framing design as a woven tapestry in this way avoids any need for reduction to simplistic and mechanistic definitions of design, because the systems view both recognizes the rich unique essence of any given particular design problem and simultaneously offers a means of addressing the underlying complex indeterminacy. So, while the complete definition of a design problem can never be fully stated in empirical terms, the matrix of design issues that arises along with their interrelated dynamics can all be seen as a natural and vital condition within which design operates. And while the most obvious examples of such complex systems are found in living organisms and molecular biology, architects can still readily align their designerly thinking to systemic principles such as irreducible complexity, rich ambiguity, and robust response to the environment.

From this description of complexity and chaos, it is a short jump to the related notion of systems and on from there to the full depth of complex

Table 2.2 Characteristics of complex dynamic systems

Interdependent parts or agents	Autonomous and choiceful independent actions without any centralized control or communication but with an overall adherence to a global purpose, such as stock market fluctuations driven by independent investors
Potential	Systems are sustained by an exchange of energy and/or information with their environment. As such, they stay in states of flux, hysteresis, and oscillation. This is sometimes referred to as the "far from equilibrium" state of a system
Organized flow	Systems exhibit purposeful and organized flows of energy, matter, or information, such as in the flow of forces in a structural system
Feedback from environment	Cybernetic responsiveness to frequent events, such as the behavior of an organism to its surroundings
Adaptive behavior	Robust and self-correcting patterns of behavior that advance and sustain the global purpose of the system
Emergent behavior	Large-scale aggregate behaviors that are not the property of any of the components or agents of the system, such as the orderly convection patterns of boiling water
Self-organizing	The development of new structures in a system that exhibit qualities which are greater than the sum of its parts, such as the growth of a mushroom
Sensitive to initial conditions	Dependency of interaction and outcome on initial states even though operative rules of interaction and behavior are predefined
Deterministic but unpredictable	Behavior according to rules but without foreseeable outcome or being traceable to initial conditions
Non-linear behavior	The linkages of input-to-output or cause-to-effect are not obvious or predictable
Autocatalytic	The ability to produce new higher order structures from within existing lower order structures, such as the vortex of a hurricane
Self-replication	The product of emergence that enables an evolutionary adaptive system to make copies of itself, such as in living organisms, DNA, and certain proteins

dynamic systems. Table 2.2 describes the characteristics and behavior of complexity, systems, and their embodiment in dynamic systems. Later sections will deal more specifically with some of the more technical and scientific definitions.

Tandems, Tangles, and Tapestries

From these characteristics and behaviors, we understand that cybernetic feedback is an essential element of how a system purposefully adapts to its environment. In the general case of natural organisms, the purpose is survival and the environment is nature. The tension between a system's environment and the system's purpose is thus a generative dialectic. Without it the system will perish.

Consider the human mind as such a system. In pre-scientific philosophy it was assumed that some controlling mechanism rather like a computer's central processing unit (CPU) was required to regulate brain function. This mechanism was explained in the form of a homunculus or "little man in the brain" who was assumed to be a complete but miniature person intelligently regulating input and output of the brain processes. We understand today that there is no such "ghost in the machine" ordering mechanism or, to use the phrase from theater, no "deus ex machina." The human mind is of its own accord entirely emergent, self-organizing, and self-regulating. The brain is just a body organ. The mind is an adaptive and dynamic system that achieves animation. The difference between the brain organ and the emergent animated mind is complexity, and the essential role that complexity itself plays in organizing is a vital response. That difference then is what we know as consciousness and mindfulness.

By analogy, the left and right hemispheres of the human brain are comparable to the physical and strategic aspects of design. The brain/mind distinction is thus a model of animation and complexity in the Two Spheres formulation of architecture. The interaction and complexity of brain functions is what leads to higher order mindfulness. Without the interplay of such generative factors, however, the feedback and resolution that leads to that mindfulness would never occur. To that end, the notion of tandems can be added to the previous discussion on tangles and tapestries.

Using the terms in Table 2.2 then, it is also the case that there are many paired sets of tandem concepts that should be considered as generative aspects, tensions, or dialectics in the complexity of architectural design. These tandems are key to understanding the Two Spheres implications in design. Table 2.3 lays out some paired concepts and generative tensions as were initially implied in the corresponding discussion in Chapter 1. To be synthetic, of course, these tandem aspects of the Two Spheres must be seen in a positive way as complementary, generative, and dynamic rather than antagonistic, mutually exclusive, or otherwise negative and divisive.

Just as in cybernetic feedback and as illustrated by the LH + RH model of the emergent human mind, these corresponding paired aspects of the strategic and physical design spheres demonstrate that a complete and whole design can never be achieved without integral inclusion of both aspects. Each of them is a vitalizing dialectic, a tandem. It is not so much then that each tandem represents a conflict, but rather that each is a continuum along which different design decisions must be made and for which consequences will result. The difference between each end of the continuum is simply the driving potential that perpetuates a balancing dynamic act between them. So, not only are these tandem opposites not mutually exclusive, they are not at conflict to begin with; they are indeed sympathetic and synergistic. Compromise is not the issue; integration is. Isolated sphere left brain thinking or right brain thinking

Table 2.3 Tandems: Paired aspects of the Two Spheres perspective, some generative and dynamic tensions in design with reference to the left versus right brain hemisphere (LH and RH) model of the human mind

Strategic Design Aspects	Corresponding Physical Design Aspects
Left brain rational effect	Right brain emotive affect
Measured	Immeasurable
Foresight	Immediacy
Intelligence	Significance
Globally systemic	Locally experiential
Deep interaction, and interdependence	The direct thing itself
The real	The ideal

are, for example, not even possible unless one is totally schizophrenic or has a surgical hemispherectomy. It is likewise impossible to design with one isolated pole of any Table 2.3 tandem. Nor is the difficulty of design truly ever composed of any such either/or propositions; but rather by how each tandem is resolved, balanced, and made whole; and by how the forces are woven together in a tapestry rather than simply untangled from one another. In design we are of course always using our complete brain rather than some isolated fragment of it, but our thinking is not automatically synthesized, integrated, or complete. It must be directed mindfully and made whole through the cognition that is design thinking. However critical any one isolated component of our thinking may be, that particular physical or strategic piece of the puzzle may be necessary, but it will never be sufficient without its complement from the other sphere.

Examples of this sort of synthetic resolution are readily evident in our everyday tandem pairings of nutrition and cuisine, exercise and rest, risk and safety, work and play, reflection and exploration, and so forth across every facet of life. Given the design choice, for instance, who would optimize their own daily nutritional food intake without an integral appreciation for culinary flavor, aroma, variety, texture, and customary habit, not to mention the rituals of shared meals and setting of the experience? And who, likewise, would wish to do the opposite by consistently focusing on epicurean pleasures with little concern for ease of digestion and healthy sustenance? The whole ideal of human diet then is conditionally inclusive of both nutrition and cuisine, just as life is a tossed-salad blend of exercise and rest, work and play, and all the other dialectic tandems that dynamically drive the variety and oscillation of life.

Such paired choices are not just abstract dichotomies used to conveniently and academically explain away difficult choices; rather they are some of the real dynamics that shape and drive life. In regards to each pair then, as well as to the whole enterprise of life, success is not dependent on choosing one aspect or the other as if they were somehow mutually exclusive; but rather in how the two are carefully and intentionally assimilated and made into one whole thing that sustains a healthy and self-actualizing lifestyle. The answer always shifts along a continuum of the possibilities between the two extreme positions. It takes more than just picking one, or simply combining the two; it requires an integrating act of maintaining both a generative dynamic and a balanced equilibrium. It takes design. Kahn's tandem of measurable and immeasurable phases of a great building is an obvious design application.[7]

And so it is with the Two Spheres in architecture. The careful and intentional assimilation of physical and strategic aspects demands that design be brought to bear on the synthesis of dynamic pairs, for design is always evident in the careful application of human intent. And design does not reside in a hierarchical ranking or preferred ennoblement of the left or the right spheres, but rather in how we bridge from one side to the other and back again in a way that elevates the result to more than the simple sum of its left and right component parts. For the strategic and physical spheres, for the measurable and the immeasurable, the bridging is ultimately accomplished by how we connect the real and the ideal. The act of bridging is thus what we call design. To embody the resulting artifact of design with human significance is then to recognize its aesthetic value as vested in Scruton's "interconnection between our understanding and our appreciation"; in other words, in the interconnection between the real and the ideal.[8]

Louis Sullivan's famous dictum on form and function is another obvious example of such design thinking accomplished through the dynamics of a tandem pair.[9] Should the design be purely sculptural at the expense of function? Or, on the contrary, should the design be dominated by efficiency and pragmatics at the loss of all direct and immediate emotional appeal? Both of these demands are actually straw-man fallacy-type questions as they assume a black-and-white, mutually exclusive problem that is dichotomous and dualistic. But design is a loving dance, not a forced march. The real question must rather be as to how both can be realized in a manner that authentically bridges between them. The answer is complex of course, and will require more than rational or intuitive thought can provide alone.

Generative Dialectics

Without dynamic tensions working as generative tandems then, it is clear that the rich ambiguity that lies tangled among any paired aspects of the two spheres could not be exploited in design. To show how such active ambiguity becomes a generative and dynamic component of design, consider Figure 2.1. As long as generative tensions are at play, then systemic conditions remain dynamic; oscillations of the polar factors at each boundary swing around; feedback causes adaptation; and the ambiguity between the poles is constantly explored, investigated, and plumbed. When the tension slacks, however, then dynamics are weak, oscillation slows, ambiguity abates, and the issue essentially dies. Without the driving differences inherent in their paired aspects, the dynamic cannot be sustained, feedback disappears, adaptation ceases, organisms hibernate, systems collapse into homeostasis, conversation and debate go silent, and design ceases to operate. Following Figure 2.1 then, this model of generative dialectics can be applied to any issue configured as a tandem pair.

As Figure 2.1 illustrates, whole things are complex and dynamic; complex things prevail as coherent systems; and coherent systems involve ambiguity, oscillation, interaction, interdependence, and, lest we forget, complexity. Clearly the dynamics we observe in these tandems are that of the complex systems perspective. They have all the defining elements of a system: oscillating feedback, dialectic boundary conditions, rich middle-ground ambiguity, and continuous adaptation. To use the dynamics of discourse as an example of how this oscillation animates an exchange and breathes a life of its own into conversation, consider Gadamer's insight to the dialectic of dialogue:

> When one enters into a dialogue with another person and then is carried further by the dialogue, it is no longer the will of the individual person, holding itself back or exposing itself, that is determinative. Rather, the law of the subject matter is at issue in the dialogue and elicits statement and counterstatement and in the end plays them into each other.[10]

On Being a Systems Thinker

Most people are already, consciously or unconsciously, given to systems thinking. Life in the everyday matrix of information, interaction, context-driven problem solving, and uncertain outcomes has brought us collectively into postindustrial manifestations of the systems approach.

Generative Dialectics and Active Ambiguity

histeresis

Imagine a group of animals in a long rectangular building. At one end of the building the environment is very hot. At the other end the environment is very cold. The animals will naturally move from one side to the other and settle somewhere in the middle, where the density of square feet per animal will be smallest. As the temperatures vary on either end of the building, the animals will search for lower areas of stress and their concentration will oscillate

ideal organism

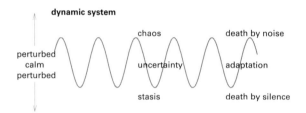

The ideal organism oscillates between the epicurean state of calm relaxation and comfort and the adventure state of seeking new resources. As the environment varies through the seasons and through the day, the organism will move from safety to risk as appropriate

dynamic system

The teleologic and autopoetic forces of a system keep it on the edge of chaos in a state of ambiguity between stasis and chaos. A system adapts to uncertainty in response to driving potentials. Like many dialectics, one pole is death by homogeneity of potentials and the other pole is death by randomness and failure of order. A continual or periodic perturbance is needed to keep the dynamic flowing

discourse

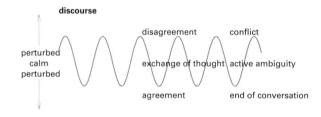

A range of active ambiguity is also what keeps discourse at a productive and generative level of energy and motion. Again, when the potential of exchange is removed, the discourse ends in lack of energy ... when the potential meets total disconnection, then discourse ends in conflict

design

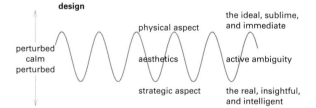

Ambiguity in design rests in the level of complex interaction between the ideal and the real. This ambiguity is served by aesthetic bridging between the two aspects of immediacy and foresight

Figure 2.1 Tandems, generative dialectics, and active ambiguity.

If you love the spontaneous forest more than you do a cultivated tree farm, then you are quite likely already something of a systems thinker. If you favor contingent and flexible solutions over rigid ones, then you are even more of a systems thinker. If you prefer indeterminate open-ended explanations over fixed and deterministic answers, then indeed, you are a systems thinker. If you believe more in principles and wisdom than you do in experience and expertise, then again, you are a systems thinker. If you realize that the universe is not a deterministic set of cause-and-effect rules, but is instead more like a dynamic and complex set of fluid interrelationships, then you are a bona fide and confirmed systems thinker.

If none of these choices identifies you as a systems thinker, then perhaps there is something about the many current perceptions and approaches to systems theory that is still too confusing and mysterious to be convincing to you. Most of us today, however, are native systems thinkers; not because we have a deep scientific understanding of systems theory, but rather because the world around us is full of natural organisms, contingent knowledge, open-ended explanations, deep wisdom, and complex relationships; none of which make much sense from a narrow deterministic, cause-and-effect, machine-driven mode of explanation. The world is just too marvelous to reduce to the machine, so it has to be the system. Science agrees. Art concurs. Philosophy confirms.

To amplify a bit, the reason the tree farm is not a system has little to do with its visual organization of neatly spaced rows and trimmed branches; those are just visually apparent symptoms. At the underlying level of deep relation and organization, a system is inherently robust, self-organizing, self-emergent, self-sustaining, self-regulating, and self-restorative. A machine is none of those things. In short, systems like a forest are authentically animated, but artifacts like a tree farm are just machines. Consequently, while the tree farm will require ever-increasing amounts of fertilizer and pesticides to produce an ever-dwindling supply of increasingly poor-quality wood, the forest will go on perpetuating its own rich and complex network of processes, relationships, and flows. And if lightning strikes and they both burn down, only the forest will reconstruct itself from the ashes.

Another radical distinction between tree farm-style mechanistic devices and the naturally complex forest system is manifested in the corresponding difference between symptomatic and systemic relations. To use a more direct example, consider the patient who presents at the doctor's office with chronic headache discomfort: the doctor who prescribes a pill for the pain is dealing with the situation at a reductionist symptomatic level. On the other hand, the doctor who asks the patient when was the last time they had an eye health exam at the optometrist is looking for some underlying systemic root of the situation where the essence of the condition actually originates. Note that one doctor prescribes, while the other doctor inquires.

One more layer to this insight is offered by different scales of relation that differentiate the pill-pusher doctor's insight from the root-cause doctor's thinking; what physicist David Bohm called local and non-local order.[11] The pill-doctor takes a deterministic Cartesian cause-and-effect view of what is involved. This mechanistic perception and explanation occurs at the local scale of reality where our direct and immediate perception of events will obscure the real complexity of what is going on. The root-cause doctor on the other hand recognizes that each patient situation is unique, complex, and messy; full of interacting events and beyond reduction to superficial cause-and-effect understanding. One doctor pretends to tame the complexity; the other doctor simply embraces it.

Looking Outward: Complexity and Science

Given that design problems can be understood as complex, indeterminate, and wicked, it follows that architecture can be approached with the same general principles used by other disciplines which embrace complex problems. Those general principles are called cybernetics, a science that dates to the 1940s and a way of thinking conceived by Aristotle around 350 BCE. This section frames the relation of cybernetic science with postindustrial society and shows their relevance to progress in the field of architecture.

Our interest in cybernetics stems from work in fields of information theory, control, feedback, and communication. The term "cybernetic" itself is derived from the Greek word for steersman, *kybernetes*, and so refers to how intelligence navigates in a self-correcting manner. Through Latin, the word has also come into the English language to mean governor in both the political and the mechanical feedback senses of the word. An architectural perspective on these various ideas is set forth here to illustrate their importance in strategic design.

First, it must be strongly emphasized that complexity theory is not a speculative, conjectural, or purely theoretical discussion. Complexity is real and it is the best perspective we have today on how the everyday world around us actually operates. The systematic principles involved in dealing with complexity have been applied to common practice in every conceivable discipline and profession. The foundational literature supporting complexity is enormous and pervasive. Any brief survey of contemporary business management articles, for example, will illustrate that systems thinking and cybernetic processes are being brought to bear on even the most practical and pragmatic of problems. Cybernetics is not just the esoteric stuff of laboratory research and cosmological philosophies.

While early interest in cybernetics dealt with engineering control systems and artificial intelligence, the field is primarily concerned with the general principles of interrelated actions, organized flows, or events that comprise systems. It has become an interdisciplinary field of study involving diverse traditions such as mathematics, technology, biology, philosophy, and the social sciences. Likewise, its implications toward systemic problem solving have been extended to psychology, ecology, and management. Sociologist Walter Buckley published *Sociology and Modern Systems Theory* in 1967; Stafford Beer published *Cybernetics and Management* in 1959; G.E. Hutchinson presented a paper entitled "Circular causal systems in ecology" in 1948.[12] The entire field has also reached popular consciousness through Whole Earth Catalog advertising; literature such as Stephen Hawking's *A Brief History of Time*, the cyberpunk genre of science fiction writers like Bruce Sterling and William Gibson, and the widespread media coverage of fractal images, chaos theory, and non-linear physics.[13]

Cybernetics is more specifically the study of information and communication in animals and machines. It is concerned with complex systems that exhibit dynamic and self-adaptive behavior toward some goal-oriented condition, such as the survival of a species or the balance of a gyroscope. This behavior is present in a wide assortment of organic and inorganic systems; it is in fact the prevalent model. Cybernetics is thus a close cousin of General Systems Theory and Systems Research. Gregory Bateson noted that cybernetics was concerned with pattern and form rather than with material and energy.[14] Margaret Mead called it a way of looking at things and a language for expressing what one sees.[15] This entire area of thinking emphasizes holistic interactions and connectedness among system parts and is thus quite different from the reductionist analytical approach that tries to understand problems through the behavior of its individual pieces. The affinity of strategic design to cybernetic thinking is rooted in this holistic approach to the understanding of complex problems.

Examining the world at this systems level reveals that most of the predicaments we confront are actually wicked problems; that is to say, they exhibit dynamic complexity. Everything about such predicaments is bound up together in non-linear relationships whose outcome can only be understood in terms of probability and extreme sensitivity to starting conditions. A popular conceptualization of this has been called the "butterfly effect" whereby a butterfly softly stirring the air in one part of the world can be said to be inter-acting with a typhoon on the other side of the world. The "Butterfly Effect" is often ascribed to Edward Lorenz. In a paper in 1963 given to the New York Academy of Sciences he remarks: "One meteorologist remarked that if the theory were correct, one flap of a seagull's wings would be enough to alter the course of the weather forever." By the time of his talk at the December 1972 meeting of the American Association for the Advancement of Science in Washington, DC, the seagull had evolved into the more poetic butterfly—the title of his talk was: "Predictability: Does the Flap of a Butterfly's Wings in Brazil set off a Tornado in Texas?"[16] Staying with the atmospheric systems for a moment, in the late 1960s the British chemist James Lovelock began to compare the atmosphere of Mars, which he observed was in a state of dead homogeneity, while the atmosphere of Earth was in a constant state of dynamic self-correcting, self-evolving, and self-regulating equilibrium.[17] This led him to propose the controversial Gaia Principle, which considers Earth as one immense interactive living system, every part of its complex workings affecting every other part: the Earth as one organism of which we are all autonomous agents.

Turning to a more formal scientific perspective, Heisenberg's 1927 Uncertainty Principle of quantum mechanics has shown that complex relations are much more prevalent than the simple mechanistic ones we can perceive and understand directly.[18] The late Polish mathematician Stanislaw Ulam even remarked that "To speak of non-linear physics is like calling zoology the study of non-elephant animals."[19] The undeniable fact is that we live in a non-linear universe. That around us which appears to be simple and mechanistic is largely a consequence of the mistaken belief that our first order, local scale of linear cause-and-effect perception is somehow comprehensive and holistic. This habitual simplification is the only way our bounded rationality can functionally filter through the real complexity in moment-to-moment existence. In the more reflective state of design thinking, however, those heuristic rules of continuous simplification must be set aside: the true underlying complexity and unique essence of the situation must be probed instead.

In postindustrial society, the language of cybernetics, global econo-mies, systems thinking, and advanced physics is now spoken all around us. Chaos, dynamic complexity, cybernetics, feedback, artificial intelligence, neural networks, indeterminism, deep interrelatedness, non-linear behavior, and stochastic processes are just a flavor of the lingo. There are a great many such concepts, and for each one there are also multiple interpretations and defini-tions. Within all that, there are still a great many overlapping boundaries and territories yet to be argued over by thinkers central to each discussion. Sorting all that out will be a great philosophical project for many years to come, and so, although the concepts are vital to the proposition of Two Spheres, a final resolution of all these myriad schemes is not part of this present architectural project. On the other hand, meaningless oversimplifications will not be offered here as a substitute for clarity and profound understanding. Attempting to make either exact distinctions or ready simplifications where so much fuzziness exists and continues to shift about is simply futile and quite probably useless. An accurate sketch of the concepts is necessary to develop insights of course, but precise definitions will not be argued here. See Table 2.4 for a rough overview.

Table 2.4 Complexity, cybernetics, and systems thinking in architecture

Complexity Term	Rough Definition	Strategic Parallel	Architectural Examples
System	A collection of interacting parts forming a complex whole. A system cannot be understood in terms of a mere collection of its individual parts	Organization of flows: material, energy, people, information, water, etc. (after Churchman 1968)	A structural system organizes the flow of gravity through a building to maintain static equilibrium
Synergy	The whole is more than the sum of its parts (Aristotle, *Metaphysics* 1037)	The difference in effect gained by the designer's intended interaction of parts, which is greater than the total effect of what the parts or components achieve independently	This is a general goal of all design
Cybernetic	Use of feedback for control and regulation of a system usually involving circular causation of input-reaction mechanisms between a system and its environment	Capturing streams of information for continual adjustment of building response	Interactive or responsive building components that change in response to conditions, such as shading devices, operable windows, daylighting; also could include moving or changing components of the building such as switchable glazing or operable walls
Complexity	The non-linear behavior of many parts in a system whose future state is determined by their interactions	Client + Site + Code + Budget + Time + Vision + Unknown	Sustainable systems are complex interactions. Building criteria always form complex indeterminate problems for which there is no clear approach or definitive solution
Dynamic	A system wherein the relationship between cause and effect is very subtle, especially in considering the impact of an intervention over time or over different scales of application	Combinatorial or "detail complexity" arises from the number of possibilities to choose among. It is much less difficult to address than dynamic complexity, which relates to interactions of the system's components over time	Optimizing the current arrangement of a floor plan is much easier than allowing for growth and change of user areas over time

(Continued overleaf)

Table 2.4 *Continued*

Complexity Term	Rough Definition	Strategic Parallel	Architectural Examples
Interrelatedness	A networking of connected components whose states are dependent upon and have impacts on one another	Size, quality, and time in a design problem are always interrelated	Any change in the size, cost, or appearance of a design has a ripple effect on the other two aspects
Scale	Local, micro, and macro scales of impact, only the local scale of which is commonly and directly perceptible to human senses, but as the local scale is largely symptomatic rather than essential	Cause and effect are not always closely related in time and space. Changes at one time, level, or scale may have unnoticed repercussions elsewhere in the system	Aside from the matrix of macro climate, regional climate, site micro climate and interior climate, there are also the scales of cosmology and biology that elude direct perception
Attractor	The point or goal toward which a system tends to move, even if it behaves in a non-linear (chaotic) manner. Equilibrium is an attractor in thermodynamic systems	The architectural design intention and the suggested, but ever transient, character of its solution, which is only resolved by exploration, interpretation, and iteration	Design concept, scheme, intention, or other distinguishing ambition
Emergence	Difference in the behavior of individual elements within a system within their limited freedom and the behavior of the system itself which may be more complex	These are qualities which arise out of the collective dynamic of the relationship and configuration of design elements. These qualities were not present in the separate elements.	The whole is different from the sum of its parts, and is ideally something more than the sum of its parts
Entropy	The degree of randomness or disorder in a system	Architecture is inherently anti-entropic as it is (1) aligned against the degenerating forces of change and (2) intended to impose and maintain a particular state of order	After Mostafavi and Leatherbarrow's book, *On Weathering* (1993)—Is the building set to patina or to stain?
Edge of Chaos	Tendency of dynamic systems to remain roughly midway between static and random states	This is where the prospect is in design, invested in the areas of the problem which are neither settled in an unalterable given condition nor lost in random meaninglessness	The problem space of architectural design resides in the rich ambiguity between program determinates and meaningless noise
Hermeneutic Cycle	The interpretation or translation of a text or a situation for the purpose of deriving a new or more correct view	The iterative reading and reinterpretation of a design condition while spiraling down to the attractor of design intention	Design propositions are always abductive, as are the propositions of scientists and artists
Perturbation	An external force acting on a system which may produce an immediate or long transition shift in state	Seasonal change, occupancy levels, weather conditions	Changes in use, occupants, weather, energy costs, institutional model

Feedback	Control link from the output of a system back to the input in order to maintain the current state (negative feedback) or to diverge to another state (positive feedback)	Data collection and sensing, two-way communication with equipment, performance monitoring	Control systems, building automation, intelligent buildings, passive thermal response
Systemic	The antonym of symptomatic. The essential and radical source of behavior of the whole in concert with its environment	Are today's problems the result of yesterday's solutions?	Sets of organized flow: light, air, heat, gravity, people, products, information . . .
Bifurcation	Theory on how dynamic systems can affect large qualitative changes in response to small changes in its environment	Small changes can have big results	It can be difficult to leverage the impact of change if the delay in the result or the scale of the result is not first understood
Scenario Planning	Modeling or simulation-based exploration of future states based on current conditions and anticipated influences	Creative imagining of different possible futures amongst which choices can be made proactively	This relates to the idea of proactively inventing the future rather than trying to reactively predict it
Structures	Organizational principle of how a system's patterns are physically embodied and purposefully realized including their traits, values, shapes, and efficacy	The qualities and characteristics of components in response to the intended purpose	Building systems including site, structure, envelope, services, and interiors
Processes	Principle involving the steps, stages, or interactions performed to accomplish an organizational pattern in such a way that the outcome is cohesive	The selection, configuration, deployment, and integration of components	Functioning of a building and its systems in terms of use and performance
Patterns	Organizing principle of a general solution approach to a categorically generic problem, from which a specific problem may be addressed	Problem-solving procedures	Design theory or design method
Holistic	A focus on the overall big picture of structures, patterns, and processes as the reality of a situation rather than on individual parts, aspects, or symptoms of the situation	Strategic plan for deployment of tactics and resources to meet objectives and goals	A complete design realized as a built work of architecture

Looking Back: Complexity and Postindustrial Progress

Despite the ephemeral and nebulous concepts involved in complexity science, there are nonetheless a surprising and reassuring number of vital connections between postindustrial concepts and the timeless aspirations of architecture. Seizing upon them will not be a great feat once the groundwork is laid. Consider, for example, the similarities between postmodern and postindustrial rejection of straightforward, mechanistic positive objectivism versus contemporary science's insight to the uncertain behavior of non-linear systems. This section will focus specifically on those connecting commonalities.

Here are some of the key events tying complexity to the evolution of a neotechnic postindustrial condition:

- 1782—Immanuel Kant publishes *The Critique of Pure Reason*, establishing the problematic of noumena versus phenomena, or between the thing itself and our limited experience of them through observation of their appearances[20]
- 1922—Alexander Bogdanov publishes *Tektology: Universal Organization Science*, perhaps the earliest treatise on the part/whole relationships in systems. He proposed that physical, biological, and human sciences could be unified as systems of relationships with underlying organizational principles[21]
- 1924—Max Wertheimer publishes *Gestalt Theory* and, along with Kurt Koffka and Wolfgang Kohler, founds Gestalt psychology.[22] Their students included Kurt Lewin, who founded social psychology along with the hermeneutic cycle of action research. Another of their students was the theorist and artist Rudolf Arnheim, whose major books include *Visual Thinking* (1969), *Art and Visual Perception* (1954/1974), *Entropy and Art* (1971), and *The Dynamics of Architectural Form* (1977)[23]
- 1947—Warren Weaver outlines a taxonomy of system complexity in his paper "Science and Complexity"[24]
- 1959— Stafford Beer publishes *Cybernetics and Management*[25]
- 1963—Karl Popper publishes *Conjectures and Refutations*, establishing falsification as the true realm of conjecture and scientific explanation[26]
- 1964—Roy Ascott publishes *The Construction of Change*, on the relationship between art, systems theory, cybernetics, and human behavior[27]
- 1967—Walter Buckley publishes *Sociology and Modern Systems Theory*, the first substantial exploration of General Systems Theory as applied to social systems published by a scholar who was not aligned with the cybernetics or general systems movements[28]
- 1973—Friederich Hayek publishes *Law, Legislation and Liberty*, distinguishing between cosmos and taxis as that of spontaneous emergent order and intentional made order[29]
- 1980—David Bohm publishes *Wholeness and the Implicate Order*, using quantum physics to describe the "enfolding and unfolding universe" as an unbroken whole of "implicate and explicate order."[30]

Karl Popper's Three Worlds

Karl Popper's framework of Three Worlds is useful for reintegrating the notions of systemic complexity with those of postindustrial evolution (Figure 2.2):

First, there is the physical world—the universe of physical entities . . . this I will call "World 1". Second, there is the world of mental states, including states of consciousness and psychological dispositions and unconscious states; this I will call "World 2". But there is

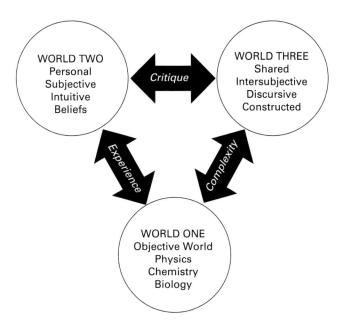

Figure 2.2 Popper's Three Worlds.

also a third such world, the world of the contents of thought, and, indeed, of the products of the human mind; this I will call "World 3".

(Popper & Eccles 1977: 38)[31]

- World One—Objective reality, what Kant calls noumena or "the thing as it is."[32] Bohm would term this the non-local implicate order.[33] Hayek would say it embodies spontaneous order.[34] At this level, however, the human mind is not capable of seeing things as whole because reality is inherently complex, deeply interrelated, and messy. Order exists, but it is non-linear and dynamic. This is what we now understand as the systems basis of the real universe "as it actually is." In the postindustrial context, World One must be approached with theory and principle rather than with tools and expertise; everything is networked and globally connected; and outcomes are always anticipated in flexible terms of scenario planning and backcasting.

- World Two—Subjective perspectives of the private individual, or what Kant calls phenomena: to Bohm this is the local explicate order of perception, what we are restricted to by our senses and limited cognition. Aldus Huxley describes this in *The Doors of Perception* and Herbert Simon relates it to "bounded cognition."[35] This is the world of personal intuition gained through the lens of experience and the cloud of heuristic shortcuts. For Hayek, this is intentional and artificial order.[36] World Two is full of first-hand knowledge that we draw on instinctively from our own internal resources; but this knowledge must be recognized as only shorthand approximations of reality filtered for quick and easy response to the constant rush of waking conscious experience. On the other hand, without such contingent knowledge, we cannot achieve much in the way of higher understanding or participate in intersubjective discourse. To

Plato, the World Two realm of subjective perceptions is like the shadows we cast on the walls of the cave while pointing at them as fires burn behind us out of our sight. In postindustrial thought, World Two is the world of symptoms which signal toward but only hint at underlying dynamics.

- World Three—Intersubjective knowledge based on shared constructions of complex realities: for Popper, this is the world of discourse and falsification. As a rude example, we only know that sulfur stinks because there is a preponderance of agreement on the matter; so it is accepted as factual. The postindustrial position maintains that this underlying complexity is always the true description of reality we should embrace, even though that reality is dynamic, contingent, non-linear, and seemingly nondeterministic. Dealing with this complexity is thus recognized as a "hermeneutic" process of interpretation by iterative cycles: observation, learning, adductive proposition, trial test for fit, and back to observation. Finally, World Three is the realm of inclusive person-to-person relation and discourse; inclusive in that it involves: people as mattering in observation, people's perceptions in the definition of problems and projects, and people as not only shapers of destiny but also as stakeholders in the destination. It is thus a team world rather than a hero world. The adductive and hermeneutic basis of World Three operates much in the way that we describe design. The construct of design is itself, for example, a clear product of World Three formulation, as is the construct of architecture. Both design and architecture are, therefore, products of human discourse. As individuals we may have private beliefs and values about design and architecture, but until we participate in the defining discourse at a World Three level our private values and beliefs are meaningless to society at large.

This World Three basis of dynamic systems and complexity science demands a rethinking of today's often negative attitudes concerning the relation of science and architecture. As all forms of human pursuit are now fully given over to systems thinking and the realization of the ubiquitous nature of embedded complexity, it is essential that architecture not remain a discipline in denial (see Table 2.5).

Table 2.5 Postindustrial professions

Physics	Quantum mechanics and the Unified Field Theory (Bohr, Heisenberg, Hawking)
Engineering	Non-linear and chaotic systems
Psychology	Self-actualization and psychosynthesis (Maslow, Graf)
Sociology	Knowledge-based culture (Kuhn)
Business	Industrial Organization Psychology
Medicine	Holistic health and mind/body healing (Chopra)
Agriculture	Organic gardening and beneficial insects (Rodale)
Economics	Life-cycle costs and externalized accounting (Henderson)

Source: After Bachman (2003).

Looking Within: Complexity and Philosophy

> our experiential relationship with architecture is fundamentally of a different order from that of the other arts. With architecture, we are submerged in the experience, whereas the relationship between us and a painting or a symphony is much more one of simple exposure . . . our aesthetic experience with architecture is one of submergence rather than passive and contemplative exposure, as in the case of art.
>
> (James Marston Fitch 1988: 4)[37]

Instrumental Versus Constructed Experience

Every architect operates from a personal position defined by a set of beliefs and values that collectively make up their philosophical beginning points in design. In short, everyone has a set of guiding theories and principles from which they operate. This is true regardless of where an individual lands on the scale of intellectual to pragmatic attitudes about architecture, because even the most straightforward and applied approach to design will entail some discrete set of beliefs and values that, in principle, exclude other beliefs and values.

A connection is also possible to Heidegger's relational notions of personal *zuhanden* and public *vorhanden*:[38]

> For Heidegger, our first relation with things in perception and action is an integral ecological relation with things "ready-to-hand" or *zuhanden*. On the other hand we also construct spaces of relations with things in the world which makes them communicable and part of our knowledge. This is our relation with things "present-at-hand" or *vorhanden*.
>
> (Stephen Read 2008: 9)[39]

Looking Forward: Complexity and Architecture

To relate the hidden dimension of complexity to architecture we can observe that the designer is always required to reduce intolerably complicated requirements into a single well-resolved, finite, and easily constructed building form. Rather than surrender to those intolerable requirements as a rationale for reductive simplicity however, architects typically find that the true richness of the design lies in transforming complication into complexity. There is no reason the solution should be a static one simply because its features must be condensed to the legal detail of construction documents.

This discussion does not imply that reality is only a construct of our imagination or experience; quite the contrary: chaos theory is not about disarray and confusion; it is just a deeper order, nature's order. Rudolf Arnheim,[40] the noted Gestalt psychologist who has focused on architectural aesthetics, has said: "a tendency to attain order is by no means absent from inorganic systems . . . in a world replete with systems of structural organization, orderliness is a state universally aspired to and often brought about." The complex systems all around us are always ordered, patterned, and well behaved according to some set of complex relationships. It is just that those ebb and flow relationships are so interwoven that they transcend our direct perceptions or cause and our corresponding understanding. Like the form of a tree or a cloud, they appear to behave spontaneously, when in fact they are shaped in every detail by an endless web of deeply interrelated determinate forces. The agents of formulation, consequence, and resulting product operate independently and far beyond the collective global local order we can see.

To deal with complex systems then, it is clearly necessary to deal holistically with the overarching patterns of their behavior and not surrender to intuitive, first order, superficial, or mechanistic manipulations of separate pieces of the puzzle. When direct causal linkages are not evident, human recourse is to operate by principles and theories rather than by experience, expertise, or intuition. This again is a manifestation of postindustrial progress and civilization in general: to look beyond the first order appearance of things to our everyday direct perceptions and heuristic shortcut reasoning; and to seek the underlying relations and complexities that animate the true essence of our world.

It is obvious then that the true complexity of a problem will never give rise to a simple deterministic solution. This suggests that strategic understanding of complex problems is most appropriate as a beginning point for the adductive insertion of design intention and as a regulating tool for evaluating physical design—further implying that strategic design and physical design are both separable and compatible.

To relate the hidden dimension of complexity to architecture we can observe that the designer is always required to reduce intolerably complex requirements into a single well-resolved finite form, but also that there is no reason the solution should be a static one simply because its features must be condensed to the legal detail of construction documents. The corresponding alignment of science, architecture, and postindustrial society was shown in Table 1.1.

This suggests that strategic understanding of complex problems is most appropriate as a beginning point for the adductive insertion of design intention and as a regulating tool for evaluating physical design—further implying that strategic design and physical design are both separable and compatible.

It follows that architectural design, like all real-world situations that are examined in sufficient depth, will reveal systemic problems of both detailed complexity and of dynamic complexity. On one hand, selecting and combining materials or colors will involve detailed complexity. These details all act at the local level of human perception and their operations are relatively intuitive and mechanistic. On the other hand, thermodynamic stability, construction sequence, ecological balance, occupant satisfaction, flexible expansion, and most other problems of strategic design will always entail feedback loops and dynamic complexity. Like the tree and the cloud, these dynamic systems all operate at non-local levels of reality which are not directly discernible to human perception. They are inscrutable to intuition; be they the micro scale of molecular heat transfer or the macro scale of long-term ecological balance. Although dynamic systems operate outside of direct human perception, they do nonetheless have real and consequential impacts. Using local scale perceptions to make non-local scale decisions can therefore lead to unpredictable, unintentional, and entirely dysfunctional results, even if those shortcomings are not revealed in the initial stages of operation.

Turning now directly to architecture, Precept Four of Chapter 1 described the strategic and physical spheres of design as the dynamic tandem that leads to holistic and mindful architecture, wherein the whole is different from the sum of its strategic and physical parts. If the whole is synergistic and greater than the parts, the idea is that a building is thus potentially animated by complexity and an identifiable character of architecture will emerge. Like all the other tandems illustrated in Figure 2.1 then, the physical and strategic spheres of design can be seen as a dynamic system of generative difference, oscillation, hysteresis, feedback, ambiguity, and purpose. And like the shared constructions of World Three in postindustrial terms, physical and strategic spheres of design are themselves constructions that are needed to comprise a higher order construct: architecture. In the range of higher and lower order constructs then, we eventually reach a point where terms must be operationalized in concrete measurable units. This is necessary in order to facilitate the highest order discourse. That operationalizing of the two spheres is what follows. To link complexity in design with complexity in the world, Chapter 3 will then advance an examination of buildings as to their own complex, bimodal, and deeply interrelated systemic nature.

The physical sphere has already been characterized in this discussion as that element which evokes a direct and significant human response. This affect of physical immediacy is how architects embody sublime, transcendent, non-ordinary experience of the world into human occupation of the built environment. In evoking direct experience, physical design is that which elevates our perception of the world from an everyday numb experience to a feeling of being in the moment. The physical element essentially provides meaningful place rather than functional space. It is the Zen equivalent of seeing rather than just looking, hearing rather than just listening, tasting rather than just eating, and feeling rather than just touching. Martin Heidegger's existential perspective is a congruent touchstone for this, given the many comparisons of his work to the characteristics of Eastern thought. In this sense, physical design differentiates the higher order construct of architecture from mere buildings because architecture is that which succeeds in all those ways of bringing us into the immediate world.[41] Building further on Heidegger and his assertions from the 1920 *Being and Time*, Dasein is the consciousness defined as caring about what it means to be in the world. Clearly we can designate the architect as the Dasein consciousness in this description of physical design.

The strategic sphere, by contrast, has been described here as a collection of activities conventionally but mistakenly relegated to "predesign" and other secondary levels of status. As an amalgamation of design tasks, the list of strategic activities would include planning and programming, constructability and serviceability, adaptability and flexibility, sustainability and a host of other words ending in ability. More recently the components of professional design services have also been extended to include continuous commissioning that starts before design and runs through the life of the building. Likewise, the concerns of post-occupancy evaluation constitute a new design service intended to verify and validate design intentions.

Taken collectively, all these strategic design concerns are related to one single goal: How does architectural design embody human intelligence in the built environment? That is the role of the strategic sphere.

Comparing the two spheres of design in this systems perspective of mindful architecture, it becomes obvious that architects endow the built environment with qualities that form a complementary whole. Physical design is the endowment of human significance, while strategic design is how architects embody human intelligence. These are, again, literally comparable to right brain and left brain thinking as our rationale and emotive hemispheres. In another complementary sense, physical design is about immediacy while strategic design is about foresight. The immediacy of physical design is vested in direct experience, while the foresight of strategic design is manifest in human intelligence.

We now return to the question of how strategic design and physical design are brought together to form a whole that is greater than the simple sum of the two spheres. Taken negatively, antagonists dedicated to one sphere or another of design might argue that the opposite sphere lacks veracity, or that some danger is inherent in the basic assumptions of whatever is not wholly acceptable physical design to some, or something falling short of independently viable strategic design to another. In either case the argument here will be that pluralistic thinking is required to achieve an integral whole, for while devotees of physical design or strategic design chauvinism may be correct on many points or in specific circumstances, neither are they completely correct or accurate in a general or useful way. For the organism of design to have adaptive and self-balancing dynamic success, we must think inclusively and holistically about full-minded architecture and not engage schizophrenic babble of half-brained design. This mindfulness is more than an analogy; it is a literal example of architectural thought and the wellspring of human cognition.

There are nonetheless some notable symptoms that do arise when design loses balance and slips into a dysfunctional relation of physical and strategic dimensions. As simple reminders then, the following items should serve as beginning lists of some potential imbalances. Please note that no explicit mention of beauty or aesthetics is made here at this point of the discussion— those issues are addressed in Chapter 6.

- Physical design can zealously slip into the flawed rationale of art for art's sake,
- The epicurean pleasure principle is not an unquestioned or complete value structure,
- Design gestures alone do not guarantee that corresponding results will be realized,
- Expressive form as sculpture is not an exclusionary pursuit of architecture,
- Resolution of form must not exclude resolution of program at any phase of the design work.

Likewise, design inspirations from strategic mandates must be more than well-meaning intentions:

- Strategic design can autocratically erode into a dark utopian stranglehold,
- The yoke of efficiency should not preclude enjoyment,

- Technical precision should not exclude spontaneous expression,
- Accuracy does not excuse ugliness or justify awkward physical solutions,
- Cost does not trump value,
- Function does not guarantee appreciation.

Animation

Falling back on the comparison of the physical and strategic design spheres with Kelso's corresponding two brain hemispheres, we can extend the analogy beyond whole-minded versus schizophrenic design thinking into the realm of the animated versus the artificial. Mary Shelley's 1818 novel *Frankenstein* is a good model for this distinction between vital animation and mechanistic device, but not because of Shelley's warning on the perils of the industrial revolution or how that warning presages the postindustrial era; that theme is just ironically parallel to the present topic.[42] Instead, the Two Spheres comparison to mindful animation is meant here in a more central theme to press home and summarize issues regarding the complex whole. So, not unlike the tree farm and the forest analogy, the difference between an architecture of animated wholes versus one of nuts-and-bolts monsters can be differentiated by the presence or absence of inherent and essential complexity. Frankenstein's soulless creature "Adam" was never truly animated of course; it basically had all the right parts in all the right places, but it could never transcend its fundamental essence as a machine. The complexity from which an animated consciousness could emerge was lacking somehow. The whole was, for Dr. Frankenstein's creation, nothing more than the simple sum of its parts. The creature was assembled from a laundry list of anatomical parts, and no extent of completeness, quality, or the particular arrangement of parts could ever extend it to a complex whole. The recipe was lacking some animating ingredient.

Unlike Dr. Frankenstein's creature though, living organisms and other truly systemic organizations all around us display properties and behaviors of deeply interrelated and interacting components. They exhibit spontaneity, pattern, purpose, and intention. They are self-correcting and self-sustaining. They have meaning and, finally, they are beautiful to us. These all being qualities we wish to invest in our architecture, reason dictates that design should aspire to the same complex properties and behaviors. In our emerging neotechnic era, the opportunities to do so are definitely blossoming.

Chapter 3

Buildings as Complex Systems

> I argue that the framework based on the description of fundamental flows of energy and matter—and the ways these distend, hurtle, pause, wait, accelerate—not only illuminates the behavior of buildings, it also makes clear the relationships between the building and its site, and its wider context.
>
> (Groák 1992: 38)[1]

Chapters 1 and 2 described physical and strategic architecture in the broad terms of a designerly way of thought that captures the inherent complexity of architecture. Those two chapters are thus primarily concerned with the intellectual topic of architecture as a reflective human pursuit. Chapter 3 now turns from the reflective topic to the productive subject of the matter by turning the focus to the material artifacts of architectural design; predominantly that of constructed buildings.

The Building as Flow

In everyday experience, we naturally and commonly relate to buildings as objects in the landscape and thus, in Vitruvian terms, we appreciate them primarily as physical forms of functional, durable, and aesthetic value.[2] But this everyday sense of a building is only a first order notion that is largely limited to our direct immediate sensory perception: what has already been described here as the immediate or local scale perception dominated by sensory experiences of vision, touch, sound, and aroma. As a direct result, these immediate sensations have reflective ripple effects, evoking associations, memories, and other mental encounters. As we all know, the reflective affect is often as powerful as the direct first order perceptions, but the stimuli for both still reside in the immediate physical scale of our object orientation to the building, be it a greater building or, just the same, a lessor one. This entire local scale of everyday experience is the realm of the physical sphere of architecture: direct, immediate, sublime, and transformative.

Another level of reality, however, exists for every building. This other reality resides in a building's intangible matrix of invisible flows and relations: the building as an interactive set of dynamic forces. This non-local scale of reality is not directly accessible to our human senses, even though we experience their actions and relations. One feature of this physically impercep-tible existence, as described by Groák, is that of flow: people, air, light, heat, sound, information, water, materials, pollution, moisture, product, and so forth.[3] We are certainly aware of these phenomena of flow as they impact our senses, but no one can directly observe or detect them at the mechanical level of physical behavior. From a position on the moon, for instance, you cannot see light flowing from the sun to the Earth. We experience light only in the reflected brightness of objects, but never as the flow of luminous flux. We know how people circulate around in buildings but have only an intuitive idea about their patterns of movement. Intellectual understanding of building physics is thus distinct from perceptual experience of flow. This difference goes back again to Popper's Three World framework of World One physics versus World Two subjective realities.[4]

The easiest example in buildings is the physical sensation of air temperature versus the corresponding but inscrutable flows of thermal energy. As human vision does not extend into the infrared wavelengths of electromag-netic radiation, we cannot see heat radiating from every object in the universe warmer than absolute zero ($-273°C$ or $-460°F$). Nor can we observe molecular level conduction of heat through solid materials or the latent heat of phase change as a liquid gains enough energy to reach a vapor state. We can feel a cold draft of moving air of course, but we cannot sense the buoyant forces that drive the motion of convective heat transfer.

At this non-local, World One scale of physics then, a building is conceptually an ordered set of many sorts of organized flow. Working back-wards from organized flows to their channels through material and space, we can thereby reconceptualize a building, not as an everyday physical object, but as conceptual circulation systems composed of conduits, reservoirs, barriers, valves, switches, transformers, and other modulating elements. This non-local scale of reality is what has been described here as the strategic sphere of architecture: intelligent, insightful, responsive, and performative.

The intellectual topic of architecture taken in these complementary aspects of physical and strategic design has already been discussed as a complex and systemic issue of design and a part of what defines the construct of architecture. Interpreted into Popper's terms then, architecture is a World Three entity of shared construction, discourse, and critique (Table 3.1).[5] Likewise, the complementary strategic aspect of architectural design reveals a mode of complexity that operates in the World One realm of physics, biology, and chemistry. The circle closes in the experiential context of architecture as invoked by Fitch in Chapter 2, because personal experiences occur in the World Two domain of subjective and intuitive frames of reality.[6]

Like Groák's depiction of buildings as flow, the idea of dynamic flux coursing through a series of filters, barriers, and switches is also well described in Norberg-Shultz's seminal work, *Intentions in Architecture*.[7] More recent treatments are frequently motivated by high performance and ecological aspi-rations. John Tilman Lyle's *Regenerative Design for Sustainable Development*, for example, lists twelve basic principles of sustainability including "managing storage . . ., shaping form to manifest flow . . ., and shaping form to manifest process."[8] Although such manifestations of flow are seldom, if ever, directly observable at the local scale of perception, they are nonetheless part of a

Table 3.1 Karl Popper's Three Worlds: Some tripartite aspects as interpreted into the Two Spheres approach

World One	World Two	World Three
Objective Fact	Personal Cognition	Shared Constructions
Science	Experience	Philosophy
Strategic Sphere	Physical Sphere	Architecture
Objects, States, and Systems	Perceptions	Culture
Physics, Chemistry, Biology	Personal Intuition	Virtual Knowledge
Things as They Are	Subjective Impressions	Intersubjective Agreement
Facts	Understandings	Discourse and Critique
Data	Information	Wisdom
Knowledge	Expertise	Theory
Dualistic	Multiplistic	Pluralistic
Observation	Analysis	Synthesis
Declarative	Procedural	Structural
Truth	Conduct	Authenticity
Noumena	Phenomena	Ethos
Phenomenology	Experiential Context	Ontology
Non-local Order	Local Order	Aesthetics
Spontaneous	Intentional	Relational
Discovery	Invention	Coherence
Entropy	Order	Sustainable

building's real behavior and so are always a primary component of how we ultimately experience the built environment.

Our natural everyday object orientation to buildings is certainly a valid recognition of how we routinely encounter them in piecemeal and incidental ways, but for the architect, this easy grasp cannot substitute for the complete, complex, and whole reality of the built environment and all the meaningful ways in which we experience and occupy buildings and landscapes across time and circumstance. Architects cannot afford the ready-made satisfaction of local experience and photogenic imagery alone—that would be superficial. Nor can the gap be closed by well-intended but otherwise inoperative symbolic abstraction. As Louis Kahn quipped, "A painter can paint square wheels on a cannon to express the futility of war. A sculptor can carve the same square wheels. But an architect must use round wheels."[9] In the end such superficial measures do not even meet Vitruvian criteria because without accommodating flow the functional, durable, and aesthetic qualities of a building would be far from satisfactory. Some ruinous evidence of this is suggested by Mostafavi and Leatherbarrow's *On Weathering: The Life of Buildings in Time*, wherein some rather famous works of architecture are shown as static objects in denial of time and nature's patina, and hence to be stained and somewhat naive regarding their role as agents of dynamic flow.[10]

The Building as Phenomena

At this point some clarification is needed to disambiguate the phenomena of building physics from the philosophical perspective of phenomenology, existentialism, and transcendentalism (see Table 3.2). Physics relates to the building as it is, independent of human perception but understood abstractly. Sensate perceptions, on the other hand, belong to our subjective experiences of the building. In the terms of Immanuel Kant's transcendental philosophy, the physics are the noumea "just as it is" and the subjective experiences are the noesis or "subjective experience." In relation to the framework of Popper's Three Worlds, physics is in the non-local realm of World One and subjective human perceptions belong to World Two.[11] Both noumea and noesis are intended design outcomes, but for the architect they pose two different sets of concerns: strategic and physical, respectively. It is useful then to discriminate between the phenomenological concept of buildings as the abstraction of flows or noumea, and the actual human experience events of those flows as the experiential context or noesis. Table 3.2 also lists some parallels in the realms of literature and art as well as, for phenomenology alone, some

Table 3.2 Philosophies that align most closely with postpositive perspectives on science

	Phenomenology	Existentialism	Transcendentalism	Existential Phenomenology
Characteristics	Subjective experience and observation as the basis of engaging objective reality, or the personal subjective and introspective consciousness of objects or events as opposed to their analytical objective descriptions	Reality as the creation of meaning via exercise of individual choice, wherein existence precedes essence and external nurture precedes inherent nature; based on a physical experience, the expression of the human condition is key	The idea that spirituality transcends empiricism and that this difference is manifested in an individual's intuition; also focuses on the distinction between observation (phenomena) and the thing itself (noumea)	Favors dynamics, engagement, and authenticity; the unified movement of existential and phenomenological thinking
Philosophy	G.W.F. Hegel, Edmund Husserl, Martin Heidegger, Alfred Schutz, Eugen Fink, William James, Max Scheler, Charles Sanders Peirce, Don Ihde	Pascal, Hegel, Søren Kierkegaard, Friedrich Nietzsche, Fyodor Dostoevsky, Jean-Paul Sartre, Karl Jaspers, Simone de Beauvoir, Paul Tillich, Maurice Merleau-Ponty, Paul Ricoeur	Emmanuel Kant, Jean-Paul Sartre, Arthur Schopenhauer, Jürgen Habermas	Martin Heidegger, Hans-Georg Gadamer

(*Continued overleaf*)

Table 3.2 *Continued*

	Phenomenology	Existentialism	Transcendentalism	Existential Phenomenology
Literature and Art	Marcel Proust, André Bazin, Christian Metz, Jean Mitry, Donald Judd, Michael Fried, Jasper Johns	Franz Kafka, Fyodor Dostoevsky, Jackson Pollock, Arshile Gorky, Willem de Kooning, Jean-Luc Godard, Ingmar Bergman, François Truffaut, Stanley Kubrick, Woody Allen, David Lynch, Michael Szymczyk, Samuel Beckett	Henry David Thoreau, Ralph Waldo Emerson, Emily Dickenson, Thomas Carlyle, Samuel Taylor Coleridge	NA
Architecture	Christian Norberg-Schulz, David Canter, Thomas Thiis-Evensen, Gaston Bachelard, Karsten Harries, David Leatherbarrow, Juhani Pallasmaa, Alberto Perez-Gómez, Stein Eiler Rasmussen, Dalibor Vesely, Joseph Rykwert, David Seamon & Robert Mugerauer, Alexander Tzonis, Liane Lefaivre, Kenneth Frampton	NA	NA	NA
Design Proponents	Alvar Aalto, Charles Moore, Steven Holl, Peter Zumthor, Daniel Libeskind, Jørn Utzon, Donlyn Lyndon	NA	NA	NA

corresponding writings in architecture and the designers most closely associated with phenomenological approaches. Table 3.3 samples some comparative perspectives from positivist and relativist philosophy.

In terms of the physics that drive these noumeal flows, architects must harmonize their schemes with the dynamic requirements of performance in use. This almost always entails thermal, luminous, acoustic, structural, ventilation, plumbing, electrical, communication, informational, and logistical flows

Table 3.3 Philosophy in the context of positivism, postpositivism, and relativism

	Characteristics	Proponents
Cartesian	Dualism which understands matter and mind as belonging to separate realms	René Descartes, Geraud de Cordemoy, Spinoza, Antoine Le Grand
Positivism	Facts and laws have truth value; there is one objective reality; human senses collect objective data; the use of induction to establish general truths; causality	John Locke, Hume, Auguste Compte, Ayer, Carnap, Hemple
Postpositivism	Realism, experimental methodology, qualitative approach to phenomena, multiple realities dependent on context and all of them are socially constructed, relies on warrants, testability, falsification, assertability	Thomas Kuhn, Michael Polanyi, Feyerabend, Hanson, Jacob Bronowski, Karl Popper
Relativism	Assertion that all truths are relative to embeddedness in culture, • language, history, or other contexts; cross-comparisons are therefore often incommensurable	Paul Feyerabend, L. Ron Hubbard, George lakoff, Isaiah Berlin, Stanley Fish
Pragmatism	A mediating philosophy that attempts to overcome the realist versus empiricist divide; works by clarifying concepts, hypotheses, and metaphysical differences of practice by identifying their practical consequences	van Fraansen, Charles Sanders Peirce, William James, John Dewey, C.I. Lewis
Quietism	A view of philosophy as therapeutic mediation between confused concepts and frameworks in other discourse and takes those confusions to constitute pseudo-problems brought about by futile misunderstandings; denies the productive role of philosophy in defining truth or producing theories	Ludwig Wittgenstein, Gilbert Ryle, J.L. Austin, Norman Malcolm, John McDowell, Richard Rorty

to hold in controlled balances and equilibriums for the safety and welfare of people occupying the building. Flow, in turn, is always generated by potential. Ventilation air flow is a result of pressure differences, for example, and thermal flow requires temperature difference.

The Building as System

At the World One level then, a fully functioning building is a complex dynamic system in every sense of the terms defined in Chapter 2. That is to say, buildings consist of interrelated parts whose composite behavior is not limited to the complete laundry list of the behaviors exhibited by individual parts. A working building is also situated in a cybernetic feedback relation with its environment and this relation occurs at many scales: from Earth–sun geometry of light and shade, to micro climatic interventions of the site, to microscopic qualities of indoor air.

Most elementally, systems are defined as sets of organized flows, and the same definition applies to architectural systems. A structural system orders flows of gravity and lateral loads to produce static equilibrium. A thermal system orders heat gain and heat loss to produce thermal equilibrium. Even the lowly plumbing system manages flows of water, waste, and vented gases to purposefully maintain hygienic conditions. Every such system in a building is concerned with flows and balances as well as with their channeling and regulation.

At the second level, buildings are systems of systems. Beyond simple thermal equilibrium, for example, there is a churning matrix of thermodynamic events going on in every building that involves many first order systems. On a cold day, for instance, heat gain from lighting systems and solar heat gain from windows in the envelope system are just two of the heat gain contributions that would interact with heat loss by mechanical ventilation from the air conditioning as well as thermal conduction through the building envelope, including the windows through which solar heat is simultaneously being gained.

As a complex and emergent structure of the building, this matrix of heat gain and heat loss leads to a set of conditions in each area of the building where heat gain and heat loss are relatively equal (Figure 3.1). Since the heat losses are all driven by temperature potential between indoor and outdoor temperatures, there is a theoretical outside thermal equilibrium balance point temperature (BPT) at which the respective building area's heat gain is equal to its heat loss. To accurately anticipate this BPT, however, it is also necessary to consider the thermal inertia and heat capacity of the exterior envelope as well as of the interior mass of the building and all its contents. Even the anticipated heat loss through the envelope is impacted by absorbed solar energy that elevates the "sol-air" exterior surface temperatures whereby a roof membrane can reach 170°F (77°C). A final complexity arises with the changing flux of occupancy levels, lighting controls, use schedules, waste heat from appliances and electronics, and so forth. Consequently, and just as in the Lorenz "Butterfly Effect," the final estimation of BPT at any one particular time is extremely sensitive to the assumed initial conditions.[12] And just as the envelope, electrical lighting, fenestration, and occupant systems are all involved in this thermal matrix, there are equally complex interactions involved in other second order systems-of-systems.

The complexity captured in the BPT example approaches the level of systems as organisms, or systems as species. This critical distinction of the Two Spheres reveals how vacuous the usual generic reference to systems as

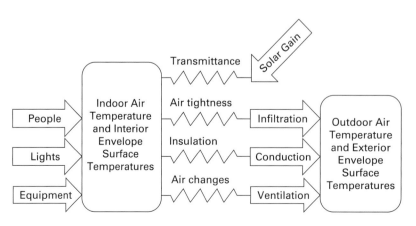

mere hardware can be, as if the system in question was nothing more than an isolated set of nuts and bolts catalog components. The more accurate notion of Systems-as-Species also transcends the slightly more enlightened views of building systems as a kit of parts, as design vocabulary and grammar, or as typological building blocks. By example of the lesser concepts of systems, we can name the kit of parts Crystal Palace and the typology of a high rise as constituted by steel frame, curtain wall, and elevator.[13]

To solidify the BPT complexity as indicative of systemic traits found in living organisms, consider that live animals maintain thermal equilibrium in nearly identical fashion to buildings, and do so in adaptive ways that respond to their environmental circumstances. A human's metabolism, for example, like that of a building, is systematically regulated to an internal temperature suited to the purpose of body function. There are internal gains from oxidation of food calories; there are thermal exchanges with the environment through conduction, convection, evaporation, and radiation; and there are regulating processes of skin response, muscular constriction, perspiration, and respiration. This is not to mention the insulation factor of external cladding with clothes.

So each organism and each building has its own unique and constantly fluctuating BPT. For humans it is usually in the range of 68 to 75°F (20 to 24°C) and is associated with normal skin surface temperature of 81°F (27°C). With physical activity and correspondingly increased internal heat gains however, BPT lowers as it must be colder outside to produce equilibrium. With additional insulation, BPT decreases again for the same reason. In small, well-insulated buildings that are surface load dominated such as a residence, BPT is usually in the 55 to 60°F (13 to 16°C) range, but for large, internal load dominated buildings with massive internal heat gain relative to their surface area, the typical BPT could actually be below freezing and the building area might consequently be in the cooling mode all year. Electrically lit interior area office zones that have no exposure to envelope heat loss are just one such building area with a typically low balance point.

Note that BPT is so complex that it is typically determined in the absence of solar gain impacts so as to control for uneven exterior skin temperature and for varying amounts of solar radiation received through various windows facing various orientations. It is not just complicated; it is complex.

A city can, in this regard, be compared to a zoo of buildings, each block full of animal organisms with specific metabolisms and a range of balance point temperatures. It stands to reason that the architect of the zoo builds different wings to provide different habitats: the cold-blooded reptiles in one wing, the warm-blooded mammals in another. Tiny birds and rodents go in one kind of environment; big cats and zebras in another. And, as the adaptive thermal regulation mechanisms for each of the creatures determines their species' characteristic behavior, the zoo architect provides warm stones for the snakes to sleep on and deep ponds for the elephants to hose themselves with.

The human occupied city is no less complex or thermally differentiated than the zoo city. Office building areas with high-density heat loads from people, lights, and equipment are poor candidates for passive solar winter heating. Houses in warm–humid climates abhor external envelope mass. For any specific design situation then, the architect must understand the subject building's thermal metabolism as well as its host environment. Then, in adapting the subject building to its setting, the thermal flows, reservoirs, capacitors, barriers, and filters can be purposefully orchestrated.

Of course, our zoo architect could simply specify mechanically controlled environments for each species in the zoo. It is doubtful that anyone would think very highly of such a design, however, for there is something essential about the relationship of the animal to its natural and systemically aligned habitat that we habitually enjoy. A series of temperature-controlled, see-through glass cages with diorama backdrops would hardly be worth the ticket. It is a wonder then why we too commonly accept exactly that same generic solution in our human city.

Expanding from temperature-driven BPT thermal complexity to a larger set of environmental issues, consider the overlay of organizational zoning principles in the amalgamation of thermal, solar, luminous, aerodynamic, and acoustic response. At the level of plan organization alone, thermal organization of independent zones is nominally made in response to solar orientation, exposure area, occupancy activity, and use schedule. Luminous zoning places visually demanding task work spaces into areas where daylight is admitted. Flat diffuse lighting from the north and direct surface modeling light from the south set apart the different tasks, and the local sky conditions are anticipated. Acoustic zoning organizes spaces internally according to their traits of noisy, quiet, silent, public, private, and buffer areas. Site conditions impact the placement of all spaces. By the time all such organizing forces are overlaid and aligned into one plan, a considerable amount of strategic human intelligence has been embedded into a complex pattern of interactive and interdependent spaces, their barrier separations, and their filtered connections. The environmental flows have been organized, at least at the scale of area configuration.

Expanding now from the building scale environment to the site scale, consider an even larger format overlay of organization as the resulting building footprint and sectional profile. Here again there are a number of environmental flows and fluxes to organize: thermal, solar, luminous, aerodynamic, acoustic, and storm water at the very least. Which form best responds to all of them? What relations are made between inside and out? What axis of elongation; what aspect ratio of length to width? Is it tall and thin, or short and compact? Where is the fenestration and where is the mass? How do spring breezes sweep through and how are winter winds diverted? How are noise, rain, and sun channeled? When and where is shade provided? Moreover, how does the building itself respond to seasonal change in harmony with the moving path of the sun and the patterned temporal variations in wind, rain, and temperature? Remember that winter days are short and summer days are long. How then, finally, do all these questions coalesce into a form that embodies strategic foresight, intelligent configuration, and adaptive response? Figure 3.2 conveys one such masterly orchestration of form in wind and shade: Glenn Murcutt's design of Magney House on the southeast coast of Australia.[14]

Invoking complexity and systems language from Chapter 2, the World One physics brought to bear on these environmental examples constitute a tangle of complicated factors that act as generative tandem dialogues. The architect must weave a tapestry from these interacting flows, and the building must be brought to life by the cybernetic adaptation of the building to

Figure 3.2 Magney House, Bingie Point, Australia; Glenn Murcutt, architect. To mention just the one most prominent feature, the roof of this residence responds strategically to its purpose and its environment. It is simultaneously an air foil, a solar eyebrow, and a rain channel. Illustration by Joseph Little, a student at the University of Houston.

its environment. The building thus achieves integrity as a holistic, complex, dynamic, and interactive system. These mandates are imperative for the Two Spheres strategic qualification as architecture as robust, animated, adaptive, and intelligent. Designs that fail to make this animating synthesis must be judged as lacking in at least one significant way. These lesser designs are, in the environmental context at least, more apt to be considered as mere buildings: mechanistic, reductive, brittle, static, and simplistic.

It is not certain, of course, that systemic environmental complexity or any other singular dimension of complexity will elevate the final design to the status of a cherished work of architecture. Moreover, the synergy of a building and its activities with its macro and micro climatic environment is a relative quality that falls somewhere on a continuum and is always arguably less than perfect. Adaptation and complexity are not dichotomous conditions of black or white, inclusive and exclusive categories. The late Arthur Bowen, a founder of the international Passive and Low Energy Architecture (PLEA) network, captured this relation most adroitly by noting that "All buildings are passive; some are just more passive than others."[15] Where the threshold is drawn on this continuum is a matter for discourse and critique of each project on its own merits and within its own context, but clearly there is a margin below which a design should be deemed unsuccessful. Ultimately then, the difference between the tangle and the tapestry is a necessary and desirable condition to architecture even if some aspect of it, such as the environmental one, is not by itself sufficient.

To summarize, environmental patterns of flow are one strategic dimension of how successful buildings behave as complex systems. To that end, the examples in this section show that complexity happens at many scales—from individual components, to zones, to massing, to site, and to the greater context of regional climate. Other dimensions of systems as flow can, in the same manner as environmental dynamics, be considered as equally necessary to architectural animation. Luminous, acoustic, structural, ventilation, plumbing, electrical, communication, informational, and logistical organization were mentioned above as inscrutable World One flows and all of them "distend, hurtle, pause, wait, accelerate" and otherwise make up experiential manifestations of a building, as Groák, Norberg-Schultz, and Lyle all suggest.[16] All of those forces of flux will shape the corresponding formal response of the building as a luminous, aerodynamic, structural, or other response system, and then interactions among the systems will establish the building itself as a higher order system organized out of the fundamental systems.

The Building as Program

Another major vein of architectural complexity originates from the way in which the overall goals of design are defined. This is the foundational problem statement phase of a project, what William Peña termed *Problem Seeking* in his seminal 1969 book of the same name.[17] Briefing, programming, and planning are all different names for the activities typically associated with problem definition in conventional practice, and, as the date of Peña's work indicates, even these rudimentary aspects are relatively new to the profession of architecture. Postindustrial change is, however, already heralding a new expanded set of concepts for this activity, and knowledge-based practices with postindustrial sounding names such as scenario planning, backcasting, and morphological analysis are increasingly finding their way into the conversation. These changes come largely from the client world of business planning, but policy analysis, military gaming, and future studies are also major practitioners. The commonality is perhaps that all of these new modes of strategic foresight follow the admonition first accredited to Dennis Gabor, who won the 1971 Nobel Prize for Physics by inventing holography: "The future cannot be predicted, but futures can be invented. It was man's ability to invent which has made human society what it is."[18]

This shift from architect-centered problem definition to an increasing focus on business model planning evokes a radically postindustrial idea— namely that the project destination is more inherently a matter of knowledge-driven collaborative road-mapping than of spontaneous and genius imaginative invention. Classic strategic planning of values and mission, goals and objectives, and then strategies and tactics, has built-in currency with the client–user world. Growing postindustrial awareness of the use of such project knowledge to produce value is a trend that reinforces the desire to plan accordingly. Such concerns also lead to new systemic methods that can be described in a linear and simplistic way as a technique of visioning desirable goals, defining how to think about getting there, measuring objective progress along the way, and continually adjusting the plan to fit changing circumstances.

Scenario planning, for example, is attributed to the futurist and noted systems thinker Herman Kahn for work done in the same mid-1960s time frame as Gabor's *Inventing the Future*.[19] Embedded in this systemic scenario planning technique is the non-linear cybernetic steering provided by feedback—from both the interim measurement of defined objectives as well as from the inevitable changing circumstances that occur sporadically in the timeline of any substantial project.

The most important implication of these postindustrial planning evolutions, aside from the fact that they are exogenous expectations imposed by clients rather than enlightened design methods developed by architects, is the virtual injunction that now requires an underlying stage of meta-design, whereby the first stage of a project is a plan for how to define the problem space and operational techniques that are used, in turn, to draw the project roadmap.

Beyond Programming

Applied intelligence also pertains to other means of shaping the architectural problem definition in the formative and developmental stages of design. This includes construction management and value engineering activities, both of which are controlled by the building owner rather than the architect. Building commissioning is yet another activity that is ever more increasingly part of managing the realization of design intent. Commissioning is a process of continuous reassessment and realignment between the manners by which the building is actually used and the ways in which building controls, operations, and maintenance are performed to most efficiently support that specified use. Commissioning not only assures that the owner's intent is being realized, it also verifies and maintains the integrated operation of multiple systems, many of which can have overlapping and conflicting functions. Finally, commissioning enhances the intelligent management of buildings by serving as an accurate operating manual that is continually updated. As such, commissioning runs ideally from predesign through all phases of the project and continues into occupancy. As the building is maintained through its useful life, the idea is that Continuous Commissioning (Cx) is in place to periodically tune the building and accommodate changes in use, efficiency of equipment, and prime opportunities to upgrade. Annual commissioning in this manner has frequently been shown to be cost-effective as a means of managing the increasing sophistication of buildings in use per their systems, operational procedures, and continuous changes in use. Note that here again this commissioning work is not controlled by the architect, but rather by a third party who typically is paid by and reports to the owner.

Another postindustrial impact on this issue of problem definition is that of enhanced stakeholder involvement. This expands the programming problem definition to broadly and frequently include the expectations of user–occupant representation rather than solely that of the building owners and perhaps upper level management. Broader representation of course suggests that conflicting perspectives and expectations will more likely emerge. Just as in commissioning, this stakeholder involvement runs from the early stages of problem definition in predesign phases and continues through the occupation of the building as Post Occupancy Evaluation (POE). POE is generally concerned with the performance of the building in use as perceived directly by the users of the building. Collectively then, POE and Cx pose a new challenge to the architect, because now their design intentions are subject both to verification on the basis of measured realization and validation as to their appropriateness in the first place.

Evidence-Based Design (EBD)

Clinical practice is commonly defined as the resolution of one case built on the resolution of many cases. Several professions have extensive clinical databases documenting very large numbers of cases that can be extracted from as applicable to a current case. Medicine has a proliferation of such databases: pharmacology, toxicology, immunology, epidemiology, and so forth. Law and architecture, on the other hand, share but one, a common term for their more limited archives which both professions refer to as "precedent." The parallels of precedent in law and architecture are actually intriguing enough to have attracted considerable scholarship into their operations.[20]

The clinical use of precedent cases in architecture has been, however, considerably less developed than of legal cases. Up until the 1980s, architects tended to use precedent studies primarily as investigations on stylistic models or functional typologies. Much has changed in the interim however. EBD is quietly gaining influence as an empirical research-based method of establishing building parameters and preferred design tactics. The postindustrial proclivity to measure has bolstered this; including metrification on factors that were previously taken as either too complex to measure or intractable to change. Newfound statistical, computational, and cybernetic capabilities stimulate curiosity and facilitate these analyses. Worker productivity, climate and weather adjusted energy use patterns, student test scores, and patient recovery time are likely just the beginning entries.

Architects took their EBD cues first from evidence-based health care delivery with its robust data collection methodology and comparatively well-funded medical research.[21] Next came evidence-based delivery of education in school design. Sustainable design metrics were not far behind, and the field has since expanded into a general mode of architectural problem definition tantamount to other postindustrial planning methods such as scenario planning, commissioning, and post-occupancy evaluation.

The Building as Robot

Postindustrial attitudes on inventing the future, multiple stakeholders, post-occupancy evaluation, and continuous commissioning all have one thing in common: a hunger for data and the value that such information contributes to the design and operation of a building. The topic of automation is similar in the value that it provides, but differs as the application of cybernetics directly to buildings, as opposed to the use of information technology to think about the design of buildings, so instead of just incorporating human intelligence in our buildings, we can also imbue them with an operative intelligence of their own.

Digital instrumentation facilitates cybernetic feedback by enabling continual measurement and verification of building use, control readings and settings, and building response to the conditions and controls. Instrumentation furthers the feedback loop by storing these measurements digitally and making them readily available for analysis in formats as simple as a spreadsheet.

At the smallest level of instrumentation are devices that collect and log readings, and the related software that allows us to convert the raw collected data into visualizations, patterns, and statistical inferences. Miniature devices capable of collecting thousands of readings across months of time or divided into designated intervals between measurements are now readily available, reliable, and affordable. They are also easy to use with interface software and university serial bus (USB) connection to a computer. With a few such devices and a good plan for how to interpret the data, it is now easy to take temperature, light level, humidity, sound, and other quantitative measurements and convert them into an accurate picture of building and occupant behavior.

At a second level of instrumentation, the everyday digital control and operation of buildings is itself a growing source of diagnostic feedback. Direct Digital Control (DDC), for example, has been in use for more than twenty years. Such systems are used to automate the control logic of buildings, signal failure alarms, and to integrate the operation of several building systems such as lighting and security or energy use. Since these systems both sense building conditions and control equipment in response, they provide two-way communication between the building and the building operators. And since DDC activity is recorded, it creates a continuous record of interactions.

A third level of instrumentation takes the building to the level of artificial intelligence. At this point, the building is a robot. These control systems learn the building's use and response patterns and decide independently how to anticipate and optimize building operation. Where features of the building are dynamic, such as operable shading devices or dimmable glazing, for example, the building as robot can calculate the optimum balance of daylight versus solar heat gain and physically adjust building components to suit.

Finally, it is increasingly likely and practical to allow for the building and the occupants to interact through a second generation of robotic interface. Feedback is provided at the Oberlin Center for Environmental Studies, for example, by a dashboard-type monitoring system located near the entry. Here even passersby can observe real-time data such as how much energy the building is producing with photovoltaics versus how much it is consuming.

Beyond this, the robot may soon become an animated genie-like avatar that appears on the building computer intranet. This building-to-occupant feedback and interaction could easily and beneficially be used to initiate occupant control of their own environment.[22] And of course the whole conversation would be a matter of record and potential diagnostics, a clinical database for better commissioning and for better "lessons learned" design of the next building.

The Building as Teleology

Isaac Newton's scientific foundation of classic mechanics held that any phenomenon could be reduced to a mere collection of parts and pieces whose arrangement and movement were governed by deterministic natural laws. These natural laws were held, in turn, to predict the behavior of the whole phenomenon within a rational and ordered universe that agreed with human first order intuition as to the behavior of the universe. This Newtonian view held sway through the eighteenth and nineteenth centuries. In 1900, however,

Max Planck proposed the quantum bridge between energy and matter. In 1927, Werner Heisenberg published the Uncertainty Principle and, along with most other physicists, began the formulation of quantum mechanics.[23] The universe was thus transformed from one of rational intuitive order to one of quantum probability and indeterminacy. Matter and energy became interchangeable and interactive. Observation directly impacted measurement and state. Light is an electromagnetic wave until we look at it, but thereafter it is a photon particle. The true workings of the universe were revealed to us as counterintuitive at the microscopic and macroscopic level of behavior. Our intuitive local scale of direct immediate perception was irreparably shorn from the imperceptible macro scale quantum workings of the universe.

By the late 1950s and early 1960s, Newton's reductionist theory was quickly eroding in the face of systems theory and new understandings on nature's spontaneous creativity, self-organizing behavior, and emergent ordering principles. The first relevant congress, the Interdisciplinary Conference on Self-Organizing Systems, was held in May 1959, in Chicago,

> to bring together research workers in the fields of the Biological, Mathematical, Physical, Psychological, and Social Sciences who have actively considered the development and growth of Systems capable of spontaneous classification of their environments . . . [and] which exhibit characteristics of organization and growth, of thought and learning, of information and communication—those characteristics which are normally attributed to intelligent organisms.[24]

Teleology, as the study of how a system purposefully achieves its goals, was a prime topic of that 1959 Conference on Self-Organizing Systems. Many of the Chicago attendees were visionary scientists working in the early field of cybernetics. Heinz von Foerster, for instance, focused on self-referential systems and second order cybernetics.[25] Similarly, the London research psychologist Ross Ashby, who published *Design for a Brain* in 1952 and *Introduction to Cybernetics* in 1956, went on to become president of the Society for General Systems Research from 1962 to 1964.[26] Ashby and von Foerster were both at the University of Illinois Champaign for some time and co-published an article on biological computing in 1964.

Teleology is actually commonplace. Any complex dynamic system is goal oriented; that is to say, it has purpose and pursues that purpose opportunistically. A living organism's purpose is to sustain its own vitality, for example. This purpose, or to use the Greek word "telos", acts as what in systems terminology is called an "attractor."

In Chapter 2, the tandem forces that drive dynamic systems were shown in several examples to oscillate around what Ross Ashby identified as a calm equilibrium point.[27] In complex systems theory, we now call that equilibrium the "attractor;" and we attribute the dynamic oscillation to self-organizing behavior that seeks that equilibrium attraction state. The section of this chapter on The Building as Flow describes the thermal equilibrium balance point as just such an attractor. Figure 3.3 illustrates this ordered behavior in the familiar example of boiling water. Ilya Prigogine, pioneer cyberneticist and president of the International Academy of Science until his death in 2003, termed this dynamic

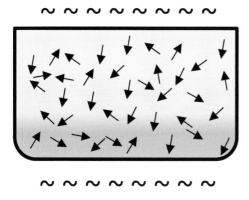

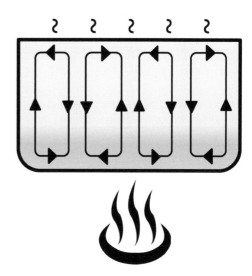

Figure 3.3 Entropy passing through a system of boiling water to produce patterned flow. Too much flow creates turbulence and too little results in homeostasis. In a cool pot of water (left), molecular motion is random and the water is in a disordered state as there is no potential of temperature difference present to produce systemic flow. In a boiling pot of water (right), each molecule becomes an autonomous agent acting locally and independently in response to the change in environmental entropy as heat passing through the pot from bottom to top. No one molecule of water has any information as to the state or behavior of any other molecule. In this heated state, self-organization always produces Bénard roll patterns of convection.

as "order through fluctuations" and compared the "Being" of Newtonian static laws with an irreversible and continuous "Becoming" of teleological behavior.[28] In all such subsequent transformations of understanding in postindustrial society and postpositive science, teleology has become a conceptual replacement for Newtonian physics and its reductive mechanical explanations.

True to the description of complex wholes, we see here what Louis Kahn, through his reading of the German philosopher Schopenhauer, called "will-existence," or simply "what the brick wanted to be."[29] Rudolf Arnheim calls this origin a center, axis, or direction.[30] In cybernetic terms this will-existence can be translated as an embryonic teleological "purpose" that drives a complex system. Teleology explains why the acorn wants to be an oak tree and how its internal organization purposefully assures it. As a drive, systemic teleological purpose is present in all complex systems including natural and man-made ones such as corporations and buildings. We might say from this that everything has some essential potential that can be actualized. This is Aristotle's Final Cause, which illustrates that the acorn's process of change and motion is ultimately, inherently, and purposefully directed at becoming an oak tree.

As this chapter shows, postindustrial society has embraced the value of well-defined problems and has also acknowledged that those problems are almost always complex and dynamic in nature. Architects though, are being swept up in this transition rather than commanding it, because their profession is, by and large, a conservative follower of the movement while their clients are the proactive leaders. Several relevant issues have been detailed here, namely: the complex behavior of buildings as sets of ordered flow and dynamic systems, the advent of architectural programming, the evolution of postindustrial planning methods, the value of continuous commissioning, and the validation of post-occupancy evaluation, evidence-based design mandates, and robotic building intelligence. In all instances, these issues relate to the building as a complex system in that they demonstrate a teleological purpose, tandem forces of motion, dynamic states of opportunistic attractors, and the feedback of cybernetic intelligence between the building and its many contexts of environment.

Part Two

Embracing Complexity

Chapter 4

Encounters with Complexity

Part One of *Two Spheres* depicted three drivers of architectural change: postindustrial society, systems thinking, and complex buildings. Part Two now examines three phases of adaptation to those evolutions: encounters, convergences, and embraces. This first chapter in the Part Two examination is a historical recounting of four architectural encounters with complexity; all originating in postindustrial transformation. That history is told through four lively tangos that architects have danced with complexity: wicked problems, messy authenticity, ordered essences, and natural ecology. Chapter 5 then illustrates some current convergences between architecture and postindustrial complexity. Chapter 6 concludes Part Two by speculating as to how these encounters and convergences might inevitably lead from a dance to a full embrace.

Introduction

Increasingly, the two histories of architectural design and complex systems are convergent, drawn together in the emerging postindustrial mandates of knowledge production, neotechnic society, globalization, economic interdependence, and ecological sustenance. But the architectural history of these encounters has seldom been couched in terms of their teleological and dynamic influences, nor have their separate operations been characterized or connected in a way that adds coherence. There has never been that full embrace of what postpositive science tells us is our best understanding of how the universe really works vis-à-vis how buildings and cities are designed to become artifacts of that reality. This chapter addresses this missing history by making explicit distinctions between each of the four modes of architectural complexity, tracing their early proponents, and characterizing their operative impacts on design.

Architecture is in fact a continuous encounter with complexity, an encounter that is inherently manifested by concerns such as initial project requirements, design goals, context of place, and performance in use. These complexities can be sketched out as:

- Design begins with a "bottom-up" need to find, identify, collect, and deductively digest vast amounts of detailed information related to user needs, site conditions, code requirements, and so forth (Peña 1969);[1]

- This bottom-up need pairs directly with an inductive "top-down" ambition for the design outcome as an authentic member of a place, a building that both has its own identity and its role in the cultural fabric (Jacobs 1961);[2]

- Next, architectural design must accommodate different sets of stakeholders and facilitate collaboration as well as be robust in the face of inevitable changes in its use, maintenance, and control (Simon 1969);[3]

- Finally, the occupied building must work as a complex organism with dynamic interactions, operations, and well-balanced flows of everything from people to daylight, information to heat, and merchandise to air (Ackoff 1968; Groák 1992).[4]

These are not just a sequence of four complicated and detail-heavy tasks that the architect must reduce and tame into manageable problems so that they are suitable for intuitive and imaginative design responses; rather, they are separate dimensions of what can be seen as the possibilities of fully mindful design. This mindfulness, in turn, is exactly what produces animated buildings that respond to their own unique essence, fit their environment, and are adaptive to change. To complexity science, this designerly mindfulness represents the cybernetic, teleological, and dynamic systems behavior of buildings as organisms. To architects, this complex mindfulness represents buildings that are authentic, elegant, and timeless.

Various aspects of architectural complexity have been previously addressed by several thinkers who will be important to how this discussion is developed (Figure 4.1). Our present-day understanding of architectural design in the context of postindustrial society certainly engages their writings from several viewpoints—sustainability, strategic planning, post-occupancy evaluation, continuous commissioning, as well as a host of other sophisticated investigations and accountabilities coming to the fore.

Despite those previous works, however, critical distinctions of architectural complexity have not been well enumerated, and in much architectural practice they are too frequently lumped collectively into work that can presumably be reduced to intuitive solutions. So instead of recognizing complexities, design investigation is generally rendered as normative problems of programming, site design, interiors, and service systems. Unfortunately, these fallback normative approaches are reductive and procedural-based activities and they are frequently organized around straightforward methods that miss the true systemic complexity underlying a design challenge. This approach has been characterized as a futile attempt to "tame complexity" by Rittel and Webber.[5] As Churchman points out in an introduction to some of Rittel's early work, this taming tact is inherently deceptive and morally wrong. He would rather that we say: "Look, I've tamed not the whole problem, just the growl; the beast is still as wicked as ever."[6]

In the more radically artistic or literary models of architectural design theory beyond normative design practice, the complex relational underpinnings of a design project can be dauntingly far beyond our intuitive ability to resolve

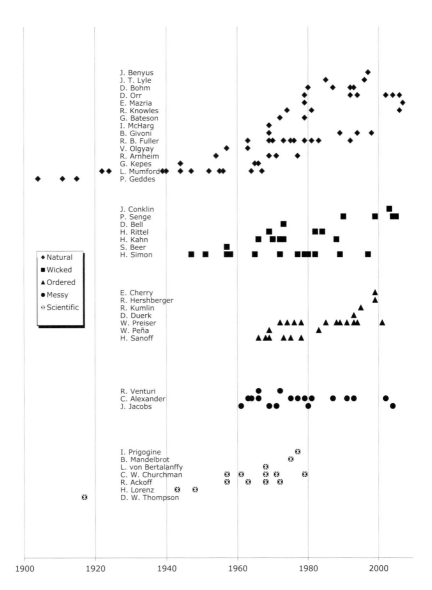

Figure 4.1 Timeline of complexity in architectural literature with some corresponding works on the science of complexity.

them into physical concrete terms. Consequently the complexity is often simply denied or ignored in favor of purely subjective or intuitive approaches. Hence, the most complex, vital, and unique essence and therefore authentic opportunity of the design challenge can be disguised, corrupted, or completely lost. To quote Christopher Alexander's *Notes on the Synthesis of Form* (1964):

> when a designer does not understand a problem clearly enough to find the order it really calls for, he falls back on some arbitrarily chosen formal order. The problem, because of its complexity, remains unsolved.[7]

To summarize this critique, we can say that architectural design has heretofore generally treated the deeply interrelated and dynamic characteristics of buildings as if they could be reduced to mechanistic problems that are readily amenable to physical manipulation as formal objects. In turn, these mechanistic problems are presumably to be solved by a process outside of design thinking that normatively consists of distilling data down to whatever intuitively seems to matter most, or else by ignoring the complexities altogether in favor of purely formalistic solutions. At best, the detail level of complexity may be recognized as an issue of complicated information, but the dynamic aspects of interaction, feedback, collaboration, and integration are still too often sublimated. It is not that architectural thinking has never encountered complexity, but rather that the normative level of problem definition in design practice seems all too frequently to avoid, deny, or dodge the issue, and thus the critical level of design thinking has yet to fully acknowledge the potential of what is latent in its own literature.

This chapter establishes a meaningful taxonomy of the encounters architecture typically has with complexity and shows accordingly that each has a separate but heretofore largely undesignated history within the discipline. The ultimate goal then is to enhance the richness of these encounters by correctly placing them inside the imaginative aspect of architectural design, rather than leave them as undistinguished routines of mechanistic data reduction.

The Four Encounters with Complexity

As per previous chapters, the scientific study of complexity generally refers to dynamic complexity wherein deep interrelations drive cause-effect events that are not directly observable or intuitively straightforward. For the purposes of this discussion, complexity includes the study of non-linear systems, cybernetics, and chaos. This differentiates dynamic complexity from the tamer pursuits of detail complexity, which is merely about complicated information or problems of combination, or optimized logistics. In short, detail complexity is about mechanistic problems with simple solutions while dynamic complexity is about systems and systemic solutions.

In this full sense of the term, complexity has seldom been directly acknowledged in built or written works of architecture. The early and rare exceptions now seem incomplete in their treatment (e.g. Jencks 1995).[8] There is, however, a literature of architectural thought that borders on the topic and thrusts toward its center, and this literature does go somewhat further than is apparent from most architectural discussion. What remains is to recognize and filter out how these architectural themes on complexity have emerged, how they are situated in the discourse of architecture, and how they may be brought to center stage. In short, the missing history of this literature can be seen, as a whole, to connect architecture's designerly thinking with the complex systems view of science.

The four encounters that follow illustrate the different dimensions in which architecture has danced with complexity in that dynamic way that recognizes an underlying systemic nature—namely that these encounters were all collectively recognized in the early and mid-1960s as clearly emergent issues and frameworks for designerly thinking. That timeline places them squarely in the origins of postindustrial change.

The actual events of these encounters overlap considerably, as does the thinking of those who led the charge. Indeed, some of the classifications offered are admittedly open for further argument as to which authors should be identified with which encounter. To that end some connective linking between the different encounters will be elaborated as each theme is discussed. For discussion purposes, however, the encounters are represented by a bibliographical sketch based on first edition seminal works for which each, at least arguably, belong to one of the four categories of architecture's encounters with complexity.

Encounter One: Wicked Problems Basis of Complexity

The wicked dimension of complexity is defined from one side by the natural limits of human cognition. The other side is that of problems whose bounds are fuzzy and indeterminate, but always made of interrelating parts. Taken together, we have the compounding condition of unstructured and limitless information being channeled through a narrowly constricted human processor. This complexity is emphasized by recognition of the social dilemmas in which they are set, and by the transformation to a primary production of value through knowledge manipulation (Bell 1973).[9]

Herbert Simon (1957, 1976) is well noted for his contributions on the practical limits of human cognition.[10] Bridging political science, psychology, cybernetics, organization theory, economics, and parallel fields, Simon received many honors including the Turing Award (1975), the Nobel Prize for Economics (1978), and the National Medal of Science (1986). His writings on "bounded rationality" and "satisficing" concerning our limited ability to collect and use data are definitional. According to Simon, we eventually run out of time, patience, or other resources for any project and must settle for "satisficing" so that our solution is good enough to satisfy sufficiently (satis-fice) without actually being able to cognitively maximize the outcome of complex tasks. This fundamental wickedness of restricted human throughput is thus established by Simon's important concepts. While Simon's interests were predominantly linked to organizational theory and economics, architecture is concerned with the same cognitive limitation, especially in the collection and use of project data, building codes, site constraints, budget targets, and user needs.

On the other side of wicked complexity is the formulation of design as a problem of indeterminate and unbounded information. To this end, Rittel and Webber published their landmark essay on wicked problems in 1973—"Dilemmas in a General Theory of Planning."[11] They described "wicked problems" as a class of problems distinct from simple or "tame" problems; some traces of Rittel's work in this area go back to at least 1967 (Churchman 1967) and the basic idea has been traced to Karl Popper.[12] Generally, however, Rittel is credited with establishing wicked problems as a wholly new second generation of design approaches. The previous first generation is characterized as a closed and linear approach to problem solving, whereas the second generation is one of open inquiry and argument. Without recounting all ten of Rittel and Webber's characterizations of this wickedness, it can be said that in this class of problems there are no defined starting points, operational rules, ending points, or universally accepted definitions. There is never a best solution, just a better or worse one. Designers never finish, they just run out of time or other resources. In fact, every attempt to solve the problem dynamically changes the designer's previous understanding of its definition. This is certainly a good description of the design activity in any domain, and it obviously applies well to architecture and planning. Wicked problems are also a close parallel of indeterminate, non-linear problems—that is to say of systems. In our postindustrial era of know-ledge- based production therefore, it turns out that wickedness is fundamental to the value of design. Design and wickedness now go hand in hand.

Aside from the term's origin in the writings of urban planning, the wicked problems construct has since garnered considerable attention and use in architecture. Wickedness is cited as a term in a broad spectrum of literature on the nature of design (e.g. Buchanan 1995).[13] Additionally, Ackoff's *Redesigning the Future* (1974) framed the idea of wicked problems as "messes" and Horn (2001) calls them "social messes," thus connecting wicked problems back to the physical and social sciences.[14]

In combination, Simon's satisficing and Rittel's indeterminate prob-lems describe wicked complexity in architectural design as an attempt to apply intelligent restraint in the encounter of open-ended challenges that inhabit a poorly bounded problem space.[15] One has to be smart enough to know when such complexity can be resolved and patient enough to work through its matrix of information and relations. Wicked problems are directly related to data, conversion of data to strategic information, and the use of that information by design decision makers with limited cognition. Wickedness is thus an essential problem of form making in the strategic aspect of design, especially in regards to how human intelligence becomes embodied in a built work. As Coyne has put it: "To summarise, we can go further than Rittel and Webber did in their 1973 article. Wickedness is the norm. It is tame formulations of professional analysis that stand out as a deviation."[16]

Lastly, wicked complexity needs to be set in the larger historical and global context that frames its formulation, namely Daniel Bell's *The Coming of Post-industrial Society* (1973).[17] Bell places the western hemisphere transition into an information society somewhere in the early 1950s. This seems to portend the late 1950s and early 1960s chronology of architectural works on complexity across all four of the encounters, but given the connections between the information society that Bell describes, the codification of wicked problems by Rittel, and Simon's description of our bounded rationality, it seems especially appropriate to recognize Bell in the context of this first encounter.[18]

Encounter Two: Messy Complexity of the Whole

Messy complexity is taken as a term from Robert Venturi's *Complexity and Contradiction in Architecture* (1966). In this text, generally recognized as a manifesto of postmodern architecture, Venturi advocated that architecture should grapple with the messy and difficult whole:

> I am for messy vitality over obvious unity . . . I am for richness of meaning rather than clarity of meaning . . . I prefer "both–and" to "either–or," black and white, and sometimes gray, to black or white . . . . But an architecture of complexity and contradiction has a special obligation toward the whole.[19]

The urban thinker Jane Jacobs (1961, 1969) weighs in here as well.[20] In her terms, an authentic belonging and sympathy to context are essential to the complex whole of design. Her work rejects the Utopian regulations and optimized land planning principles that are often associated with weaker applications of modernism:

> There is a quality even meaner than outright ugliness or disorder, and this meaner quality is the dishonest mask of pretended order, achieved by ignoring or suppressing the real order that is struggling to exist and to be served.[21]

To see complex systems in the messy authentic way that Venturi and Jacobs evoke requires a particular understanding. They argue for complexity as a kind of spontaneous order, and not as turbulence:

> The leaves dropping from the trees in autumn, the interior of an airplane engine, the entrails of a dissected rabbit, the city desk of a newspaper, all appear to be chaos if they are seen without comprehension. Once they are understood as systems of order, they actually look different.[22]

> The results of such profound confusion between art and life are neither life nor art. They are taxidermy.[23]

Or, as Peter Laurence summarizes in his detailed treatment of the Jacobs and Venturi tie:

> Apart from Jacobs's direct influence, among the parallels that emerged from their Townscape affiliations and other interests, the concept of complexity stands out, with Venturi's conception echoing Jacobs's historic introduction of complexity science into architectural and urban theory.[24]

Mathematician and architect Christopher Alexander also shares in this perspective of messy complexity.[25] To him there is an authentic natural order, self-emergent from spontaneous responses to prototypical situations. His differentiation, closer to that of Jacobs on one hand, is between artificially contrived forms that are to a large degree the architect's endogenous invention versus naturally emerging forms that are more or less an exogenous discovery. Closer perhaps to Venturi on the other hand is Alexander's language of iconic patterns, an environmental and structuralist "pattern language." This linguistic approach to form is identified in Alexander's case with a reverence to innate human associations with formal types; Alexander contends that designers should draw on these natural icons rather than seek to continually reinvent new forms solely for the sake of individual style or novelty. His notion of a pattern language thus tracts right beside the messy vitality that Jacobs and Venturi use to separate the authentic inclusive wholes from the contrived authoritarian ideals.

In Alexander's words: "We are searching for some kind of harmony between two intangibles: a form which we have not yet designed and a context which we cannot properly describe."[26] Or to rhyme back to the wicked encounter with complexity: "Complexity is one of the great problems in environmental design. Adequate information about the existing environment and about the types of place that it is desirable to make cannot be kept inside one brain."[27]

Collectively, these three positions on messy architectural complexity demand an authentic and meaningful fit within an inclusive whole. Fit here refers to the cohesion of component pieces as well as to the setting of a completed solution within its context. In closing this messy encounter then, it is worth noting that all three of the champions, Venturi, Jacobs, and Alexander, wrote from within the mainstream of architecture and urban design, and did so at the distinct departure point of postindustrial awakenings.[28]

Encounter Three: Ordered Complexity of the Essence

> Different views and approaches to the question, "what is going to count as information?" can lead to radically different problem spaces and certain kinds of view can ensure that the problem space used is not an adequate map of the task environment. It is necessary, there-fore, to examine at some length the relation between knowledge and architecture.
>
> (Heath 1984: 251)[29]

Ordered complexity can be described as the process of reeling in and organizing all the project information that designers need to digest, even as building programs are getting more and more complicated. Sanoff (1968) and Peña (1969) along with Preiser (1978) pioneered this as a radical architectural pursuit, and many practitioners of programming and strategic planning today are their protégés.[30] Work in this area of architectural complexity is principally concerned with finding the unique essence of a design situation so that its true nature can be addressed. Ordered complexity thus deals with the tasks of programming and strategic goal setting, but is also interested in collaborative problem defini-tion, participation of multiple stakeholders, and proactive scenario planning. The latter is what we associate with proactively "inventing the future" as opposed to passively following current trends. In this proactive sense, there is also an architectural connection between ordered complexity and the wicked complexity associated with open-ended problems. And, at the same time, Venturi's take on complexity overlaps with the problem definition and goal-setting agenda of ordered complexity:

> First the medium of architecture must be re-examined if the increased scope of our architecture as well as the complexity of its goals are to be expressed. Simplified or superficially complex forms will not work. . . . Second, the growing complexities of our func-tional problems must be acknowledged.[31]

Architects sometimes choose to subjugate this ordered complexity element of their work into a category of "predesign" and view it as a marginal but neces-sary distraction from their core pursuit of design as an art form. Peña actually advocates a separation between problem seeking and problem solving, precisely because of the prevalent Balkanization between the cultural artistic

silo of architecture as distinct from its social and ethical silo.[32] But this aliena-
tion is more correctly seen as a powerful dialectic that activates holistic
approaches to ordered complexity because at the core of even the most
rational mindsets in this literature of ordered complexity, there is always a
constant search for systemic solutions to what can only be called wickedly
complex problems. Behind the procedurally analytic approach of every major
thinker in architectural problem seeking is a deep structural investigation into
the root systemic problem. In other terms, ordered complexity is a quest for
the unique essence of a design situation, a generative teleological seed principle. This unique essence is like Aristotle's Final Cause, where an acorn is
potentially an oak tree. Final Cause asks, for example, why the little acorn
(much to the disappointment of hungry squirrels everywhere) does not simply
grow into a larger acorn. Teleology illustrates that the acorn's process of
change and motion is ultimately directed at becoming an oak tree. In complexity,
as in architecture, we can understand the acorn as DNA, an instruction set of
what is to be designed, but not as an edict on how to go about formalizing it.

   As a notion of design paralleling the characteristics of chaos theory,
we see that our encounter with ordered complexity can also be conceived of
as the core problem space which organizes all the facts and figures collected
in "predesign" (Figure 4.2). Surrounding this core is a negative space that can

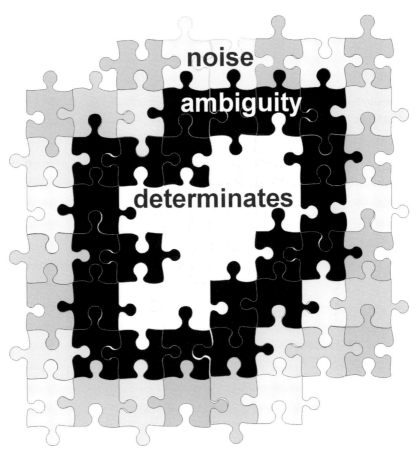

Figure 4.2 Diagram of determinates, noise, and ambiguity.

be thought of as the region of fertile ambiguity. In systems theory, this rich ambiguity characterizes what occurs on the edge of chaos where organisms adapt to environmental feedback in a cybernetic loop of indeterminate actions and reactions. Without ambiguity and the hysteresis of feedback, the system falls to homeostasis and ceases to function. In the design space and task environment of architecture, it is this very ambiguity that makes design possible.

In contemporary ordered complexity literature, the niche of ambiguity is occupied quite neatly by works dealing with scenario planning. Scenario planning and the field of strategic planning in general is fundamentally concerned with separating the problem space into core known determinates and peripheral unknowable noise; thereby revealing the region between them of ambiguity and choice (Figure 4.2). In architecture, this framework of thinking can liberate designers to focus on nascent and pregnant possibilities where ambiguity truly exists, and where design resources are not wasted in futile efforts to reframe the fixities or ponder futile impossibilities. It is for reasons such as these that design tends to modify existing solutions that promise robust precedents as opposed to exploring radically different and potentially superior ones. It is also clear which of those two alternatives is the more creative one. To paraphrase the poets:

> The primary [spontaneous imagination] I hold to be the living power and prime agent of all human perception. . . . The secondary [contemplative imagination] I consider as an echo of the former, coexisting with the conscious will, yet still identical with the primary in the kind of its agency, and differing only in degree, and in the mode of its operation [dissolve, diffuse, idealize, dissipate, unify]. . . . Fancy, on the contrary has no other counters to play with, but fixities and definites. The fancy is indeed no other than a mode of memory.
> (Coleridge 1817: 167)[33]

After unique essence and rich ambiguity, the third component of ordered complexity is a social one—that of multiple stakeholders, each with conflicting interests, varying priorities, and potentially different definitions of the design mission altogether. These stakeholders may consist of different client or user groups or of different members of the project team. A client, for example, may involve directors of different departments as well as managers of facilities, finance, human resources, and a host of other individuals with vested interests and rival responsibilities. Likewise, a hospital must work not just for doctors, but also for patients, nurses, technicians, and visitors—not to mention the hospital authority. On the team side, major building projects are led by an architect who orchestrates a group of civil, structural, and mechanical engineers, as well as a host of consultants. Each party of the team comes with potentially antagonistic priorities of their specialty and differing means of implementation and management. It gets complex very quickly: while client stakeholders represent potentially antagonistic goals of the overall project, the design team stakeholders work on individual components.

Team building in architecture is also captured in the discipline of project management. Here we have the procedural thinking that began perhaps with Frederick Taylor and developed up to the time of postindustrial society through mathematical techniques such as Program Evaluation and Review Technique (PERT) or Critical Path Method (CPM). As collaborative and collective intelligence involved in project management is expected to reflect professional attitudes and capabilities of each and every participant, it is not surprising that an element of complexity would be assumed in this combined work. A team is a system of autonomous agents acting toward a purposeful outcome after all.

The client and user side of the conflicting stakeholder issue has not been so cleanly addressed however. While some works tackle the issue of user groups and multiple stakeholders directly (e.g. Sanoff 1978, 2000), other architects are focused on the owner alone as the complete source of design parameters.[34] These particular designers are thus potentially limiting themselves to a normative translation of the owner's brief into first a program and then an agenda for design.

Despite this three-fold encounter with unique essence, scenario planning, and collaborative design for multiple stakeholders, the general history of architecture's encounter with ordered complexity does not yet adequately account for the complex underpinnings it engenders. Nor does it often fully grasp ordered complexity as a bona fide source of design inspiration. Instead, designers seem to prefer a quick overview of design parameters with just enough depth to arrive at an intuitive proposition about how to proceed. This is perhaps because the restrictive limits of known determinates are far easier to recognize than the open ambiguity of problem space or the seeds of systemic essences: determinates must be sought out and understood, while unbounded ambiguity allows for easy intuitive manipulation. Hence, most designs must ultimately repeat the same basic solution types that have been used before with only incremental and superficial adaptations. Connections back to Venturi's "inclusive whole" and Jacobs's "authentic fit" are thus weakened by reliance on robust precedents. To quote Alexander again:

> When a designer does not understand a problem clearly enough to find the order it really calls for, he falls back on some arbitrarily chosen formal order. The problem, because of its complexity, remains unsolved.[35]

Encounter Four: Natural Complexity of the Organism

> A look behind the footlights reveals that nature has no choice in the assignment of roles to players. Her productions are shoestring operations, encumbered by the constraints of three-dimensional space, the necessary relations among the sizes of things, and an eccentric sense of frugality.
>
> (Stevens 1974: 4)[36]

Finally, we turn to architecture's encounter with natural complexity, presented here as the intentions of designers to incorporate or emulate nature's own complex responses to a particular design's specific challenges. As an architectural encounter, this complexity can be described as having five dimensions—ecology, flow, morphogenesis, synergistic, and Gestalt psychology.

As discussed in Chapter 1, the ecological dimension of natural complexity begins in architecture with Patrick Geddes, a Scottish biologist and pioneering urban ecologist who initially worked with Thomas Huxley.[37] Geddes is also closely associated with the work of his protégé, the prolific historian Lewis Mumford.[38] Together, Geddes and Mumford describe civilization in successive phases of paleotechnic, technic, and then neotechnic eras of design, foretelling Bell's observation of our current postindustrial era transition into a society of knowledge-based production.[39] Their neotechnic era also portends the ascendance of information and cybernetics over machine production, resource depletion, and pollution.

Further elaboration of the ecological branch of this encounter arose most prominently with Victor Olgyay's *Design with Climate* (1963) and Ian McHarg's *Design with Nature* (1969).[40] These works came on the heels of Rachel Carson's *Silent Spring* (1962) and signal not only an emergence of green design imperatives, but also a corresponding set of design tools.[41] Other primary works that were formative to this aspect of design thinking would include Givoni (1969) and Knowles (1969, 1974, 1981, 2006).[42] Then slightly later Mazria (1979; Mazria et al. 2007) and Lyle (1985, 1994).[43] None of this environmentally inspired thinking has withered in the years since publication and all the volumes mentioned are still foundational reading.

This ecological approach is principally one of seeking harmony with the complex patterns, relations, interactions, and forces of nature. It recognizes environment as context, treats climate as a resource and inspiration, and it seeks to discover form that is self-emergent and responsive rather than trying to willfully invent it. In terms of architecture's encounter with complexity, the ecological approach treats built artifacts as if they were themselves an organism of nature. Referring back to Table 3.1 other connecting branches of the encounter with natural complexity are found in the noumenal and phenomenological discussions on architectural philosophy as well as in the experiential context more directly present in buildings.

Very close to this ecological theme is the dimension of natural complexity as organized flow in buildings, as discussed in Chapter 3. Steven Groák (1992), for example, imagined that a building may be considered as a system of flows—people, light, air, heat, information, products, gravity, sound, and so on.[44] The building's components then assume metaphysical description as reservoirs, conduits, capacitors, and—to use Norberg-Schulz's (1966) original terms— filters, barriers, and switches.[45] As an architectural encounter flow also connects strongly to the ecological theme in design literature. Lyle (1994) laid out twelve strategies relating design and flow.[46] His most relevant points were to use intelligence to replace energy, allow multiple pathways for complex flows, use form to embody process, and shape form to accommodate flow.

Finally, flow also inspires morphological principles toward the appropriation of biological order into artificial objects. Christopher Alexander argued this in his *Notes on the Synthesis of Form* (1964), a work for which he was awarded the American Institute of Architects' Gold Medal.[47] Janine Benyus's *Biomimicry* (1997) is perhaps the most acclaimed recent work in this theme.[48] In general, these works are derived from the self-organizing and self-emergent form we find in nature as it is now understood to be the purpose-driven result of shaping and regulation by systems of organized flow. From snowflakes to skeletons to the stars, in the organized convection flow of boiling water, the choreography of a flock of birds, or the rippled crests of sand-dunes, pattern and structure in nature always arise to embody their formative flows.

The next dimension of natural complexity after those of ecology, flow, and morphogenesis relates directly to the difference between the whole and the sum of its parts. Buckminster Fuller (1963, 1969, 1981; Fuller and Applewhite 1975) popularized this as the "synergistic" quality of how the behavior of systems differs from what can be expected by examining their separate parts.[49] To Fuller, synergy was more than a principle, it was a cause leading to the "ephemeralization" of a problem by doing more and more with synergistic design that required fewer and fewer resources. His own architectural projects, such as the Dymaxion House (1948) and his dome for the American Pavilion at Montreal's Expo '67, illustrated this through what he labeled "tensegrity," the building of strong structures from thin triangulated members. As a connective note to wicked complexity, tensegrity is also used in management science as a concept in deliberative structures, for which Beer (1994) developed a "syntegration" method for looking at collaborative deliberation.[50]

The synergistic dimension of natural complexity is also encountered in Bohm (1980)[51] as a coherence of "implicate and explicate order" where we find "undivided wholeness in flowing movement." On the less esoteric side is anthropologist and cyberneticist Gregory Bateson (1972, 1979)[52] and his abductive or propositional view of examining patterns and relationships. More toward architecture, but still not purely design focused is Orr (1979, 1992, 1994, 2002).[53] In mainstream architectural literature, synergy is often discussed in terms of integrated building systems (Guise 1985; Rush 1986; Bovill 1991; Bachman 2003).[54]

The final dimension of natural complexity is found in the branch of Gestalt psychology that focuses on art and architecture, most prominent in the work on aesthetics by Gyorgy Kepes (1944, 1965, 1966) and Rudolf Arnheim (1954, 1969, 1971, 1977).[55] This theory of mind holds that the human perception of order recognizes holistic and self-organizing tendencies as well as dynamic interrelationships. Kepes was the director of the Center for Advanced Visual Studies at MIT, where he investigated the unity of nature and technology. As a longtime friend of Laszlo Moholy-Nagy, Kepes was also an influential participant in the Bauhaus school. Arnheim had a similar agenda for unifying nature and technology and is best known for his landmark book *Visual Thinking* (1969). To quote:

> Order makes it possible to focus on what is alike and what is different, what belongs together and what is segregated. When nothing superfluous is included and nothing indispensable left out, one can understand the interrelation of the whole and its parts, as well as the hierarchic scale of importance and power by which some structural features are dominant, others subordinate.
>
> (Arnheim 1971: 1)[56]

Or,

> The aim of science we now see is to find the relations which give order to the raw material, the shapes and structures into which the

measurements fit . . . the relations which the facts have with one another—the whole they form and fill, not with their parts. In place of the arithmetic of nature, we now took for her geometry: the architecture of nature.

(Bronowski 1965: 56)[57]

In summary, architecture's four engagements with natural complexity provide phenomenological and experiential linkages between built form and the complex operations of buildings. This natural complexity is manifested by ecological responsiveness to nature, ordering of flows, morphogenesis, synergistic integration, and human cognition of meaning through order that harmonizes with the natural world. Natural complexity is also architecture's closest encounter with scientific complexity because of the direct connection of built form with environmental performance and the physics involved in achieving such design intentions. As a consequence of this proximity to science, natural complexity comes ready with more instrumental design tools than do those encounters related to defining problem space—wicked problems and ordered essence. Likewise, natural complexity is more instrumental than the rich, messy complexity of Jacobs, Venturi, and Alexander.

Despite this instrumentality and affinity with science, natural complexity is also the most ennobled of the four encounters. Current professional design standards have, for example, strongly embraced the ethic and the engaged pursuit of sustainable design. It remains to be seen, however, if scientific understandings of the building as a complex system will be fully acknowledged. At this point, architects are still developing the tools and agility to incorporate basic procedural advances in this area.

Discussion

Summary illustrations are offered here to clarify the main points and chronologies as discussed in the four encounters. Table 4.1 lays out a knowledge map of each mode of architectural complexity as well as a corresponding column on the scientific view. Figure 4.3 sketches the major aspects of each encounter and identifies their primary advocates.

Table 4.1 Complexity science and four modes of complexity as encountered by architecture

	Scientific	Wicked	Messy	Ordered	Natural
Proponents	Ackoff, Arnheim, Churchman	Simon, Rittel, Bell	Jacobs, Venturi, Alexander	Peña, Sanoff, Preiser	Geddes, Kepes, Olgyay
Postwar landmarks	1957	1957	1961	1965	1963
Realm	Cosmology	Society	Culture	Institution	Organisms
Objective	Adaptation	Intelligence	Spontaneity	Essence	Responsive
Organization	Dynamic	Cybernetic	Organic	Collaborative	Holistic
Order	Interactive	Managed	Authentic	Discovered	Emergent
Problem	Evolve	Bounded rationality	Identity	Reduce data	Flow
Agents	Systems	Decision makers	Citizens	Stakeholders	Systems
Application	Behavior	Organization	Urban	Definition	Design

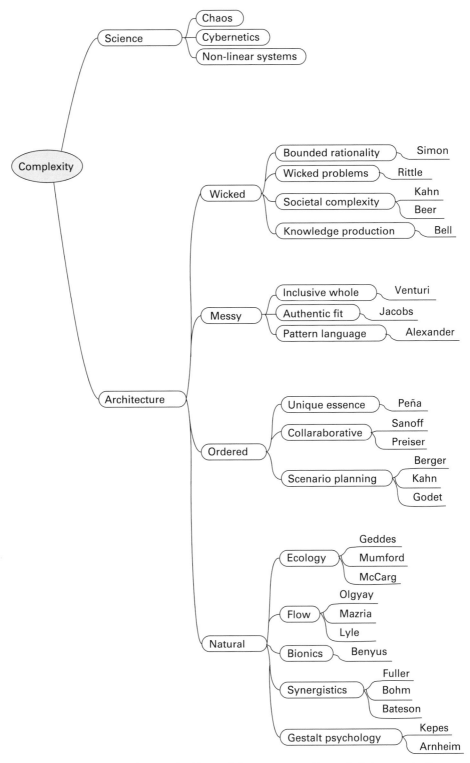

Figure 4.3 Knowledge map of architecture's four encounters with complexity (composed with FreeMind, available at http/freemind.sourceforge.net/).

The motivation for sketching out this missing history originates with the recognition that architectural design has indeed been engaged in significant encounters with complexity, but that these events have never been drawn together or given coherence. Such coherence will only be sufficient when designers recognize how far their skirmishes with complexity have ventured into realms of complexity science and how far there is yet to go. Perhaps as the two histories continue to converge, architecture will accept that these are shared realms and will commit to its own program of wicked, messy, ordered, and natural design investigations. This is not to say that architecture and science are merging or that one is minor to the other, but it can be argued that both disciplines operate and coexist within the same parameters of a complex and dynamic reality. We may thus expect that they have some common basis in complexity.

In closing, there are two points of difference between architectural complexity and complexity science to reinforce and perhaps clarify. The first is the difference between systems and symptoms: in the era of postindustrial knowledge production and mounting accountabilities such as sustainability, post-occupancy evaluation, and continuous commissioning, architecture will be challenged to provide systemic solutions to increasingly wicked problems in a world of diminishing robust solutions. Formal gestures will not suffice. The second point is that of scale and representation: complex systems operate not just in the local scale of human perception, but also in the non-local scales of micro and macro forces far outside direct human experience. The architecture of this non-local world is clearly not amenable to the sort of physical representation that architects associate with personal authorship in their most cherished productions. A different and decidedly more postindustrial vision is required.

The gift that architecture brings us, however, is an endless faith and capacity for the translation of relations into abstractions, abstractions into ideas, and of ideas into forms, places, situations, buildings, and cities. It is to this faith that architecture must turn when it finally chooses to embrace systemic complexity on its own wicked terms.

> We must face the fact that we are on the brink of times when man may be able to magnify his intellectual and inventive capacity; just as in the nineteenth century he used machines to magnify his physical capacity. Again, as then, our innocence is lost. And again, of course, the innocence, once lost, cannot be regained. The loss demands attention, not denial.
>
> (Alexander 1964: 11)[58]

Chapter 5

Converging into Complexity

Introduction: Encounter, Converge, and Embrace

Architecture's four historical encounters with complexity are situated within our current and emerging postindustrial context by a corresponding set of overlapping convergences: four fundamental evolutions we experience in postindustrial society as technical, societal, economic, and environmental forces that impact architecture. Those four convergences into complexity are the subject of this chapter.

- From the wicked problems basis of design there is a convergence with technology wherein human rationality and computer cybernetics are conjoined,
- From an isolated mechanistic perception of local scale events we are absorbed into a dynamic system of interrelationships, macro and micro scale reality, and globalization,
- Likewise, from an economy of short-term profit we converge into a broader concern with long-term value and human capital,
- Finally, the encounter with natural complexity leads out of industrial era resource consumption and into a sustainable neotechnic regard for environment, equity, and economy.

Figure 5.1 diagrams these four postindustrial conjunctive events. Note that each convergence is a transition away from technic industrial era perspectives and closer to an assimilation of neotechnic and postindustrial values. The attendant personal intuition and first order gratification of bygone days will not disappear from the essential human condition of course, but they are increasingly augmented by our equally human reliance on the complex tools and technologies we create. By the same token, at each of the four convergences there is a confluence of the physical and strategic spheres of design. The ultimate result is that our short-term, local scale, direct, and immediate scale realities of the industrial era are inevitably meshed with the longer term foresight of postindustrial knowledge society. Architecture must increasingly rely on this strategically embodied human intelligence to advance the human condition within a supportive built environment. The Two Spheres ascend together, and they converge.

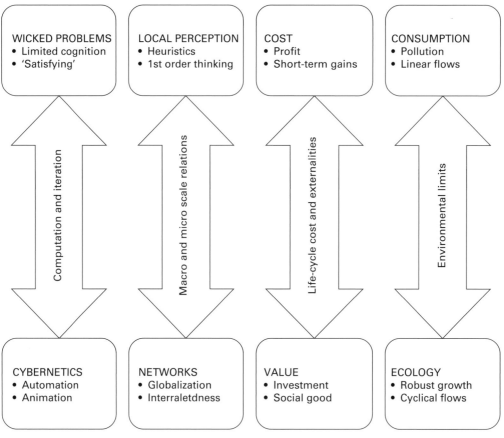

Figure 5.1 Four post-industrial convergences with complexity.

Convergence One: Bounded Rationality Meets Computer Cybernetics

Postindustrial technology impacts both the ends and the means of architecture: that is to say, both the design artifacts, and the act of designing. Toward the built end-result artifact, our techné of materiality, systems, and construction defines a vocabulary and grammar: the architect's solution space. As the means of production, the corresponding techné of information, communication, and documentation shapes the processes and frameworks within which architects compose: the problem space of architecture. Architecture inevitably evolves then as the problem space and the solution space of those techné evolve. This evolution is inherent to architecture's progressive roles in civilization, society, and culture. The sublime and transformative physical sphere of architecture transcends this progressive role and is forever sacred, yes. Timeless qualities of that physical dimension of architecture persist and prevail in even the simplest architectural structures and in archeological treasures where technology now seems absent. Working forward from any point in architectural history though, the full potential of what and how we design always requires the full technological complexity of what is now, or was then, practically possible. That technical requirement is as true for any architect of the past as it is for the architect of today.

As to the ends of architecture, technical advances in the materials and methods of construction are readily apparent to anyone observing the ever-evolving solution space of built architecture. Architecture's laboratory is the built environment and that is where the architect's vocabulary of progressive innovation is realized. This evolution of solution space has been a historical constant in architectural design. In regards to the architect's means of working in that laboratory, however, postindustrial technology has led to a radical convergence where wicked messy problems are met with cybernetic advances in information, communication, and documentation. While the ends of architectural design remain timeless then, the means have begun to change exponentially.

Sydney Opera House

A landmark architectural convergence of human intuition and cybernetic augmentation is clearly substantiated in the Sydney Opera House and its soaring, sail-like, shell-shaped roofs (Figure 5.2). When Jørn Utzon won the international competition for the project in January 1957, the firm of Ove Arup and Partners wrote to Utzon offering to partner on the project. Coincidentally, both Utzon and Arup were Danish, as was an Arup partner, Ronald Jenkens. It also happened that Jenkens was an expert in the calculation of thin-shell structures, and the Opera House conceptual design initially suggested exactly that structural approach. Utzon accepted the Arup proposal and the work began with abundant shared enthusiasm for their collaborative abilities to meet the challenges of this unique design. The ensuing difficulties were, however, to become a pivotal point in the Two Spheres confluence of physical design genius and strategic information technology. It has even been noted that "if there is a historical point of departure for the evolution of a new structuralism, Peter Rice locates it in the relationship between Jørn Utzon, Ove Arup and Jack Zunz in the structuring and materialization of the Sydney Opera House."[1]

Figure 5.2 Sydney Opera House, Sydney, Australia; Jørn Utzon, 1957–73; photo by Adam Jackaway, via the Society of Building Science Educators.

The freeform roof-shell structures led to immediate difficulties. By 1963 the team had gone through no less than twelve unsuccessful structural schemes. The fundamental problem was that the irregular shapes of Utzon's original design led to indeterminate structural forces—having no equation for the shape meant that there were no methods for straightforward calculation of their structural loads. Undeterred by this difficulty, Arup and Partners, under the leadership of Jack Zunz and with the notable contributions of Peter Rice, set about applying novel computer techniques to the problem. The computing capabilities of the day were put to full application at Arup and Partners, but years later they had reached no practical solution. In 1969, Zunz estimated that Arup and Partners had already spent 415,000 man-hours and 2000 computer-hours engineering the project.[2] They used British-made Ferranti Pegasus and Sirius computers drawing 18kW of power each from dedicated generators. This 1959 vacuum-tube era, £50,000 ($1 million in equivalent US 2010 currency) technology provided Arup with roughly the computing power of a 1999 hand-held calculator. Along the way though, in 1961, Utzon finally reverted to a regular roof form composed of uniform spherical sections; a move which not only simplified structural calculations to triangular spherical patches, but also allowed for prefabricated construction by precast concrete components rather than poured in-place thin-shell concrete roofs, along with all the necessary erection of vertical formwork on which to construct in-situ concrete.

By the time the roof shells were solved though, the Opera House's structural foundations had already been poured and these proved inadequate for the new design. They had to be demolished and replaced. Further such complications, apparently including many injected by the governmental client, led to cost overruns and an ongoing critique of Utzon in the Australian press. Construction costs that were grossly underestimated at an initial $7 million in 1957 grew to $22.9 million in 1966 and an eventual final cost of $102 million. From the original completion date estimate of something between August 1964 and March 1965, the ultimate date was October 1973. Utzon's name was not even mentioned at the formal opening. He had resigned from the project in 1966 and it took thirty-three years for the client and the architect to reconcile.

The architectural success and formal mastery of the Sydney Opera House has, of course, been justly recognized. Utzon received the Pritzker Architecture Prize in 2003. The United Nations Educational, Scientific and Cultural Organization (UNESCO) granted the Opera House World Heritage Site status in 2007. This is definitively seminal architecture. In its time, the practicalities of cost and construction were overcome by the insight and experience of those central to the work who steadfastly believed the result would be worth the investment. They have ultimately, in this one important instance, been proven quite correct. Fortunately, the ongoing confluence of human intuition and computer cybernetics promises to alleviate this sort of difficult struggle and replace the old problems with newfound capabilities.

Today, it is doubtful that the difficulties of a project such as the Opera House would be so seriously underestimated in the emerging postindustrial problem space formulations of architectural design. Project planning and strategic foresight are no longer left to that level of intuition and faith; certainly not as they were in the Opera House Competition days of 1957. Consequently, it is equally unlikely that so much conflict, delay, and expense would be

encountered or tolerated. This does not mean that Utzon's Sydney Opera House design would be rejected by hyper-rational postindustrial information technology though; quite the contrary! Increases in computing capability since 1961 have in fact greatly magnified the architectural imagination, not dampened it. As William Mitchell, Dean of Architecture at MIT, wrote in 1999 comparing the Sydney Opera House with Frank Gehry's 1997 Museo Guggenheim in Bilbao, Spain (structural engineering by Skidmore, Owings & Merrill), "Gehry had no need to seek heroic simplifications, like Utzon's resort to spherical patches. The gap between what could be dreamed of and what could be produced had been narrowed dramatically."[3]

This example of postindustrial convergence is thus a decidedly positive one: the architect's intuition is merging with cybernetic exploration and digital information management, so bounded human rationality is being complemented by superhuman computational power. The ability to translate visionary ideals into mindful reality is thus enhanced. Other architectural examples that illustrate this technologically magnified imagination abound in the early days of the new millennium. They exemplify a tapestry of wicked problems woven into cybernetic insight rather than a tangle of imaginative ideas set against practical restrictions. To mention a few prominent examples:

- Gehry's continued work at the Los Angeles 2002 Disney Concert Hall (Figure 5.4) and the 2004 Pritzker Pavilion in Chicago (Figure 5.5), both with Dowco Consultants Ltd. as structural engineer,
- Libeskind's 2007 Royal Ontario Museum in Toronto (with Arup), with its crystalline interlocking forms (Figure 5.6) not unlike the Sydney Opera House,
- The Beijing Olympics "Bird's Nest" National Stadium (Figure 5.7) by Herzog and de Meuron (with Arup).

Figure 5.4 Disney Concert Hall, Los Angeles, CA; Frank Gehry, 2002, photo by Sheila Ellen Thomson, adopted for use via the Creative Commons license.

Figure 5.5 Pritzker Pavilion, Chicago, IL; Frank Gehry, 2004; photo by Terri Boake, University of Waterloo, via the Society of Building Science Educators.

In the Two Spheres perspective then, Herbert Simon's "satisficing" and Horst Rittel's "wicked problems" definitions from the late industrial and early postindustrial cusp are concurrent with and parallel to the Opera House structural design.[4] Utzon and Arup's transformative 1957 to 1964 encounter with complexity was initially a tangle of intuitive vision and technical complication, as if the two were competitive aspirations, only one of which might prevail. Resulting conflicts over the Opera House design, materiality, strategy,

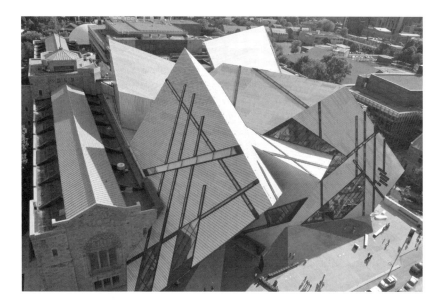

Figure 5.6 Royal Ontario Museum, Toronto, Canada; Daniel Libeskind, 2007; photo by Terri Boake, University of Waterloo, via the Society of Building Science Educators.

Figure 5.7 Olympic National Stadium "Bird's Nest," Beijing; Herzog and de Meuron, 2008; photo by Terri Boake, University of Waterloo, via the Society of Building Science Educators.

cost, and timeline are now legendary parts of the project's emblematic status. The sometimes acrid struggle for control over design decisions had a profound impact on the project and on the future careers of everyone on the team, most especially Utzon. In this antagonistic condition of early postindustrial convergence then, the Two Spheres were divided between the real and the ideal.

The physical sphere of Utzon's idealized and idyllic vision for the sail-like shells under the Harbor Bridge are direct reminders of Kahn's immeasurable quality, but the veracity of their realistically measurable structures was strategically difficult and problematic. Moving the project from immeasurable vision to measured working performance and then back to a great building of immeasurable quality was a heroic journey of Homeric proportions: an Odyssey.

The ending of the Opera House story was mostly happy-ever-after, but the price was unnecessarily high and the effort excessively consuming. Finally though, whatever culpability one assigns to various team members for the difficulties, this project's eventful account certainly marks a signal event in the transformation into a postindustrial epic of architectural history. From the tangle of conflicting vision versus reality, architecture moves on to a new tapestry of postindustrial information society and the value of knowledge production—a tapestry woven from cybernetic silk.

Cybernetics and Moore's Law of Integrated Circuits

> Three technology laws are bringing about an advance in civilization that has significant and far-reaching consequences. Moore's law (exponential increase in processing power), Gilder's law (exponential increase in communications bandwidth) and Metcalfe's law (exponential increase in connected intelligence).
>
> (Pinto 2000)[5]

Moore's Law is a key postindustrial cybernetic principle named after Gordon Moore, a co-founder of the Intel™ corporation. At about the same time as the Sydney Opera House structures were being resolved, Moore predicted in 1965 that integrated circuit hardware would double in physical density of transistors every two years without increasing substantially in cost.[6] Not only has this forecast proven to be exceptionally accurate, it has also been successfully applied to many other facets of digital technology, such as processing speed, memory capacity, instrument sensitivity, fiber optic capacity, software productivity, and camera resolution. All of these information capturing, storing, processing, and communication technologies are thus improving at an exponential rate and, when tracked even closer, exhibit an exponential rate of acceleration in the exponential rate of improvement.

To demonstrate the rapid pace of progress in cybernetic capabilities, Table 5.1 tracks the exponential growth curve of information technology. Each round of technical advance uses new tools and new thinking developed in the previous round.

The Sydney Opera House and Frank Gehry's Bilbao Museo Guggenheim structures are separated by some thirty-six years of evolutionary progress in information technology. By Moore's Law of two-year increments, that is eighteen doublings of power or a multiplying factor of 2^{18}. In other words, the affordable computing power available in 1999 for Gehry's Bilbao museum is something like 260,000 times more advanced and powerful than that available for Utzon's Opera House. That progress spans the evolution of computers from the IBM 350 RAMAC mainframe to the 64-bit laptop. It took the combined expertise and skills of the world's most advanced project team four years to decide they could not directly translate Jørn Utzon's vision of sail-like shell structures into material form. By 1999, any architect could probably sit at the airport and wirelessly download free software for calculating indeterminate structures on their laptop. Figure 5.8 portrays this exponential pace of information technology as predicted by Moore's Law. Further convergence will likely be propelled by continued exponential growth in computing power. Some

Table 5.1 The exponential growth of information technology as a function of computer power

2000 BC	Greek geared calculator	The Antikythera
500 BC	Counting boards	Roman Calculi
300 BC	The oldest surviving Babylonian counting board is discovered on the island of Salamis	The Salamis Tablet
1200	Use of the abacus is chronicled in China	Suan-pan
1500	Rediscovery of mechanical computation after the Dark Ages	Astrolabe
1670	Blaise Pascal devises a mechanical calculator that can add and subtract	Pascal's Calculator
1801	Mechanical loom controlled by punched cards	Jacquard Loom
1842	Ada Lovelace, Lord Byron's daughter, designs a computer program for one of Babbage's Analytical Engines	May 24 is Saint Lovelace Day as she is the patron saint of programmers
1860	Telegraph systems with routers form a network	"Texting" begins
1870	Telegraphs transmit images	"Faxing" begins
1885	Charles Babbage designs a steam-powered mechanical computer	The Difference Engine No. 1
1890	Herman Hollerith develops mechanical computers used in census taking	The Hollerith Automatic Feed Tabulator
1924	Herman Hollerith leaves the Census bureau and starts International Business Machines™	IBM™
1930	Electrical motors used to power mechanical computers, increasing their speed 1000-fold	The Difference Analyzer
1937	Digital symbols and vacuum tubes used	Atanasoff-Berry Computer
1938	Konrad Zuse invents a binary computer	The Z-1
1939	Konrad Zuse upgrades to floating point math	The Z-3
1939	Alan Turing develops a code-breaking computer	The Bombe
1943	Vacuum tube computer decrypts secret codes in World War II; ten were made in England	The Colossus
1942	Alan Turing describes the complete design of a computer that would store programs	The Turing Machine
1942	IBM™'s first purpose-built computer made for the atomic bomb project, it was 51ft long and 8ft high	The Mark I
1946	Use of the Williams Tube cathode-ray technology to provide a type of random access memory (RAM)	The Baby (Manchester Small-Scale Experimental Machine)
1948	First electronic, digital, programmable computer is developed at the University of Pennsylvania	ENIAC (Electronic Numerical Integrator and Computer)
1948	John von Neuman proposes a new computer configuration still used today	Von Neuman Architecture
1951	Application of commercially available computers to regular office work	LEO (Lyons Electronic Office)
1951	Computer predicts Eisenhower election victory	UNIVAC I
1952	First IBM™ mainframe computer	IBM 701

(Continued overleaf)

Table 5.1 *Continued*

1953	Smaller IBM™ still weighs over 900kg and its attached power supply 1350kg. It costs over $4 million (2010 $US)	IBM 650
1953	Transistors replace vacuum tubes, reduce size and power requirements	University of Manchester's Transistor Computer
1956	Disk drive peripheral device introduced	IBM 350 RAMAC
1957	Optimized compiler programming developed	IBM Fortran
1960	Dr. Grace Murray Harper develops a high-level programming language and software compilers	COBOL
1960	Network of defense computers manage nuclear defense	SABRE
1968	Apollo moon lander guided by computer	AGC (Apollo Guidance Computer)
1969	Labor Day, the Internet is turned on	ARPANET
1971	4-bit microprocessor chips	Intel 4004, Texas Instruments TMS 100, Garret AiResearch
1971	First personal computers	Kenbak-1
1972	8-bit microprocessor chips	Intel 8008
1972	Internet email	user@computer
1973	16-bit microprocessors	HP BPC, Intel 8086
1974	32-bit microprocessors	Pentium Pro
1976	First personal computer using a single-processor chip	Altair 8800
1977	Personal computers debut with 4kB to 48kB of RAM	Apple™ II, Commodore PET, Tandy Corporation™ TRS-80, all 500 times slower than their 2010 counterparts
1980	32-bit microprocessors, busses, data paths, and addresses	AT&T™ Bell Labs
1981	First portable computer weighs in with 5-inch monitor and 23.5 pounds	Osborne 1
1981	First computer with mouse, hard drive, network connectivity, screen icons, and laser printing	Xerox™ Star
1982	Personal 16kB computer for $1600 (US 1982)	IBM™ PC
1983	First folding form factor laptop	Gavilan SC
1984	Color display laptops	Commodore SX-64
1988	High-resolution "VGA" laptop displays	Replaced CGA and EGA
1992	64-bit microprocessors in commercial market	DEC Alpha
1994	First Initial Public Offering of Dotcom era	Netscape
2001	64-bit microprocessors in personal computers	Itanium 1
2004	Social Network era begins	Facebook, et al.
2007	The first netbook	Asus™ Eee PC 700

Source: data compiled from several sources.

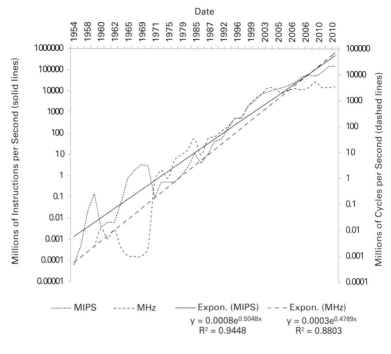

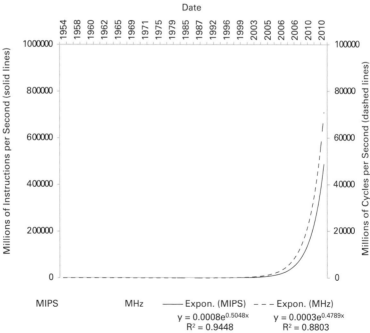

Figure 5.8 Exponential and linear scale plots of performance for some sample computers that were marketed from 1954 to 2011. The same data sample is graphed in both plots. Processor calculation speed in Millions of Instructions per Second (MIPS) is given along with the processor bus speed in Millions of Cycles per Second (MHz) and the exponential trend lines are a close fit to the technical timeline. Other factors of computing power are not shown here, such as bus width and cache memory. Also, note that in the linear scale plot, progress seems slow and incremental until the exponential growth curve races away. (Data taken from many sources.)

futurists and artificial intelligence researchers seriously anticipate that the modest laptop computer of 2030 will have 1,000 times the computing power of a human brain, and by 2050 will attain the combined intelligence level of the entire human race.[7]

Our postindustrial information society is deeply invested in the value of cybernetics and knowledge-based decision making. The transition of design processes from Sydney Opera House to Bilbao Museo Guggenheim in the relatively short timespan illustrates the corresponding architectural buy-in. We will increasingly see the same cybernetic knowledge basis of design value in other empirical activities of architects and their design teams. The influence of these information era approaches are already at least faintly familiar to most practitioners:

- Building Information Modeling, BIM—"digital representation of physical and functional characteristics of a facility creating a shared knowledge resource for information about it forming a reliable basis for decisions during its life cycle, from earliest conception to demolition,"[8]
- Integrated Practice, IP—often associated with Integrated Project Delivery in construction; the architectural focus of IP involves the collaborative effort of all project team leaders working in synchronized and asynchrosis modes through digital media from the inception of the design to its completion and ongoing commissioning,
- Evidence Based Design, EBD—use of empirical evidence, statistical relations, and interacting variables in the weighing of design decisions, with the intent of maximizing both qualitative and quantitative levels of the intended results,
- Continuous Commissioning, Cx—periodic confirmation that a facility is operated, controlled, and maintained to best suit and most efficiently meet the present and changing uses of that facility,
- Post-Occupancy Evaluation, POE—verification and validation of design intentions through the direct qualitative evaluation by the actual users as to the relative success of the realized design intentions in use, including their actual design appropriateness to the needs and perceptions of those same users,
- Performance Modeling—simulated behavior of a proposed building scheme and its systems, often compared to a base case or to other design alternatives so as to evaluate relative fitness, cost, efficiency, or other critical factors.

Note that unlike the Sydney Opera House example of early convergence, none of these definitively postindustrial processes are performed "after the fact" to simply confirm intuitive and associational design decisions that the architect has already made. On the contrary, all of these up-and-coming knowledge, evidence, and algorithmic complements to the architect's thinking are necessarily deployed in step with the architect's formulations, from conceptual beginning through continued occupancy and use. To reference Popper again, World One and World Two operations are, in these cybernetic complexities, carried on simultaneously and cross-checked continuously so as to maximize and assure a high level of World Three outcome: so the World One physics, biology, and chemistry are checked iteratively as the World Two subjective insights are explored; all in search of an ultimately positive result in the broader public realm of World Three shared discourse and criticism.

Other Factors

So, as answers to complex design questions become more accessible, the underlying questions become more significant and we are more apt to enquire into the depth of their nature. Computer simulation, database operations, optimization procedures, and other tools of the postindustrial information age are having just that effect. These same tools open new design possibilities by offering "what if" and "push–pull" explorations that were previously too time-consuming and mind-numbing to be practically investigated. Indeed, there is now an entire literature on the use of data analysis tools just for visualizing complex information. Cleveland and Tufte are among the best sources on visualizing information today, but the origins of the field are usually dated all the way back to William Playfair and his 1786 Commercial and Political Atlas.

Beyond what the tools of information cybernetics avail for us directly, we are entering an era in which architectural design, engineering, production, and assembly are increasingly unified by shared computer-model workspaces. This leads to a number of intriguing potentials for future development, a few of which will suffice to close this section on the convergence of bounded human rationality and the augmentation of computer cybernetics.

First is the advent of mass-customization of building components, the impact of which will likely exceed that of industrial age economical and modular mass-production. In the mass-customization scenario, the designer's digital drawings become the engineer's parametrics. Several iterations and refinements later, the same data document becomes the manufacturer's production requirements as well as the machine instruction set for precision, computational-driven, custom fabrication. Along the way, the actual design of a component or even of the building form in general might be shaped by computational algorithms that capture aerodynamic response, minimal structural thicknesses, or other influential flows. The resulting form of the building or building component would be one that embodies a great deal of information and intelligence, and then reproduces the appropriate response with elegant precision, along with the actual component hardware for assembly.

Along another line of computational cybernetic convergence, the dynamic automation of building performance is fast replacing our safety-factor-driven reliance on over-design for static conditions and one-way automatic controls. In short, the same cybernetic intelligence we use in designing architecture is also being embedded in our constructed designs as artificial intelligence. Buildings are thus themselves becoming nothing less than intelligent robots. We will soon design our building automation systems to interact with occupants through publicly visible "dashboards" or genie-like avatars of the building smiling up at us from our computer screen view port. These prospects for how information animates the design and operation of buildings are unbounded and have already been unleashed.

In the aftermath of this convergence of computer cybernetics and bounded human rationality, it is also worth noticing that building design has lost most of its historical insulation from objective accountability. Architecture was described in the limited terms of a creative art only for so long as its investigations and productions were considered to be much more the result of inspired genius than of deliberate intelligence. The complex basis of postindustrial architecture reverses that balance. Now, instead, a clinical database on the intelligent design of intelligent buildings is being cataloged from the accumu-lating documentation of post-occupancy evaluations, commissioning studies, sustainable design experience, evidence-based design, and a host of high-performance building case studies. By example of just two public institutions working in this area, the Center for the Built Environment at the University of California, Berkeley, reported that as of October 2009 their web survey instru-ment of Indoor Environmental Quality (IEQ, for thermal comfort, air quality, acoustics, lighting, cleanliness, spatial layout, and office furnishings) had been implemented in over 475 buildings, with over 51,000 individual occupant responses.[9] In England, the 1995–2002 PROBE project (Post-occupancy Review of Building Engineering) of the not-for-profit Usable Buildings Trust (UBT) performed a landmark set of building studies notable for their full-disclosure permissions from the entire design team of each project. UBT has gone on to develop a Feedback Portfolio and the Soft Landings Framework tools.[10]

Convergence Two: Local Perception Meets Global Dynamics

Complexity theory in science, as already discussed, describes the cosmos as an interconnected set of non-linear dynamic systems. These systems entail multiple cause-and-effect chains of action and reaction that ultimately produce non-intuitive outcomes and often bewilder our limited human, intuitive, common-sense understandings. Such complex outcomes are not predictable or comprehensible by the first order thinking that relies on our immediate perception of the world through intuition and direct experience of our local surroundings. Instead, we must use higher order thinking to appreciate the special non-local order of chaotic patterns, strange attractors, and bifurcation.

Thus, in our present understandings gained through the higher order physics of quantum mechanics, many of our first order impressions from clas-sical Newtonian physics concerning causality, locality, matter, energy, and reality in general are set on their head. Heisenberg's Uncertainty Principle of 1927 is the founding event. Eddington referred to this same work in 1928 as the Principle of Indeterminacy. Bohr, Schrödinger, Popper, and Einstein all contributed to the early development on this line of thought, and the work continues today. In essence, quantum mechanics reveals that however much we know about the current state and initial conditions of a situation, its future state is not predictable by linear, deterministic, causal rules. Instead, the future states of such a system are strictly probabilistic. Lorenz demonstrated this around 1960 in his studies on weather patterns and the Butterfly Effect: small variations in initial conditions and interactions of complex factors determine future behavior and thus allow for a range of possible outcomes for which we can only have probabilistic expectations.

The thrust of this quantum effect is that classical Newtonian physics are only superficially satisfactory and only so at the immediate and everyday level of human perception and experience. We do not need to calculate the likelihood of a quantum anomaly with every step we take. At the deeper level of invisible interrelations and multiple interdependencies, however, our linear mechanistic explanations fail. Referring back to Chapter 2 and Mandelbrot's work with fractals beginning in the late 1970s, this quantum indeterminacy is an essential and natural ordering principle, one that is drastically rougher than the visibly smooth form and regular mathematic geometry humans give to their artifacts and to the world of human perception in general. In the end then, causality must be understood as non-linear, complex, and non-deterministic.

Personal and Societal Level Consequences

Some implications of this quantum non-local reality, complexity, indeterminacy, and systems theory in design were discussed in Chapter 2, especially in the sections dedicated to complexity and philosophy, the differentiation of phenomenology from the experiential context of architecture, and in Popper's Three World model of knowledge. Those concepts apply to this present conversation at two levels. First, at the personal level, our World Two subjective, intuitive, and heuristic formulations of World One reality are all imperfect cognitions and artificial constructions. You cannot really tell much about complexity by looking at its surface representations in the world. Humans are fallible and live by roughly accurate generalities and usually reliable heuristics rather than by precise measurement or relation. We often confuse normative expectations for the way things seem to be or should be, with the prescriptive knowledge of how they actually are (Hume's Is/Ought problem). Imperfect human perception then, along with bias, fallacy, passion, habits of mind, and limited cognition, all combine to necessitate a distinction between the world as-it-really-is versus the artificial reality we each create as our own personal and highly interpretive reality.

That said, it may be superficially adequate to allow that "perception is reality" at the everyday local scale of immediate experience and direct affect, but the non-local reality of complexity is a different case. And while the individuals and societies that occupy the built environment may coexist with architecture very successfully at the level of immediate perception, the architect's acuity must be more abstract, relational, and critical, and it must span both the local and the non-local scales. Buildings are complex and require complex understandings. The Two Spheres model of mindful architecture always dictates that the physical immediacy of local affective direct experience be fully coupled with the non-local strategic intelligence of effective foresight. In the Two Spheres mode of postindustrial complexity, Venturi's dictum is realized: architecture simultaneously embraces the "difficult complex whole" of both spheres.

Moving discussion to the macro societal level, our globalized world increasingly reflects the same interconnectivity, interdependence, and non-linear relations as are exhibited by the natural world of non-local quantum physics. This globalization reveals our interconnectedness of culture, economy, and trade, and it illustrates how worldwide society behaves increasingly like a set of non-linear dynamic systems. The underlying interdependence of geographically and temporally separate events shows that our typically local perception of events and their shallow association with direct cause-and-effect outcomes needs to be reconsidered.

For a historical perspective on globalized interconnections, the first two-way global network was the telegraph, circa 1850. Then, around 1860 came the telephone, and finally in 1970 the World Wide Web we call the Internet. Print, phonograph, radio, movie theaters, and television filed in between with one-way media networks providing news, ideas, entertainment, and advertisements. Just as in the advance of computer-based cybernetic information technology, these human communication networks and their interconnections among all the populations of the world are ever more embracing, inclusive, immediate, full, and natural. We are now all connected into and coupled together by a continuous stream of flowing intelligence. Second order information tools are proliferating to filter, analyze, and interpret data flow. The devices we use to stay online in this stream have become constant and even sacred totems of our every waking moment.[11] In the USA, for example, more people now use their mobile device to check the time than those who use a watch.

Lloyd's of London Example

In 1977, Richard Rogers and Partners won the competition for a new Lloyd's of London Headquarters (Figure 5.9). At that time Lloyd's owned two computers, both of which were used in mundane ways to store client records. Rogers's design strategy though was based in large measure on accommodating Lloyd's continual office space growth as well as their uptake of new technologies. The competition entry was more of a system for accommodating the future Lloyd's operation than it was a physical edifice. The final design, true to Louis Kahn's articulation of served and servant spaces in works such as the Richards Medical and Salk Institute laboratories, featured the robust flexibility of several adaptable components: modular service towers, permanent service cranes, raised floor access systems, and individual controls for each workstation.[12]

Between the Lloyd's competition scheme and the completed 1986 building, Rogers's formative strategy for project flexibility was repeatedly

Figure 5.9 Lloyd's of London, London, UK; Richard Rogers and Partners, 1986; photo by the author.

validated, even as a work in progress. From the original two computers, Lloyd's selection of information technology expanded to include personal computer workstations, an office intranet, and a building-wide video network. At the 1977 project inception, technology was just entering the age of personal computers with the Commodore PET™ and the Radio Shack TRS-80™, but by the 1986 completion date the PC was in widespread use as portable VGA laptops sporting the IBM 80386™ processor. In the span of this one project's design, computing advanced several generations—about five doublings of capacity by Moore's Law, or a multiplier of 32.0. Meanwhile the client's requirements evolved in-vitro and the systems technology had to mesh with the building service provisions. Information management is obviously critical for an insurance brokerage like Lloyd's whose viability depends on taking calculated risks. As such, the Lloyd's Headquarters epitomizes the ascent of postindustrial knowledge society and the vital nature of the information economy. That was 1986 though, and even more has happened since.

So, in this confluence of local perception and global dynamics, architecture must be designed in service to a massively networked world; a world of neural connections, infinite databases, open source libraries, social networks, instant communication, and collaborative intelligence. Or, as journalist and author Thomas Friedman asserts, "The World is Flat" and the playing field has been leveled to the point that we must either join in the triple convergence of governmental, corporate, and individual globalized empowerment or we should find another way to remain competitive and viable.[13] This also impacts the means by which the design problem space is construed, because it inevitably means that more teamwork will occur, that team members will work in remote and asynchronic modes, and that more teams will compete for the work to begin with.

Architecture must accommodate both dimensions of this convergence: of local and non-local scale events on one hand, and the new realization of their collective invisible micro and macro scale interdependence on the other; i.e. the non-local scale of relations, and the global scale of interrelated networks. The immediate perception of a building's apparent "commodity, firmness, and delight" must now be supplemented with an acute awareness of its long-term and far-reaching impacts. In other words, the qualities we perceive in a building through direct, sublime, immediate experience are only the physical sphere of the building. The strategic sphere of non-local, relational, and intelligent foresight is equally elemental to good architecture. Both are necessary, but neither will ever be in any way sufficient in and of itself to what will count as architectural achievement.

Convergence Three: Cost Meets Long-term Value

A cynic, as Oscar Wilde reminds us, is someone "who knows the price of everything and the value of nothing."[14] As a postindustrial notion, we see this idea of cost versus value gaining currency in attitudes favoring long-term investment rather than short-term profit. This reflects the principle that value is produced by knowledge workers employing the intelligent collection, interpretation, and inference of information. It is also in contrast to the quick commodification of data into cost avoidance and instant profit that typifies the industrial age.

A secondary consequence of this convergence is an increased emphasis on postindustrial shifts toward social progress and, to cite from Chapter 1, away from private dispensation of resources for individual gain. This change is what Patrick Geddes and Lewis Mumford saw as the evolution away from paleotechnic industrial profit priorities and toward neotechnic investment in the public good.[15] It is also what Daniel Bell predicted as the rising primacy of human capital.[16] Furthermore, on the terrain of Friedman's Flat Earth, this convergence of value structures is also part of a technically driven social empowerment that rebalances the priorities of progress: away from shared cultural values and experiences and toward our shared social institutions and infrastructure. For architecture, this shift re-centers attention away from epicurean pursuits and more toward the bull's-eye of service to society. As Garry Stevens concludes in his Favored Circle social analysis of the architectural profession, the predicament of architectural practice has often been complicated by the economics of the architect's occupation. Stevens also points to a closely related "cultivated habitus" as being key to the hero status of many high-standing architects, complaining that such star status is often founded on a network of cultural advantage:

> The ancient social function of the architect, I have argued, was to produce buildings of power and taste for people of power and taste. This is still the function of the sector of intellectually dominant architects. The networks I have described acted and still act as a primary mechanism.[17]

The qualitative dimension of this twin economic and social value convergence is being realized in our postindustrial willingness and newfound abilities to include human factors in the calculations of value and cost. This human dimension is no longer an abstract externality; it is part of the equation in the long-term strategic planning and daily operations of organizations large and small. Building design is caught up in this as well: strategic planning, life-cycle economics, organizational psychology, learning organizations, value engineering, and high-performance sustainable design are frequent examples of longer term thinking that is normatively considered to be ultimately superior to immediate gain. The fundamental realization that building construction costs and operational expenses are almost insignificant compared to their monetized impact on occupant satisfaction or productivity is also a long-overlooked aspect of this. So, as the clinical evidence of these relations grows and the research methodology for validating them continues to gain ground, the veracity of arguments about the value of architectural design will morph too.

In the Two Spheres perspective, this emerging focus on individual empowerment and social investment seems to predict a growing concentration on strategic foresight and thus promises a more balanced wholeness of the strategic and physical aspects of architecture. As a pointed critique of industrial age architecture, this rebalancing is obviously aimed specifically at those aspects of the profession that now seem to have been overly culture bound and excessively dominated by epicurean gratification. That is perhaps the critique that progress always brings, and the hindsight bias of looking backward is clearly tainted by oversimplification. But the lessons of the past must be learned from and applied to current thinking, and it is certainly fair to say that going forward most architects have a boundless ambition for the human and social dimension of places, cities, environments, and the world at large. It is probably equally fair to say that this same architectural ambition carries with it ample discontent with the current results of industrial era production and the deteriorating condition of the built environment. At the same time however, it is also critical to remember that cultural and societal values are complementary and not mutually exclusive—like the strategic and physical aspects of architecture that embody them, social and cultural value spheres are tantamount and equally necessary to the whole: tangles, tandems, and tapestries.

To close this polemic, it is worthwhile to recognize how the postindustrial convergence of value structures is happening not only within the architect's practice, but also more broadly in how these structures reshape the context within which architecture is practiced to begin with.

Industrial Organizational Psychology

Industrial Organizational Psychology (IO) is an applied branch of psychology that has evolved in the junction of social psychology and organizational science. IO is essentially the psychology of people working together. From a business productivity perspective, IO is greatly concerned with the value of human capital. Human capital, in turn, is a term related to the embedded value of workforce knowledge, education, health, training, and other person-specific traits that increase their individual and collaborative productivity within the organization, business, or society. This capital is termed human because it is not freely transferable from one person to the next; that is to say, people in the workforce are not replaceable plug-in components of the organization. Investing in human capital is therefore a growing strategy for success. As a postindustrial invention, the value of human capital also reflects the emerging concept of the information society and the knowledge worker.

In business, these IO increases in workforce productivity help entrepreneurs understand and quantify the value of individuals within the organization. Human resource departments and human resource management systems are increasingly set up to help institutionalize this process. IO psychologists do research and operate within organizations to maximize these outcomes. The corresponding risks associated with human capital investment are also a concern, so issues such as job satisfaction, employee retention, prospects for personal growth, vacation, health insurance, and fringe benefits are part of the equation. Furthermore, the rapid transformation of commercial products and business practices in the increasingly volatile global market has led to a need for fluid organizational flexibility: A company making widgets in Baltimore today might be buying and selling gadgets in Singapore next week. A business might be organized in small teams today and in competing workgroups tomorrow. This need for robust flexibility in the global economy has led to a human resource concept of "learning organizations" wherein the workforce, including its leaders and entrepreneurs, remain competitive and viable by constant transformation. As the term "learning organization" implies, the human capital investment required for this dynamic flexibility is ongoing and educational in nature.

Architecture, given this postindustrial value focus, is elemental to the workforce environment and an essential component of the investment in human capital. From an economic perspective alone, the ongoing costs of the human workforce will generally exceed the first cost and operational expenses of the building in which the work is done. This increases the importance and value of architectural design that in any way enriches human capital. Good architecture is thus a good investment, not just a costly expression of image and status. As a new generation of post-occupancy studies and commissioning reports validates this connection of architectural design to human capital, it is increasingly likely that the architect's postindustrial problem space will be dominated by criteria of human capital in the programming, human factors, design, execution, and flexible operation of buildings. To date, it is generally the client base of postindustrial society that is leading the way in this while architects follow behind. The business literature on human capital and human factors is plentiful, for example, but the corresponding architectural writings are quite slim. Some of this discrepancy may result from the closed and competitive nature of marketing practices and planning services that architectural firms do not publish, but until architects declare their profession's engagement in this area of human capital, their profession will not be broadly recognized as part of the value equation.

There is, correspondingly, a new emphasis in facility planning and office design that adds architectural currency to this focus on human capital. Within such building programs there is an increasingly generous allotment of resources for employee convenience, family, and recreational enjoyment. This new approach greatly exceeds the industrial age corporate paternal attitude toward staff benefits such as cafeterias and locker rooms. Daycare facilities, gymnasiums, health centers, meeting rooms, swimming pools, and the like are now standard issue for organizations that wish to build and protect an investment in the people that embody so much value to their sustained operations.

Norman Foster's 1975 Headquarters for Willis Faber and Dumas in Ipswich, UK, is an early exemplar of this design thinking. To attract and retain a capable workforce from London to the east coast market town of Ipswich, a generous amount of space was dedicated to employee amenities despite the very restricted site. A swimming pool and exercise spaces dominated the entire first floor of the dense building plan on its tight site in the vertically restricted historic district. A skylit café on the top floor looks out to a roof garden covering the entire building footprint. Open escalators provide social space and allow daylight into the center of the plan.

Kevin Roche's headquarters in Houston, Texas, for petrochemical industry Conoco (1979–1985) provides a similar precedent and a poignant update. This suburban, 1.2-million square-foot office in the garden sits serenely as a series of three-storey pavilions surrounded by water and lush landscape. Parking is kept to the perimeter sides of the campus and open walkway connectors communicate the indoor environment with the outside spaces.[18] The flexible service core spine of the long, narrow buildings is flanked on both sides by daylit perimeter offices in a design configuration that has accommodated a long series of technical systems updates and office space reorganizations. More recently, however, Conoco built an addition on the west end of the campus to include a very high level of quality amenities that mesh closely with generous human resource provisions and family-oriented policies (Design architect: Picard Chilton; Interior architecture and programming: Planning

Design & Research (PDR); Architect of record: Kendall-Heaton; Landscape architect: Office of James Burnett). This addition complements the original campus cafeteria and replaces its original basement exercise room with the new catalog of features.

At the organizational institution scale then, corporations are emulating the high regard for human capital found at the global level in the prosperous Scandinavian countries, where postwar and postindustrial transformation has long been a matter of governmental policy and national pride. Scandinavia is an especially good example of the broader global empowerment of individuals in social networks of community participation. The value structure embodied in these new societal patterns enfolds the convergence of industrial era cost-and-profit thinking with our emerging postindustrial invest-and-sustain perspectives. Industrial organization psychology takes this changing social construct from the global scale and projects it into the arena of the built environment where design can directly enhance our productivity and prosperity.

Mission Building

A second, but related value factor in which architectural clients are leading their architects is in strategic planning at the level of visionary mission building. The architect's equivalent practice components do exist of course, primarily as programming, master planning, strategic services, or related work. But architecture has yet to make broad and vital links between these lesser functional prescriptive efforts and the more robust sort of mission-building practices that are becoming common process-level activities in commercial and institutional organizations.

While the implications of mission building as a value structure are just as important as the human capital value structure, the rudiments are more familiar and straightforward. In short then, institutions game their future success by simulating the transition from their current status to their aspirational future goal status. The fundamental ambition is to intentionally invent a new and desired future, as opposed to a more conventional, passive, and hopeful reliance on tracking current trends into a more vague and serendipitous outcome. The former is clearly a postindustrial construct, while the latter is a vivid reminder of industrial age thinking.

Mission-building terms such as scenario planning, backcasting, road-mapping, and the like are all part of the field of futures studies, or futurology. Much like the field of design, futurology is concerned with the selection and advancement of favorable future outcomes. This is in fact a definition of design that is sometimes used in business and other pursuits where design skill is being adopted as a component of their disciplinary knowledge. In 2011, for example, some of the fifty or so university business schools in the USA that were teaching design in this mode included Berkeley, Columbia, Carnegie Mellon, Harvard, Massachusetts Institute of Technology, Northwestern, and Stanford.

Architecture's power to envision and realize desirable futures needs to catch up with the mission-building powers of society at large and corporate penthouses in general. There is no architectural monopoly on designing the future and the postindustrial convergence of proximal cost-driven decision structures into more distal complex accountings of value have marginalized some of architecture's territorial dominance and its claims on primacy in design value to society. Closing this gap between the architect's functional programming and the process-driven programming of client institutions is, happily, probably not a tremendous undertaking or deeply rooted conceptual shift. It may well be that this is just as it should seem—that the social engagement of inventing the future is not at all foreign to architecture.

Convergence Four: Consumptive Growth Meets Environmental Limits

Architecture's encounter with natural complexity was discussed in Chapter 3 as biological ecology, channeled flow, mimetic morphogenesis, integrating synergistic, and meaningful Gestalt psychology. The confluence of that natural complexity with the contrasting patterns of industrial era growth has generated a new ecological design paradigm for architects, and has in turn founded an environmentally motivated design movement. The evolution of this movement is progressive to the point that it must constantly change names along the way in order to reflect its advancing condition. What started out as solar design soon became passive solar design to differentiate it from active solar systems such as wind, photovoltaics, and solar–thermal collector technology. Green architecture, sustainable, regenerative, net-zero energy, net-zero carbon, and other titles have been adopted in rapid succession since.

All the changing environmental design labels and green building rating systems have failed to capture the full scope of this movement. It hardly matters though, as such labels are always more indicative of aspirations than of current realities. What does matter is that few architects would today proclaim that they were setting out with a new design project to make it as non-sustainable, energy-intensive, and dark brown as possible. Even if they did, society has changed the building code regulations drastically enough to make such a design intention unattainable as an occupied building. Society wants health, safety, welfare, and a green future as well. The mandate has changed. Welcome to the convergence of consumptive growth and environmental limits.

This convergence of natural complexity with the late declining industrial era of resource depletion and environmental degradation has, in postindustrial society, revealed just how fractured architectural design had become in the schizophrenic chasm of beauty and accountability. The Two Spheres of physical and strategic aspects were laid open and the cracks began to appear. At the worst and most cynical divide, it is quantifiable environmental performance versus immeasurable sublime transcendence. This is, of course, a quintessential and false separation of strategic foresight and physical immediacy. The convergence must make them whole again.

As five billion more members of our global population begin to enjoy the industrial prosperity that only one billion of us benefit from today, the limits of available resources for us to consume are being stretched. Earth's carrying capacity for waste pollution from this consumptive growth is deteriorating even faster. Then there is the matter of one or two billion new people to serve as healthcare spreads, life expectancy lengthens, and population expands.

Historical Perspective

In the framework of Geddes's and Mumford's three epochs, our paleotechnic era was that of agriculture and mining.[19] Progress and the production of value depended directly on the bounty of natural resources and the patterns of climate. People thus necessarily lived in a direct relationship with nature wherein our more limited tools and technologies kept society in awe and subjugation of the natural world. As the environment seemed infinitely abundant, however, the pioneer attitude of resource harvesting was deemed adequate for our survival and sustenance. Nature was a resource to be tapped as suited our needs, even as our explanations of natural events were founded on their sacred origins.

In that paleotechnic preindustrial society, the complex results of such exploitive attitudes were largely beyond concern. The repercussions of long-term environmental degradation seemed negligible. As first order and local scale thinking, the observable chain of mechanistic cause and effect was explanation enough. Local scale thinking predominated because it was representative enough to predict observable outcomes and short-term consequences. On the other hand, these collectively large-scale interventions into natural ecologies were constantly perpetrated in the name of progress. The introduction of new plant species and livestock into the New World, for example, was seen as a means of taming and commodifying the vast wild landscape. The consequential long-term devastation was seldom considered because in the pioneering spirit existing ecological interrelations and interdependencies were imperceptible and incalculable. For so long as our technology and our population were limited, this paleotechnic preindustrial model was functionally adequate. Nature as resource satisfied the individual's prosperity as well as societal progress. Nature was there to be gotten.

The shift from these paleotechnic era attitudes about natural complexity to the next stage of society in the technic industrial age is demonstrated by corresponding evolutions in life expectancy and mortality rates. There was a fundamental transition from diseases of nature to diseases of industry (Table 5.2). Since 1900, for example, the average lifespan in the United States has lengthened by about thirty years, and some twenty-five years of

Table 5.2 Health and demographic transition in the United States

Factor	1900	1998
Life expectancy, males	44	74
Life expectancy, females	49	79
Leading cause of death	Dental infection	Cardiovascular
Death rate per 100,000 population	1,719.1	864.7
Birthrate per 100,000 population	3,010.0	1,420.0
Cancer deaths per 100,000 population	64.0	201.6
Heart-related deaths per 100,000 population	137.4	271.6
Infant mortality rate per 100,000 births	11,080	720
Fertility rate, average births per woman	3.56	2.01
Total population	76 million	270 million
Population growth rate	1.9%	0.9%

Sources: Center for Disease Control: http://www.cdc.gov/nchs/data/lead1900_98.pdf. The dental infection issue is from Pfizer Inc. (2006) "Oral health: Looking back", Chapter 9 in *Milestones in public health: Accomplishments in public health over the last 100 years*, p.169, New York: Pfizer Inc.

that increase come from advances in public health.[20] The twentieth-century era death rate decline in the USA from 1719 fatalities per 100,000 people to 865 fatalities confirms the progress. But along the way, death by infections, flu, pneumonia, malaria, diarrhea, tuberculosis, measles have been replaced by obesity, cancer, diabetes, cardiovascular and cerebrovascular failure. So the now treatable diseases of nature have been wholly replaced with diseases of environment, pollution, and chronic behavioral issues that became endemic in modern industrialized society. Even though we have advanced from quinine, morphine, aspirin, and digitalis to heart transplants, chemotherapy, magnetic resonance imaging, and gene therapy, our industrial stage of development has apparently not resulted in a society of proportionally increased vitality. Figure 5.10 shows the exponential growth curve for world population.

Another part of the transformation from preindustrial to industrial society relates to demographic transition, wherein underdeveloped societies with high rates of both birth and death undergo socio-economic progress to the point that they eventually transform into populations with low rates of birth and death. This demographic transition also reinforces the Chapter 1 sketch of postindustrial transition from rural agrarian production to urban service economies. In 1800, for example, 94 percent of the US population lived in rural areas and the average white woman gave birth to seven children. By 1940 only 43 percent of the populace resided in rural areas and the average white woman gave birth to two children. To amplify, in 1800 less than 10 percent of white females lived in cities and those urban women aged 20 to 44 years were raising an average 0.8 children each under the age of 5 years. At the same time, the other 90 percent of white women in the same age bracket lived in rural areas and were raising an average of 1.2 children under the age of 5 years.

A comparison of current world population shows that demographic transition in the USA and Western Europe has now entered later stages where low death rates and low birth rates have stabilized to the point of holding those

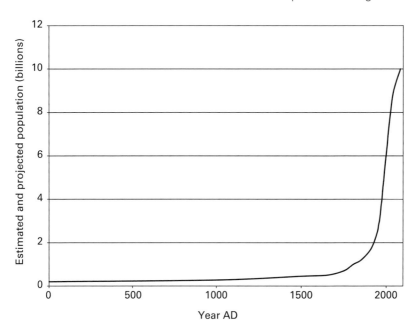

Figure 5.10 The exponential growth curve of world population since about AD 1. This plot is for the most likely scenario in which world population is projected to reach 8.9 billion by 2050. The projected high and low end scenarios for 2050, which are not plotted here, are put at 10.6 and 7.4 billion. Source: US Department of Commerce and United Nations Department of Economic and Social Affairs (2004). Population Division, World Population to 2300, United Nations, New York..

countries' population levels flat, with perhaps zero growth or even a decline. Many developing countries are still in stage one of transition however. In 1998, the birth rate and death rate per 1000 total population in the USA was about 14 and 9 respectively. In Kenya those same 1998 numbers were 32 and 14. The relative impact of technology on demographic transition and the shape of different societies is clear.

Like the era of preindustrial society from which the great civilizations of the world arose, our industrial age of progress produced its own set of impressive milestones. Using the millennial dates from the representation of modern health advances in Table 5.2, the corresponding accomplishments of science and technology in the twentieth century are sketched in Table 5.3.

Table 5.3 Some of the significant technical accomplishments of the twentieth century

Date	Event
1900	Telephone
1901	Petroleum production
1903	Manned flight
1903	Steam turbine generator
1905	Special Theory of Relativity
1906	Air-conditioned offices
1908	Model T Ford car
1910	Light bulb
1913	The assembly line
1913	Discovery of the atom
1913	School of psychology
1920	Radio broadcasts
1922	Insulin
1924	Galaxies discovered
1926	Television
1928	Offshore oil drilling
1928	Penicillin
1931	Air-conditioned homes
1934	Nylon
1940	Blood banks
1940	Ceramics
1944	Public water fluorination
1945	Dialysis
1945	Atomic bomb
1947	Transistor
1950	Leukemia drugs
1952	Polio vaccine
1954	Kidney transplant
1955	Nuclear power plant

(Continued overleaf)

Table 5.3 *Continued*

Date	Event
1959	Float glass developed
1962	Communications satellite
1969	Moon landing
1970	Earth Day
1972	CT and MRI scan imaging
1975	Personal computers
1976	Fiber optics
1982	Artificial heart
1990	Human Genome Project
1992	The World Wide Web

Source: Data compiled from several sources.

But here again, in retrospect, the repercussions of first order and local scale thinking are exposed in the industrial age of mechanistic extension and consumptive waste, just as in the preindustrial era of pioneering against nature. Two steps forward, one step back. After conquering most diseases of nature we then regress to self-inflicted diseases of industry brought on by pollution, profit-taking, commercial exploitation, and short-term planning. After taming the land with limited understandings of the resulting large-scale consequences, we next proceed to use our environment as both the material resource and the waste dump of industrial production. The list of environmental crises is long, and the related human woe inflicted by the consequential damage to our living environment is dire. We read about them every day:

- Resource depletion—non-renewable sources are dissipating and the waste stream is filling up.
- Global climate modification—the measured levels of atmospheric carbon dioxide containing the 13C carbon isotope from old buried carbon we have dug up and burned since the industrial revolution is the smoking gun of anthropocentric climate forcing; there are few remaining climate change skeptics anywhere among recognized scientists.
- Energy—costs go up, supply is challenged, utility infrastructures are outdated and overloaded; pollution is produced; new generating capacity has to be built; by 2030 world energy use is predicted to rise by 60 percent of which two-thirds will be for developing countries; if US energy use continues to increase at its current growth rate, the US Department of Energy estimates that 300 new power plants supplying 260,000 megawatts of new electrical generating capacity will need to be built across the country by 2030.
- Pollution and low environmental air quality—if the Earth were the size of a basketball, our atmosphere would be the enveloping thickness of a single sheet of newspaper; the daily weather report now has almost as much information about air quality and allergens

(much of which is industrial micro dust from burning and cutting processes) as it does about the chance of rain; sulfur oxides, nitrogen oxides, carbon monoxide, carbon dioxide, chlorofluorocarbons, ammonia, volatile organic compounds, particulate matter, and toxic metals are primary sources of air pollution; ozone and peroxyacetyl nitrate are formed with particulate matter in secondary pollutants, mostly as smog; in 2008, 126.8 million US residents lived in a county with air quality concentrations above the level of the health-based National Ambient Air Quality Standards.

- Species and diversity losses—about 75 percent of our crop plant varieties are now extinct and another 50,000 or so additional ones are lost each year; some 90 percent of all plant species are restricted to Africa, Asia, and Latin America, developing countries where land use for economic development is in high demand; as much as 50 percent of the world's exclusive 200 nautical mile fishing zones are overfished to the point that, for 2004, the consequent reduction in actual fishing yields was estimated to be on the order of 10 million metric tons.[21]

- Deforestation—the 2010 Report of the United Nations Food and Agriculture Organization (FAO) indicates that our global conversion of forest land to other uses is still some 13 million hectares (50,193 square miles) per year, down significantly from 16 million hectares (61,776 square miles) per year in the 1990s; with replanting factored in global net forest area loss is estimated at 5.2 million hectares (20,077 square miles) per year for 2000–2010, so an area of forest about the size of Costa Rica is still disappearing each year; for 1990–2000 annual net losses were more on the order of 8.3 million hectares (32,046 square miles); the world's total forest area, defined as having more than 10 percent tree cover, is presently about 4 billion hectares (15.4 million square miles) or some 30 percent of total land area; for the period of 1990–2010 only China and Europe managed a net growth in forest area.

- Water resources and water pollution—agriculture represents 70 percent of freshwater use globally but drinking water and sanitation are also critical needs as are ecosystem wetlands and animal life; as the quality and quantity of potable water sources is decreasing, the struggle over water rights and pollution of shared resources is intensifying; increasing development and population increases the strain; the World Health Organization (WHO) reports that global access to water for sanitation jumped from 41 percent to 53 percent during 1990–2006, but some 2.5 billion people still have no access to any improved sanitation of any kind and must rely on open defecation; from 1990 to 2010 the number of people worldwide with improved drinking water sources increased by 1.6 billion and less than 1 billion now rely on unimproved drinking water; meanwhile, every calorie of food requires a liter of water to produce it (about 3000 liters of water per person per day)[22] and from 1950 to 2010 world population grew from 2.5 billion to 6.5 billion as irrigated land doubled and irrigation water use tripled; 20 percent of the world lives with physical water scarcity where there is inadequate water for everyone's needs; unsustainable groundwater pumping is rampant; aquifer depletion is imminent in many areas;[23] industrial pollution, runoff pollution, sedimentation, and other water quality issues compound the problems.

- Population—as more nations achieve higher living standards, and as population increases everywhere, the pressures on our environment grow; exponential population growth thus means exponentially diffi-cult issues.
- Technology—we must make technology a lever that reduces and heals our damage to the environment, not a winch by which we continually multiply the harm; the built environment, where so much of our natural resources are presently consumed, must be a part of the solution.

Postindustrial Convergence of Consumptive Waste and Environmental Sustainability

Given our present advantage of hindsight, the unbearable environmental, social, and economic costs of our past pioneering and industrial means of production are becoming clear. Throughput conversion of natural resources into raw materials and on into the chain of manufacture, use, and disposal has reached a dead-end junkyard. Large-scale commodification of the environment is now understood to cause non-local and macro scale devastation. Nature's limits have converged with the bygone days of wasteful consumption.

As we willingly accept the spectacular milestone accomplishments of the industrial age, we must also fess up to its astonishingly short-sighted repercussions. The built environment will have a large role in this reconciliation of the good and the bad, because the primary interface of human civilization and the natural world happens there in our constructed cities, buildings, houses, and landscapes. This is not an indictment of what has come before, however; it is rather a call to action in the face of inevitable change.

The virtues and excesses of the last century of modern architecture can be elaborated on as readily as that of the broader industrial age milieu in which architects have been operating. As we forever recognize the architec-tural accomplishments of the past we must also fess up to its astonishingly short-sighted repercussions too. Neither of the two polarities need expansive attention here as they are well chronicled already. But such hindsight bias should probably be avoided in favor of a progressive and proactive view on where we go from today. It would be specious and disingenuous now to say that we knew better all along; we did not. Instead, this fourth two-sphere convergence of consumptive waste arrested by environmental limits is an event that begs for a new, radical departure from our "paleotechnic" and indus-trial age lineage of harvesting, production, consumption, and pollution. The old model was linear, simplistic, and mechanistic. The new "eotechnic" model is liberating in its abandonment of mechanistic local scale perception and in its favor for the non-local, non-hierarchical, complex, and deeply interrelated. In short, we are abandoning machine-production practices and opting for holistic approaches that recognize interconnected and dynamic relationships. We finally see that the world is not a machine made for our immediate gratification and quick profit; it is rather a complexly animated system in which we can either participate and flourish, or flounder and perish. What design challenge could be more richly motivating to architects than that?

Eotechnic architecture will necessarily follow two models of complexity: the systems model of tangles, tandems, and tapestries; and the cybernetic model of dynamic flow, environmental feedback, and responsive adaptation. Chapter 6 describes how the physical and strategic spheres operate and cooperate in these two models as the architectural embraces of complexity. Following the four historic encounters of architectural complexity as wicked, messy, ordered, and natural, there came the four present convergences of wickedness and cybernetics, local and global perspectives, cost and value constructs, and finally consumptive waste and environmental limits. We now turn to four embraces of complexity in the Two Spheres: hermeneutics, unique essence, animation, and aesthetics.

Chapter 6

Embracing Complexity

> We've allowed too long the idea that the world is "out of control"—
> be it our cities, the economy, or technology. We've filled the world
> with complex systems and technologies that are hard to understand,
> let alone shape or direct. But we are people, not ants.
>
> (Thackara 2005: 225)[1]

Postindustrial transformations have served in this discussion to emphasize the increasingly complex nature of buildings and of building design. And, while this convergence of society and complexity in our early eotechnic phase seems to begin in the 1960s, it is also clear that this complexity has always, in some measure, involved architecture. Having covered that, the central question of the Two Spheres is now tendered: How do we now authentically embrace complexity in building design rather than seeking to master it falsely or reductively tame it into sets of oversimplified problems? Four possibilities are suggested, and all of them are, not so surprisingly, already implicit in how architects describe what they do. But as Thackara implores us, the past skirmishes, encounters, and convergences with architectural complexity will no longer suffice. For these four authenticating possibilities of the Two Spheres to mature into full and intimate embraces, they must be explicitly addressed by the architectural profession and then loudly celebrated in their practices:

- Hermeneutics—a cyclical process of abductive inference and iterative interpretation is inherent in dealing with dynamic complexity, wicked problems, deep relations, and non-local interactions,
- Unique Essence—teleological cause, systemic purpose, and autopoietic distinction all demonstrate that, at the distilled core of any complex form, there is a root essence from which an authentic generative shaping may be pursued,
- Animation—the distinction between mechanistic and systemic conditions is that of animation, such as found in the difference between those prima facie appearances of first order, local scale satisfaction versus authentic, complex, and vital traits,

- Aesthetics—just as creativity and innovation require a confluence of whole-minded cognition, aesthetic consideration always entails a bridge between the physical and strategic sphere aspects of design.

Hermeneutics

> The issue for design is not merely "aesthetic" or "technological," if by these terms we understand exclusive, autonomous values. Rather, the issue is primarily ethical. . . . What kind of speech can, therefore, be postulated as a primary meta-discourse? We propose that a solution might be found in recent hermeneutic ontology.
>
> (Pérez-Gómez 1999: 73)[2]

The hermeneutic embrace is a cognitive framework for designerly thinking that is neither bottom-up deductive nor top-down inductive. Instead, hermeneutics are abductive in the sense of an iteratively repeated cycle of beginning observation, then learning, proposing, testing of fit, and then beginning again with a new understanding of the fundamental problem statement. Fortunately this abductive thinking is a process with which designers are already implicitly familiar as an approach to complicated levels of information on the criteria and programming of a project in its early design phase. This early phase work is usually a tacitly understood and normative method for dealing with complicated information. Elevating this to a critical means of managing complex relations begins by recognizing the propositional basis of all design innovation and creativity in general: architects do not deduce how all the facts and ideas add up to a design. Nor do architects inductively shoehorn a design into a favorite theory. Instead, like all works of innovation and creativity in art, the humanities, and in science; what architects really do in practice is size up a complex situation, arrive at an understanding that allows for a propositional attempt at the design, check for fit of the proposition against the parameters of the situation, learn about the response of the design to desired outcomes, and then loop back around to create new understandings leading to further developed propositions.

A Design Hermeneutic

> We cannot start with a whole that has no parts, and we cannot start with the parts until we understand the whole. This paradox does not imply that the circle is vicious, but merely that logic is inadequate to the task of understanding the working of understanding. Yet understanding occurs.
>
> (Snodgrass and Coyne 1997: 72)[3]

Hermeneutics describes the iterative cycle of abduction—from observation to learning, to proposition, to testing, and through redefinition of the problem back to observation again (Figure 6.1). As a branch of contemporary philosophy and science, hermeneutics is also a practical approach to recognizing the very real limits of bounded human rationality pressed against the wicked complexity

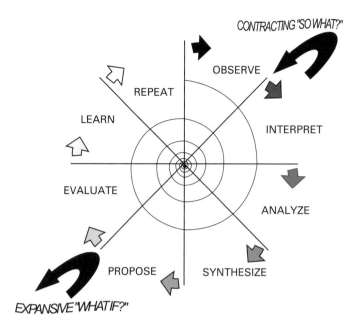

CONTRACTING "SO WHAT?"

OBSERVE

REPEAT

LEARN

INTERPRET

EVALUATE

ANALYZE

PROPOSE   SYNTHESIZE

EXPANSIVE "WHAT IF?"

Figure 6.1 The hermeneutic spiral, the gravity of the strange attractor, and the activating forces of expansive and contracting design questions.

of building design. An architectural design version of the process is readily construed as a bona fide approach to complex, messy, dynamic, and deeply interrelated problem spaces. In short, hermeneutics can be embraced because it is inclusive rather than reductive, complex instead of mechanistic, relational rather than hierarchical, and, lest we forget, propositional rather than presumptive.

Because this architecturally construed hermeneutic is cyclical and iterative, the process can be thought of as a constant circular spiraling down toward a final solution point at which the unique essence of the design problem waits like the "strange attractor" of chaos theory. We can also imagine in this design hermeneutic that there is a pair of dialectic forces at play in propelling the design work: a centripetal inward pull and a centrifugal outward tug. Each of these forces is powered by a persistent questioning attitude in design problem space: "What if?" is the outward tug of force that always expands possibility in the opportunistic quest for better and richer alternatives. "So what?," on the other hand, is the contractive force that draws the design gradually toward final realization. As suggested by the spiral path, there is no straightline, direct, and immediate connection between the wickedly tangled problem and the tapestry of its complex solution. Rather, a constant questioning and continuous cycle of learning are required, as well as a willingness to constantly adjust the problem statement. These two forces also depict the pitfalls of unbalanced forces: when architects wander too far on the vector of "what if?" centrifugal exploration, the strange attractor loses its gravitational pull and the design whirls off into the void. Conversely, when the architect plows directly toward an immediate centripetal "so what?" solution, there is only one opportunity to hit dead-center on the unique essence of the attractor—a narrow miss sends this second architect off into the void as well.

The Two Spheres in the Hermeneutic Context

According to Benjamin Bloom's critique and William Perry's principles of ethical and cognitive development, a dualist perspective would necessarily see either strategic or physical aspects of design as having the "right" answer and would reject one or the other sphere as false.[4] A multiplistic view, although more open to differences in approach and suspicious of single-source authority, might still be hopelessly mired in the endless search for some right and absolute way to resolve the differences between the two. Pluralism on the other hand allows us to accept that both strategic and physical spheres of design are equally valid and essential, without having to first resolve their seemingly incommensurable principles. Where dualism is simplistic and multiplistic consideration is complicated, pluralism is complex. Likewise, these levels of cognition can be fitted to the taxonomy of questions: declarative questions of right or wrong ask what, where, and when; procedural questions of expertise ask how, for these are the measurable reality; structural questions of wisdom ask why, and there lies the immeasurable ideal.

A couple of observations will give this idea more relevance. First, it should be noted that the hermeneutic cycle is very much akin to Thomas Kuhn's model of paradigm shifts, and to Rittel and Webber's approach to "wicked" indeterminate design problems.[5] As such, the hermeneutic approach might already feel intuitively familiar to anyone engaged in the adductive basis of architectural or ecological design propositions. Furthermore, the learning feedback loop inherent in hermeneutic iteration, paradigm shifts, wicked problem approaches, and adductive design propositions can all be logically connected to the basic notion of indeterminate problems, cybernetics, teleological processes, self-organization, emergent form, and thus to complex dynamic systems.

In further context of the Two Spheres, hermeneutics is the natural designerly means of addressing complexity, whole-minded cohesion, and dynamic systems. The physical and strategic aspects of design always appear as complex, complementary, and generative tandems that seek the unique essence of their strange attractor (Table 6.1). These tandems must be welcomed proactively and explored enthusiastically if the Two Spheres are to make a whole-minded unity. If architects should instead mistakenly confuse the Two Spheres as complicated, antagonistic, and inhibiting problems, then they will ultimately miss the strange attractor and may well be lost in the void. A deliberate interpretive hermeneutic approach leads us forever and forever,

Table 6.1 The Two Spheres tandems

Right Brain Physical Aspect	Left Brain Strategic Aspect
Affect	Effect
Immediacy	Foresight
Significance	Intelligence
Emotive	Rational
Immeasurable	Measurable
The Ideal	The Real

not to centrifugal or centripetal bifurcation, but to the strange attractor. Or so we might, at least, pray.

To summarize this embrace of complexity, we can say that architecture is congruent with the interpretive and assimilative method of hermeneutics because of the:

- Implicit nature of design knowledge wherein understanding and interpretation are superior to empirical fact alone,
- Adductive basis of hermeneutics which is already native to propositional design thinking,
- Oscillating engine of expansion and contraction in design between "What if?" and "So what?" thinking,
- Pluralistic perspectives that designers maintain about what qualifies as good architecture,
- Divergent perspectives of multiple stakeholders involved in architectural projects,
- Multiple scales of overarching order at the macro-inductive scale and integrity of individual details at the micro-deductive scale,
- Indeterminate or "wicked" nature of design in which there can be no linear or procedural recipe for solution,
- Cybernetic nature of information feedback systems in complex problems of design and the iterative effect this has on continually redefining the problem space,
- Principles of natural teleology, which cybernetics and Aristotle describe as the Final Cause, and
- Incomplete nature of knowledge and finite limits of human understanding in any complex problem, conditions leading to Herbert Simon's description of "satisficing" as the good-enough solution in favor of the perfect one.

Unique Essence

For the hermeneutic spiral to lead us to the strange attractor in design problem space, we must first know the unique essence toward which we will be drawn. That essential attractor becomes the design intent and it must be embraced. From Aristotle's Final Cause in Chapter 2, the teleological relation of the acorn to the oak tree should be understood in architecture as a search for a singular unique essence to which design can respond. Without first identifying this essence, design work will wander, guess, and assume rather than understand, structure, and respond. The questioning attitudes of expansive possibility and contracting solution will have no sound basis of response. While the more inventive side of human intention is vital to the translation of the essence into built form, that teleological essence of the acorn is first required.

Programming Ambiguity

In the Two Spheres context of postindustrial architecture, the unique essence of problem space is defined in the design phase of programming. Chapter 4 discussed architecture's encounter with ordered complexity in this context as principally concerned with finding the unique essence of a design situation so that its true nature can be addressed. The tasks of strategic goal setting and collaborative problem definition, multiple stakeholder engagement, and future scenario planning fit that ordered complexity. In a normative technic era framework, these tasks of programming might have been negatively considered as reductive acts of delimiting what a design should be. In the complex frame of postindustrial architecture, however, problem space construction in programming is a critical act of teleological definition. Discerning the normative from the critical here, programming has never been the mere complicated tangle of collecting and organizing design determinates. That oversimplification misses the larger tapestry of insight and foresight embodied in the deeper modes of programming. Rather than, as Martin Pawley has aptly put the reductive definition, "taking stenography" from clients then, what architectural programming actually affects is the distinction of three territories in design problem space: known determinates, irrelevant noise, and fertile ambiguity (Figure 6.2).[6]

Comprehensive preparation of known determinates of course includes the client brief of wants, needs, and resources as well as site information, climate patterns, code information, and so forth. Determinates such as these are essential for a program of any complexity, but they are not the essence. Determinates are dead and static, not rich and fertile. The disambiguation of irrelevant and impossible noise is also essential, but only as excluding from ambiguity those vectors that are beyond feasible consideration.

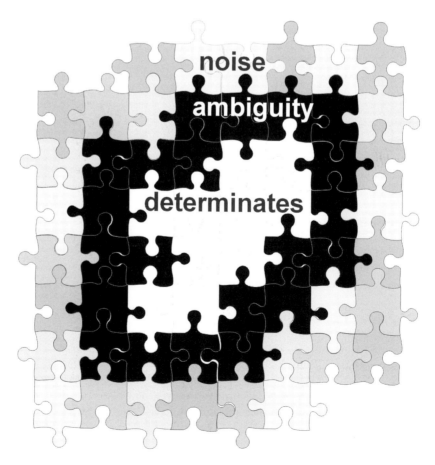

Figure 6.2 Mapping the three territories of design problem space as a primary task of architectural programming.

There is only marginal design possibility in the many possible alternative combinations and arrangements of complicated determinate data, but there are no possibilities in the excluded zone of noise.

All three territories are essential and important elements of programming, but the unique essence of a particular design exercise is always an enigmatic character of its ambiguity. For the act of design to proceed, we must first know by projection the essential place where the exercise will ultimately arrive. This projective knowledge formulates the statement of architectural intent, the design concept, the inspiration, or some other central idea that steers the process from problem space to a task environment. As a conceptual rather than prescriptive device, the unique essence becomes the seed of thought that propels design out of the impossibility of an arbitrary quest through the void, and toward an ambiguous but fertile strange attractor. The territories are the problem space, ambiguity is the task environment, and the strange attractor of the unique essence draws the architect continually toward solution space. Within that framework, design proceeds and complexity emerges.

Design operates in ambiguity, that region of problem space bounded by known determinates and encircled by incoherent noise (Figure 6.2). This rich and fertile zone of ambiguity is where possibility lives, where tandems oscillate, and where complexity breathes. Ambiguity is where windows of indeterminacy exist, possibility is nascent, and where design intentions can be most productively channeled. On the other hand, noise degenerates to chaotic turbulence and determinates die in quiet uneventful silence. But in the precious core of rich ambiguity, a unique essence lives. It must be embraced.

The Two Spheres, Complexity, and Unique Essence

Here again, in the unique essence just as in hermeneutic abduction, design embraces systemic complexity. Ambiguity at the edge of chaos is what allows for adaptation and change in any organism or system, while static equilibrium or chaotic turbulence are certain death. Correspondingly, without ambiguity in design problem space there is no complex order and no possibility for animation, emergent order, or new adaptive patterns; all one can do is rearrange the deck-chairs of predetermined requirements. In complexity, however, the tandem boundaries of determinates and noise always map out an amorphous region of design space where the nebulous essence awaits and anticipates Aristotle's Final Form.

As a Two Spheres construct, identifying ambiguity in design problem space is the primary task and ultimate goal of architectural programming. Physical and strategic influences to this process involve all the generative tandems listed in Table 6.1. Note first that nothing about this bounding of ambiguity is reductive of design possibility. In progress, of course, the transitional handoff from the analytical fact-gathering to the synthetic solution work is necessarily complex and requires further abductive hermeneutic iteration to distill out the unique essence. The generative tensions between physical and strategic spheres of the design ambiguity thus become an ongoing element of project management. All these tasks are design work, and all of this is architecture. There are no lesser or greater parts to the whole.

Relating back to architecture's four encounters with complexity, it is clear that an embrace of unique essences relates to ordered complexity and programming, and also thus back to architecture's encounter with wicked problems complexity. In messy complexity, the unique essence engages our sense of particularized and authentic place within a community fabric. As for the encounter with natural complexity, the embrace of essence situates the ecology, flows, morphogenesis, and synergy of a design as a unique organism within a natural habitat.

Unique essence also partakes of architecture's four convergences into postindustrial complexity: as a device of design vision, the essence engages cybernetic intelligence toward its realization. In global networks where stakeholders and design teams alike are more comprehensively involved in design processes, the essence is a socially constructed outcome. Value structures are also relevant to this embrace as they capture the essence of human capital and our lives in buildings. Finally, environmental convergences are important to unique essence in the special setting of any design within its particular site and climatic context.

Animation

Chapter 1 considered the human brain and mind as an analogy for complexity in design. The brain is nothing more than an organ like a lung or a kidney; the mind, however, is something quite different that emerges out of complex inter-actions within the brain's neural network, especially between its rational left hemisphere and its emotive right hemisphere as facilitated by the mediating membrane of the corpus callosum. In the end, however, the mind is self-emergent and self-ordering; it does not even reside in the brain (Kelso 1995).[7] The self-emergent mind is part of the animation of life, the difference between the whole and the sum of its parts. It is the complexity.

The Model of Animated Architecture

Along the same thread, the last section of Chapter 2 discussed complexity and architecture and included animation as distinct from mechanization. Mary Shelley's 1818 character of Frankenstein's monster, Adam, was contrasted with Kelso's Dynamic Patterns of the emergent mind to illustrate the distinc-tion.[8] We know the difference between the soulless monster and the vital mind as that of dynamic animation. We understand that this difference is vested in deep systemic complexity.

Since early modern history when natural philosophy evolved into modern science, the borders between animate and inanimate states of being have seldom been delved. Recent advances might, however, provide new possi-bilities for thinking about how those borders are crossed over and softened. Science fiction's depiction of sentient computers and real-world robotic machines around us are drawing closer together in their effective behavior. We are still far from animistic belief that robots or automated buildings could ever have souls, but there is plenty of room now to think about how much further the literal anima-tion of buildings might soon progress. Digital interfaces between buildings and people are also advancing, and such interconnected communication lines will blur future distinctions between where the building leaves off and the sentient intel-ligence begins. Can an inhabited building have a conscious intelligence?

For the present, we currently have some buildings that successfully resolve conflicting needs, ideas, values, and priorities; they address all modes of complexity and arguably attain fully mindful animation as dynamic systems.

On the other hand, we have another set of buildings which respond only to simple criteria, pleasant appearances, and symptomatic evaluation. Again and again these later buildings, however pleasant they seem in the local scale of prima facie perception, will ultimately become Frankenstein's monster when macro and non-local scale awareness is at the castle gate. If, as science and literature seem to claim, complexity is essential to full-minded animation, then building design must embrace all modes of this complexity.

Chapter 3 advanced the position that buildings are complex dynamic systems. That attitude complements the assertions in Chapter 2 that the idea of architecture is a complex construction and design is a complex activity. Amidst all that complexity, the next Two Sphere task is to show how the embrace of animation through systemic complexity facilitates the architect's design work.

Organic, Sane, Sentient, and Neural

Frank Lloyd Wright's instigation of organic architecture as a design philosophy prefigures the Two Spheres depiction of animated buildings. This early mode of organic architecture, in Wright's oeuvre, implied a sympathetic character among site, building, materials, and human habitation. The result of this common spiritual nature was to evoke a unified design expressing harmony of nature and habitation. Wright's Fallingwater, the Kaufmann Residence, is probably the best literal and figural representation of this integration (Figure 6.3).

Figure 6.3 Fallingwater, Bear Run, rural Pennsylvania—the 1935 Kaufmann Residence by Frank Lloyd Wright; photo by Abraham Yezioro, Technion - Israel Institute of Technology, via the Society of Building Science Educators.

Other Modernist interpretations of organic architecture are related to formal and morphological departures from orthogonal structures. Still other organic classifications belong to vernacular and indigenous aesthetics. Finally, in the pursuit of a sustainable design philosophy, organic architecture has come to be associated with performative ecological alignment more than with the visual sympathy of site, building, and habitation patterns.

Thinking forward from those variations on organic architecture, design in postindustrial complexity will continually advance both the affective character of harmony with nature and the effective alignment of building ecology within the encompassing natural patterns of flow. That is to say, both the affect of physical sphere and the effect of strategic sphere pursuits. As developed in the Chapter 5 Converging into Complexity discussion, the future also promises other kinds of alignment that will occur in the cybernetic convergence of bounded human cognition with digital technology.

Beginning at a fundamental level then, the Two Spheres analogy of mind as an archetype for mindful architecture can be applied literally: buildings should, even in something less than full sentience, exhibit sanity. A sane building is complex in this way, because it demonstrates a coherent sense of where it is and what it is doing. Despite the apparent naivety of that goal, there is a vast portion of the built environment we might find lacking in the proliferation of non-specific designs for generic buildings. Many examples clutter the landscape. They could just as easily be somewhere else; they seem arbitrary and generic. These buildings are not mindful, they are not animated; they are not sane. These buildings mostly belong to Dr. Frankenstein; they lack complex order and adaptive form that responds to an essence.

From sanity to sentience, or at the very least, embodied intelligence—advanced sophistication and digital automation in all phases of design, construction, and controlled operation of buildings is a positive aspect in the design of our increasingly complex buildings. If this is not a measure of the sanity and intelligence of buildings, then it is most certainly empirical evidence of embodied human intelligence. This sentience extends from the software used to articulate building design work, to the robots used to mass-produce building components, to the computer-driven control and management of completed buildings. Even in construction, tools are evolving such as laser survey marking that draw directly from the architects' digital documents and projects onto the site layout. Compared to a mere twenty years ago, it certainly seems like the robots are taking over. And, of course, that same magnitude of change is expected to occur again within the next ten years or so.

The Adam Joseph Lewis Center for Environmental Studies (LCES) at Oberlin College, Ohio, exemplifies yet another dimension of cybernetic animation as interactive feedback. William McDonough + Partners completed this project in 2001 as a facility and self-demonstrating resource for a new, student-initiated, multidisciplinary degree program (Figure 6.4). The building is located directly on the pathway from student dormitories to the main library with circulation directed through the LCES lobby. Just inside the front door, the design team placed a dashboard-style display of the building's current performance levels. Those same data were later made directly available for view over the Internet with separate tabs to display energy, water, geothermal, and other real-time data as well as historic performance. Here is a building with a direct

Figure 6.4 The 2001 Adam Joseph Lewis Center for Environmental Studies (LCES) at Oberlin College, Ohio, by William McDonough + Partners; photo by Marc Schiler, University of Southern California, via the Society of Building Science Educators.

communication link between its embodied intelligence and its inhabitants. This is a robot talking to its human companions.

Building automation of controls, sensing, and adaptive learning has usually been a back-of-the-house engineering and facilities management function. The LCES monitoring system extends that to a front door dashboard so the building can interact with resident and passerby alike. The two cybernetic paths of progress here lead to more and more animation. There are advancements in the control systems, and there are advances in the human interface. Control systems are increasingly used to monitor, automate, and integrate building operation as Building Automation Systems (BAS). The sophistication of these controls allows for features such as two-way sensing, where control signals are augmented by feedback signals. A thermostat, for example, can sense room conditions and send on/off signals to a cooling system; while the cooling system can simultaneously reply with its compressor performance level. Operation can be automatically optimized for comfort and economy. Alarm levels and automatic shutdown can be programmed if failures threaten costly breakdowns. The system can even learn to match space occupancy schedules to the daily weather forecast. Any level of logic imaginable can be programmed into such a system. Neural networks and artificial intelligence are already being employed in such BAS systems. So sanity, sentience, and feedback are just the beginning of this cybernetic animation.

At the utility scale, new "smart grid" technologies are being implemented to provide this same level of communication between buildings and humans everywhere. Additionally, this new interface allows remote controls so that building equipment can be monitored and controlled by the utility service provider. Monthly billings will summarize some of the same data that the LCES captures in real time. Eventually we can anticipate that every operating appliance will have its own email address, and that data for each appliance's energy use will appear on the monthly statement. If each appliance also has a text-to-voice capability, then we may soon find ourselves talking to the coffee pot—and having it answer us back. This event may be the kind of animation that reminds us more of an animated cartoon than of vital intelligent animation, but it should not be taken too lightly. At the far, but fast-approaching, end of the spectrum are fully automated buildings with high levels of artificial intelligence, neural networks, and the ability to adaptively learn behaviors, anticipate daily patterns, and manipulate building systems accordingly. The dynamic moving structural components of Santiago Calatrava's architecture, such as the 1992 Kuwait Pavilion, are probably only the beginning of the repeated transformations that animated buildings will perform in response to sun, wind, light, occupancy, and other stimuli.

The 1976 Rogers and Piano collaboration with Arup and Partners engineers on the Pompidou Center in Paris was a dramatic effort to animate in another way: flexible and adaptive interior space (Figure 6.5). Early schemes for the design were inspired by Arup's Peter Rice and his visit to the 1970 Osaka World's Fair, on his way back from a trip to the Sydney Opera House project. Rice was impressed by the megastructure technology of the fair's Metabolist architecture. This led to initial plans for the Pompidou to have operable floor plates to accommodate changing exhibit needs. These moving floors were one reason that all the service and circulation elements were pulled to the building exterior and left exposed, but, even after the floors were left in a fixed position, most support systems remained external to promote exhibit area flexibility. The Pompidou is an extreme example for its time, but robust organizational flexibility for building use is growing in importance as a design criterion. The fast-changing nature of globalized business enterprise and other postindustrial institutions assures this, and the relative value of human capital to building

Figure 6.5 Centre Pompidou, Paris, 1976, Rogers and Piano; photo by the author.

construction cost almost guarantees it. The discussion in Chapter 5 of Rogers's next project after Pompidou, the Lloyd's of London Headquarters, demonstrates that robust animation can be incorporated in much simpler elements than moveable floor plates or folding roofs. Building components such as replaceable modular elements, raised access floor systems, workstation furniture, demountable partitions, and wireless controls are readily available today.

Finally, returning full circle to organic renditions of animation, we can imagine complex buildings more fully and literally as organisms in the landscape. The systems basis of this as an adaptive set of flows in a containing environment has already been set out here. Ecological issues have also been addressed as relevant to animation. Taking organic animation further though, we can conceive of buildings as armatures for nature. So not only does the building adapt formal and material character in sympathy with the character of its physical setting, it also resonates with the actual physics, chemistry, and biology of the site. In this version of organic animation, architecture is a natural feature of the site. To cite Mostafavi and Leatherbarrow, such buildings will patina with age rather than stain and rot.[9] Beyond that though, these works will provide habitat for plants, animals, and insects. They will create seasonal microclimates by interacting with the site, and they will be tuned to the climatic variations of sun, wind, and rain.

Aesthetics

> Aesthetic consideration conveys the interdependence of our sense of beauty and our intellectual understanding.
>
> (Scruton 1979)[10]

> The ontological function of the beautiful is to bridge the chasm between the ideal and the real.
>
> (Gadamer 1986: 67)[11]

A fourth mode of embracing complexity is that of aesthetics, which is defined here in Scruton's and Gadamer's terms as the connection between our intellectual understanding of something and our sublime appreciation of it: between the effect and the affect we experience. We can also define aesthetics in this sense as how design is employed to connect the ideal with the real—or, in other words, the search for a beautiful solution within the realization of a construction. As the formal meaning of aesthetics involves the philosophy and study of human appreciation of beauty, these special architectural definitions are aligned with our normal usage. Embracing complexity thus affords us an aesthetic pursuit of connecting the idealized physical aspect of a design problem with the strategic reality of its built solution. In the process it is clear that the designer will connect his understanding of the design with his appreciation of it. If the built solution is true to these principles, there is a significant likelihood that the building will become an authentic part of its setting, neighborhood, and other scales of relation.

A fundamental redefinition of design must finally be asserted here. As suggested in Chapter 1 and demonstrated consistently thereafter, the physical and strategic spheres of architecture comprise a generative tandem set of activities in which design operates. The model of physical affect as design with strategic effect in support is rejected. Neither the sublime physical sphere nor the intelligent strategic sphere has any claim on the totality of design action, cognition, imagination, or aesthetic result. Both are necessary but neither is sufficient unto architecture. Design is a confluence of the Two Spheres, just as human creativity is always a confluence of the left and right brain hemispheres. Design is an emergent construct of the physical and the strategic, just as the mind is an emergent animation of the left and right brain hemispheres.

As for the real and the ideal in architecture, for our understanding and our appreciation we must accept that aesthetics is the bridge between their paired dimensions, and design is the act of bridging. The bridge we build must span from the ideal to the real, from the physical to the strategic, and from the sublime to the intelligent. And as Kahn proclaimed for all great buildings, that bridge must reach in both directions, for design must span from the immeasurable to the measurable—and then back again.

Restating design in this Two Spheres model is not castigation or critique of what has come before in the theory and practice of architecture. Rather, this postindustrial eotechnic articulation of design as a complex activity should expand and ennoble what architects do as society outgrows the pioneering paleotechnic and the industrial past. There are, however, some terms which have become trivialized in the industrial age of architecture and we should all protest against those habits that now marginalize the values of design. Corrections have been addressed throughout the Two Spheres rationale presented against the misconceptions of "system," "aesthetics," and "design." So systems are to be understood not as hardware, but as organized sets of flow. Aesthetics is not just the appeal of beauty, but the bridge between the real and the ideal. Finally, design is not vested in sublime and direct immediate experience alone, but in the connective bridges between those traits and the embodiment of human intelligence and foresight.

Embracing a Two Spheres Eco-Aesthetic

One example of this aesthetic bridge is illustrated by the span between ecological motivation to form and epicurean values of formalist expression. The dynamic of this tandem is an eco-aesthetic. As an emerging field of study, eco-aesthetics broadly concerns itself with the connection of beauty to the human valuation of our natural environment. Table 6.2 suggests a few of the many related paths taken in pursuit of this connection. The ensuing list of research topics related to eco-aesthetics is quite extensive: eco-literacy, eco-theology, eco-ethics, eco-justice, and so forth.

Despite these varied pursuits toward eco-aesthetic understanding, the appreciation of architecture vis-à-vis its ecological role as our place in nature is relatively unexplored. Notable exceptions exist but the exploration is young. On the surface this is not so surprising, because the formal artistic character of architecture has always been more ennobled than its performal aspects. How, after all, does one aesthetically consider and appreciate a sustainably designed building differently from one that is otherwise pleasing and meaningful to experience? Given the current ecology movement and the adoption of sustainable design

Table 6.2 Some diverse pursuits of eco-aesthetics

Nature as Subject	Nature as Object
Ethics	Art
Philosophy	Biology
Religion	Forestry management
Sociology	Landscape design

principles by architects everywhere, it might seem that a connection should emerge. Long-standing differences between architecture as art and ecology as science, however, make this a difficult bridge to build, but given the urgency of environmental limits society now encounters, perhaps a convergence is near.

Framing the Motivations to Form
At issue here are the conflicting value spheres at the core of formalism and ecology. Sustainable design favors ecological harmony whereas formalism advances the design of artful and significant human places. At risk are the corresponding outcomes that might result from their individual failures: ecologists fear a bleak future set in a spoiled natural environment, while formalists rail against a dismal day-to-day existence in a utopian but meaningless world of perfectly behaved routine. The point here is hopefully to illustrate that the two value spheres are not inherently exclusive of each other, despite their equally radical natures.

One sphere of this antagonism is that of architecture as meaningful art. The other sphere is ecology as truth and science. Tensions between the ideals of artistic design and the optimized technical performance of buildings are not new or unique; the differences are paralleled in many other aspects of society. C.P. Snow's *The Two Cultures and the Scientific Revolution* (1959), for example, was an early exposition of communication failures between the sciences and humanities in general.[12] Decades later, Alberto Pérez Gómez still found reason to complain about *Architecture and the Crisis of Modern Science* (1983) with the demotion of geometry "from its regal status as the generator of forms to being the servant of surveyors and engineers."[13] The general decline of Modernist aesthetics in architectural design was a corresponding factor. Modernism, at least in the hands of its masters, had championed a sense of meaning in the honest visual expression of essence and function. What replaced Modern architecture however might well be generalized as a rejection of any notion perceived as a threat to unconstrained formalism and a corresponding renouncement of scientific reductionism.

The advent of the energy crisis in the early 1970s and the subsequent rapid development of high-performance building technology only widened the gap. Now though, on the brink of consumer-driven demand for sustainable design, architects seem to be capitulating. Most recent Pritzker Prize architects would label their work as Green and most architectural journals currently feature newsworthy LEED projects.

At the basic level though, formalist architecture is still one thing, and sustainability is clearly something else. The prima facie distinction between them is as clear as that between civil engineering and design. For pure formalistic motivation art is the ultimate end, while factual matters are largely seen as reductive constraints. Ecological inspiration, on the other hand, seeks harmony with nature and regards artistic outcome as a consequence of honest truth. Formalism is inventive while ecology is discovered. Formalism is intentional while ecology is emergent. Formalism is authored while ecology is responsive. Before the two motivations can finally harmonize rather than compromise, we must first refine an aesthetic principle that accommodates them both. Somehow the two must be held as tantamount, equally radical and similarly beautiful.

Elaborating the Differences
Some dualistic and admittedly oversimplified distinctions of ecological and architectural motivations to form are listed in Table 6.3. These are offered as background perspective with the normal caveat that the differences are seldom so black and white as any such synopsis depicts. To summarize these distinctions though, we can say that ecological architecture advocates for

Table 6.3 Some fundamental differences in purely ecological vs. purely formal motivations

Formalism	*Ecology*
Invented form	Emergent form
Comprehensive	Integrated
Ideal	Real
Intentional	Natural
Inventive	Creative
Unique	Abundant
Emotive, adductive, and intentional basis	Rational, deductive, and optimized basis
Implicit understanding, contingent and situational truths	Explicit knowledge
Whole and integral (dominance of the whole)	Systemic and interrelated (fit of parts to the whole)
Ephemeralize (whole is more and less than sum of parts)	Actualize (reach measurable objectives)
Propositional (assertion of an idea)	Evidentiary (assertion of data)
Pragmatic (what works)	Theoretical (why it works)
Relational (so that . . .)	Causal (because . . .)
Authoritarian (supported by intuition and expertise)	Authoritative (supported by knowledge)
Traditional (inertia of 5000 years of comparative works)	Evolutionary (basis for change in existing paradigm)
Epicurean (good to you, like cuisine from a chef)	Egalitarian (good for you, like diet by a nutritionist)
Culture directed (values and experiences)	Society directed (rules and institutions)
Incorporate technology (make it useful to an idea)	Accommodate technology (make it useful to humans)

(Continued overleaf)

Table 6.3 *Continued*

Formalism	*Ecology*
The sublime sensibilities	Strategic intelligence
Dominance and control by human intention	Dominance of natural and spontaneous order
Accountability to owner	Concern for user
Creative insight	Collaborative discourse
Cost and risk economics	Value and time economics
Local scale perspectives, the here and now, Zen and Dasein	Macro scale perspectives, tomorrow and everywhere
Role of immediacy and elevated state of being	Role of protecting secure and harmonious future

nature and for science, while formalist architecture advocates for human intention and for art, or at least artifice. Perhaps as Trish Glazebrook suggests, the
most salient points are Aristotelian in that ecology is telos, a search for form
that emerges from nature's internal principles; while architecture is conventionally pursued as techne, a search for form that is invented by human will and
imagination usually external to how nature acts.[14]

Two further distinctions from Table 6.3 should be emphasized here.
These are less operational than Glazebrook's emergent/invented differences,
but just as significant in their underpinnings. First, formalist design tends to
place high value on affect, or impressions that are experienced as a Zen or
Daisen transformation of normal perception to a non-ordinary transcendent
realization of the present moment. This emphasizes the experiential aspects of
architecture in its physicality: material, space, sequence, and other direct
immediate sensory perceptions. Ecological design, on the other hand, places
high value on effect, especially in the strategic intelligence embodied in form,
and how it captures and utilizes human foresight.

A second, important, and somewhat commingled distinction worthy
of emphasis remains: scope and scale. First, it would be wrong to say that the
architecture of artistic formalism is never concerned with strategic intelligence,
just as it would be foolish to suggest that ecological architecture is never
concerned with pleasure or beauty. That said, however, the characterizations
still reflect generalizable rather than falsely stereotypical ambitions of the two
value spheres. This can be readily concluded from the main body of outcomes
that their respective practitioners continue to produce.

For scope and scale then, architecture can be seen to focus on the
local and the ideal whereas ecology is grounded in the global and the real. This
draws on David Bohm's notions from Chapter 2 of the non-local universe
where local scale impacts are observed directly but only symptomatically in
instant gratification and confirmation of immediate perception; while non-local
"implicate" effects are only known through deep systemic interaction.

> What we take for reality, Bohm argues, are surface phenomena, expli-
> cate forms that have temporarily unfolded out of an underlying impli-
> cate order. Within this deeper order forms are enfolded within each

other so systems which may be well separated in the Explicate Order are contained within each other in the Implicate Order. Within the Implicate Order one form can be both interior and exterior to another.

(Peat 1988: 304)[15]

Thus, the contrast of local/non-local is related to that of ideal/real. Local scale perception can ignore long-term and dynamic effects observed in ecological and other real systems. In other words, focusing on immediate formal experience is often only symptomatically satisfying and lacks concern for underlying systemic outcomes. Ecological perspectives, on the other hand, are governed by the inevitabilities of real and complex systemic relations at global scales and across long time spans. The purely formalist motivation is intent on immediate local impressions that promote experiences of a visionary ideal place through the physical composition of form, space, and material; while ecological motivation is concerned with long-range foresight about both visible and invisible interactions. We can conclude that ecology focuses on effect while formalism tends to focus on affect.

Aesthetic Resolution
Leaving aside the exclusive dualistic distinctions between ecological- and formalist-centered approaches to architecture, we can now return to the inclusive pluralistic definitions of aesthetics by Scruton and Gadamer that promote eco-aesthetic resolution.[16] Both of these assertions define aesthetics as a connective tissue between beauty and human intellect. Using Chapter 2 language again, the formal and the ecological motivations comprise a tandem of tangled complications engaged in a generative dynamic conversation. The aesthetic they weave is a complex tapestry. Applying this woven connection as an eco-aesthetic requires attaching it at one end to our sublime appreciation of immediate physical experience, and at the other end to intelligent understanding of ecological foresight. As such we can consider eco-aesthetics as a kind of intelligence and literacy that applies not only to physical aspects of the built environment, but also to those abstract appreciations where there is no physical element of appreciation, such as intellectual beauty and social equity.

Architecture is uniquely posed in this act of connection, and this uniqueness is explained by the spacings between architecture, art, and science. Unlike art, for example, architecture must serve function, economy, durability, and context as well as meaning, significance, and delight. Relying again on Louis Kahn: "A painter can paint square wheels on a cannon to express the futility of war. A sculptor can carve the same square wheels, but the architect must use round wheels."[17]

Allen Carlson points out that architecture also differs from art in that architecture has an ethical or moral function that is inseparable from its expressive ambitions.[18] The principle of aestheticism in art that seeks to separate the pleasure derived from objects from their moral or ethical origins simply does not apply to architecture. Carlson draws on the aesthetician Hospers to point out that any building which serves as a monument to oppression, racism, or other forms of exploitation may attain a "thin" aesthetic of superficial appearance, but will never achieve the "thick" aesthetic of transcendent beauty we appreciate in more enlightened works.

So, in the end, architecture does not operate like art. Some buildings may be as well composed and masterfully conceived as a work of art, but their manifestations are best judged by what they contribute to utility, society, and culture—not solely by their sculptural or compositional expressions or by their symbolic meanings.

But architecture is also not a science. The differences between architecture and mere buildings are what will transform our environment from everyday routine locations to sublime experiences of place. These transformations are not attained by optimization or rational deduction, but rather by informed abductive vision that can seize upon the essence of a design opportunity and align that inspiration with the tectonics of construction and the act of human habitation. So neither can we say that architecture is science.

Architecture then, is uniquely and independently architecture. It has its own aesthetic challenge, its own difficult knowledge, its own coded under-standings and subtle sensibilities, its own mandates to society and culture, and its own independent corpus of work on which to build, critique, and learn. Most importantly, however, architecture has its own beauty and, to borrow the research term, its own validity of "truth value." To return to aesthetic defini-tions, architecture is thus uniquely posed to "connect our sense of beauty with our intellectual understanding" and "to bridge the chasm between the real and the ideal." In this example, one component of the real is taken as the natural principles of ecology and a corresponding component of the ideal is taken as the sublime ambitions of human intention in architecture.

Summary

We live in nature. We can really no more say that we live in buildings than we can say that we live in our clothes. Buildings are obviously important artifacts because they embody and host our work and play, our rituals and history, but we live continually in the larger context of nature. Buildings are what we put on around us and occupy so as to partake of all the wonderful artifice of human intention. But all the while we continually draw on nature to construct those buildings, to warm and cool them, and to power all their functions. In the systemic and non-local sense as opposed to symptomatic and local perceptions, we dwell in nature.

The Two Spheres argues for an architecture of systemic unity brought forth by the holistic and abductive act of design; a unity that harmo-nizes the radically conflicted poles of ecologically emergent form on one hand and that of intentionally invented form on the other (Figure 6.6). The creative production of design is thus characterized as being necessarily both ideally innovative and systemically appropriate. In closing then, a quote from Nobel chemist, Ilya Prigogine:

> We believe that we are actually at the beginning of a new scientific era. We are observing the birth of a science that is no longer limited to idealized and simplified situations but reflects the complexity of the real world, a science that views us and our creativity as part of a fundamental trend present at all levels of nature.[19]

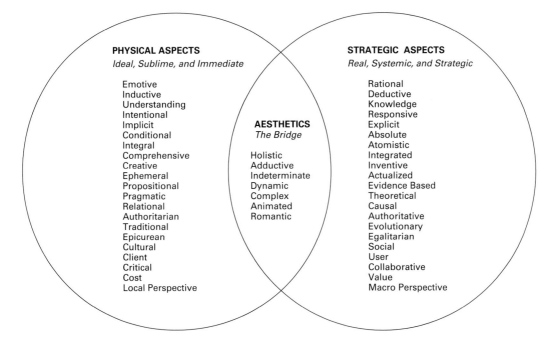

PHYSICAL ASPECTS
Ideal, Sublime, and Immediate

Emotive
Inductive
Understanding
Intentional
Implicit
Conditional
Integral
Comprehensive
Creative
Ephemeral
Propositional
Pragmatic
Relational
Authoritarian
Traditional
Epicurean
Cultural
Client
Critical
Cost
Local Perspective

AESTHETICS
The Bridge

Holistic
Adductive
Indeterminate
Dynamic
Complex
Animated
Romantic

STRATEGIC ASPECTS
Real, Systemic, and Strategic

Rational
Deductive
Knowledge
Responsive
Explicit
Absolute
Atomistic
Integrated
Inventive
Actualized
Evidence Based
Theoretical
Causal
Authoritative
Evolutionary
Egalitarian
Social
User
Collaborative
Value
Macro Perspective

Figure 6.6 Eco-aesthetic principles and the paired value spheres of intentional formalism and emergent ecology.

Conclusion to Part Two

The notion that design should serve the complex unity of the real and the ideal is not a new one, nor is it unique to architecture. Visionary quests and the urge to beauty have always inspired our imagination; while the attendant programmatic realities and logistical restraints have always spurred our ingenuity. Service to cultural advancement that is concomitant with societal need has always propelled us. Those generative tandems are inherent in all human endeavor and are especially definitional of the act of design.

The Two Spheres perspective serves that larger set of comprehensive conversations by articulating how a pluralistically enlightened embrace of complexity is important to the resolution of sublime physical immediacy and intelligent strategic foresight. Architecture's escalating encounters with wicked problems, messy authenticity, ordered programs, and the natural environment have provided the background framework of this complexity. The postindustrial convergences with cybernetics, globalization, value structures, and environmental limits have activated our subsequent urge to systemic complexity. Now, our embrace of hermeneutics, unique essence, animation, and aesthetics will facilitate design complexity. The Two Spheres will be whole-minded.

Such whole-minded consideration is shown here to necessitate an explicit articulation of architectural constructs. Some old notions of systems, aesthetics, and design have been trivialized by generic and vague repetition. In the Two Spheres model, their true complexity is celebrated and embraced. The industrial age distinction of physical and strategic spheres of architecture is replaced with an abductive hermeneutic. The aesthetic span between the real and the ideal has been bridged. The immeasurable and the measurable are joined.

Finally, the Two Spheres of architecture are differentiated here from the companion disciplines of science and art. Architecture is clearly discernible from those other two grand pursuits. Moreover, architecture is in fact a wholly different third way of knowing the world. Comparisons of architecture to the pursuits of art and science always miss this distinction, and so the true purpose of architecture is continually muddled in misdirected attempts to relegate the architect to the service of either art or science as a jealous master. Science is on the strategic bank of the river. Art is on the physical aspect shore. Philosophy flows by between them. Architecture is the bridge.

Part Three

Mapping Complexity onto the Realm

Chapter 7

Mapping Complexity onto the Profession

Examining architecture as a discipline, studying the character of architectural knowledge, reveals a fundamental dichotomy between the past procedural view of architecture as the making of the artifact and the substantive view that incorporates the effects of architecture as well.

(Piotrowski and Robinson 2000: 77)[1]

To be true to the model of holistic complexity which this book advocates as an operative theory about architecture, it is necessary now to connect the dots. Stated in terms of a Two Spheres analogy about tangles, tandems, and tapestries then, it is time to weave the tapestry together well enough to make a whole cloth. So now the threads of postindustrial complexity that have been combed through in Parts One and Two can be reiterated and spindled. And thereafter, at the risk of taking the tangled analogy too far, the intertwined design can be embroidered here in Part Three.

The Threads

Tangles

- Part One: Scoping Complexity—Postindustrial Change, Systems Thinking, and Complex Buildings

  ○ Four Precepts

    ▪ Three Epochs—Geddes, Mumford, and later Bell describe the epochal transitions from preindustrial paleotechnic to industrial technic periods of civilization; their work collectively predicts the impending forces of a third era in postindustrial knowledge society,

    ▪ The Chasm—recent consequences of postindustrial transformation are evident in the fragmentation of society in general and, correspondingly, in architecture, but these differences are complementary rather than mutually exclusive; Louis Kahn's measurable and immeasurable stages in the metamorphosis of the architect's work is key to understanding how the chasm is bridged,

- The Complex Whole—1 + 1 = 3; as the complex whole is different from the simple sum of its parts, that difference is explained by the synthesis of interrelation and interaction; systemic harmony supersedes mechanistic hierarchy,
- Two Spheres—Kelso's neurological explanations of left and right brain hemispheres and the emergent order of the complex mind are the working model for the Two Spheres explanation of strategic and physical aspects of architectural design: foresight and immediacy, the intelligent and the sublime, the real and the ideal.

○ Complexity—complicated tangles, generative tandems, and complex tapestries lead to complex and indeterminate interactions; the philosophical distinctions of phenomenology and the experiential context of architecture are connected; complexity is connected to architecture by scientific outlook, postindustrial reflection, philosophical insight, and architectural introspection; Popper's Three Worlds model serves as an explanatory framework,

○ Systems—sets of organized flow are propelled by tandem forces; systems adapt and thrive in ambiguity but die in homeostasis and in chaos; systems exhibit complex, indeterminate, and non-linear behavior,

○ Buildings—the systemic behavior of buildings entails flow as well as local and non-local phenomena; buildings themselves comprise systems of interrelated parts that behave and interact in complex dynamic ways; programmatic complexity is joined by evidence-based design, post-occupancy issues, building automation, and teleological essence in the consideration of building design as a complex activity and of buildings themselves as complex systems; there is a clinical basis of architectural practice as the resolution of one case based on the understanding of many cases.

The Tandems

- Part Two: Embracing Complexity—Encounters, Convergences, and Embraces

  ○ Four Encounters with Complexity

    - Wicked—bounded human rationality and indeterminate problems typify the complexity of design problem space (Rittel, Simon, Ackoff),
    - Messy—authentic places in the cultural fabric are a top-down ambition of design; the inclusive whole is required (Venturi, Jacobs, Alexander),
    - Ordered—programming is a bottom-up advent of postindustrial society; robust design solutions must recognize multiple

> stakeholder perspectives, inevitable changes in use, maintenance, and operation; ambiguity, determinates, and noise are bounded in the design problem space (Peña, Sanoff, Preiser),

- ■ Natural—the five dimensions of natural complexity are ecology, flow, morphogenesis, synergistics, and Gestalt psychology (Olgyay, McHarg, Carson, Givoni, Knowles, Mazria, Lyle).

- ○ Four Convergences into Complexity

  - ■ Cybernetics—bounded rationality and wicked problems converge with information technology and the exponential growth of computing power; both the ends and the means of architectural design are radically impacted,

  - ■ Globalization—local scale industrial-era thinking converges with higher order networks; the matrix of social and cultural priorities is rebalanced,

  - ■ Value—long-term value investment converges with short-term profit-taking; value is produced by creative use of information; the intelligent recipe, design, is what catalyzes the ingredients; the context of architecture shifts as commerce, government, and social organization adapt new value structures,

  - ■ Ecology—linear resource consumption models converge with postindustrial eotechnic cycles of systemic flow; technology becomes a lever to reduce our environmental footprint rather than a mechanism to multiply the damage; from the paleotechnic relation to nature-as-context and the technic era commodification of nature-as-resource, we move to the eotechnic regard for nature-as-model; the strategic and physical aspects of architectural design are highly synthesized.

- ○ Four Embraces of Complexity

  - ■ Hermeneutics—the propositional and iterative basis of architectural design matches an abductive approach to complex design thinking,

  - ■ Unique Essence—in teleological and Aristotelian terms, the final cause of a complex system describes its essential form and most elemental traits; the unique essence identifies a region of rich ambiguity between determinate data and irrelevant noise; design operates in that ambiguity,

  - ■ Animation—as in the distinction of brain organ from animated mind, the discernment of a merely satisfactory building from a vital work of architecture requires the embrace of complexity; complexity cannot be tamed,

  - ■ Aesthetics—the tandem junction of the Two Spheres is a point of inflection for bridging "the chasm between the real and the ideal" (Gadamer), and for "connecting our understanding with our appreciation" (Scruton); aesthetics is the bridge; design is the bridging.

The Tapestry

- Part Three: Mapping Complexity onto the Realm—Four Domains of Postindustrial Architecture

  - Profession—stewarding ethics, advancement, and societal values,
  - Occupation—complexity: seeking, revealing, embracing, mapping, scoping, and mining it; but never taming it,
  - Education—Popper's Three Worlds again; between the occupation and the discipline; fields and fences; standards of assessment and accreditation.
  - Discipline—research, discourse, critique, and theory in the age of knowledge production and human capital.

Mapping Complexity onto the Realm

Figure 7.1 depicts a conceptual map of the realm of architecture as a complete discipline.[2] This diagram is based on the generic aspects of most professional disciplines but also follows after Piotrowski and Robinson's *The Discipline of Architecture*, with a debt to all the contributors in that volume. To that end, the four domains of architecture are functionally described in this figure, along with the main interconnecting dialogs. Each of the chapters in Part Three explores the Two Sphere overlay of postindustrial complexity onto a corresponding domain of the realm.[3]

Discourses in the Realm

Differentiating the individual occupation of practicing architects from the collective profession of architecture as a societal institution leads to several other

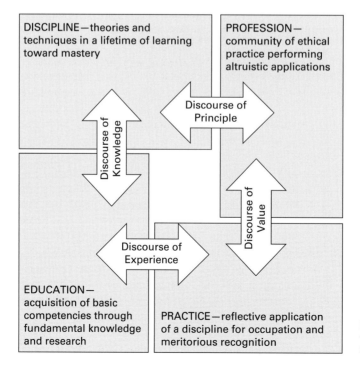

Figure 7.1 Four domains in the realm of architecture. Source: Bachman 2010.

such distinctions and also helps identify some separate yet reciprocal roles of the parties involved. First, some organizational entity must be formed to represent the profession, and that organization must operate both internally and externally. Internal operations involve cooperative agreement among architects as to ethical business practices, requirements for professional standing, and other such standardized member responsibilities. External operations concern representation to regulatory government agencies and other professions, as well as to the general populace and their public perception of what architects do. In general, individual architects support their professional organization as it works to advance their legal status, maintain fair business practices, and improve market access. That support is a discourse about the value of architectural services. Other more intrinsic goals are involved as well, such as preservation of historically significant buildings in the face of disregard and demolition, but the extrinsic goals are sufficient to define the operating parameters of architecture in its professional domain.

That value discourse between architecture's professional domain and the occupational practice domain is joined by similar relations with the educational and disciplinary domains. Figure 7.1 depicts this overall dynamic as the realm of architecture. A descriptive sketch of these discourses opens some exploration on how Two Sphere complexity impacts each domain.

First off, architecture's educational and professional domains are connected by a shared discourse of qualification wherein the profession establishes and monitors a set of nominal standards of education and experience that prequalify candidates for licensure. Schools contribute to this discourse by perpetuating both the knowledge of the profession and the future practitioners who continue architecture's service to the profession. The profession in turn helps assure that educational standards actually prepare candidates to enter the field. The profession also mentors programs that advance all stages of an architect's continuing education preceding and following their entry to occupational practice. Schools provide architectural libraries, research, peer review, schematic proposals, critique, general discourse, and future practitioners.

Second, the disciplinary domain of architecture is interposed between the educational and professional modes, relating to education in a discourse of knowledge and to the profession in a discourse of principle. The discipline domain is far from a minor intermediary in this, however, and this is true because of, or perhaps in spite of, the fact that the disciplinary domain is the most diffused mode of architecture. Of the four domains, disciplinary concern is the only one that does not have its own house. Instead, the disciplinary domain inhabits schools, practices, and professional organizations alike. In a healthy profession, these discourses sustain and nurture service to society.

Mapping Complexity onto the Profession

Every discipline exists as a culture bound together by a connective tissue of shared values, experiences, and beliefs. That tissue defines the common denominator of the discipline that unites all the realms of the domain. A multitude of subcultures with some further sets of differing beliefs and values will always circulate within the primary culture, but all those subcultures will share enough of the dominant values from the corpus of the discipline to belong to that flesh. Subcultures are positive forces because they prevent complacent homogeneity, subvert normalcy, and stimulate evolutionary adaptation to change. Further, subcultural differences provide meaningful segmentation and healthy fluidity: one can belong to several subcultures at the same time without committing to a single specific or rigid dogma. Altogether then, cultures and subcultures provide the systemic behaviors of healthy organisms: individual agents, feedback, adaptation, and organized flow.

Something about architecture, however, has gone awry along the way, and it has to do with the notion of articulating a common denominator. A representative event seems to have occurred at the 1996 American Institute of Architects Convention in Minneapolis with the release of a three-year, 172-page study entitled *Building Community: A New Future for Architecture Education and Practice*. This document, later known as the "Boyer Report," was commissioned by all five of the collateral architectural organizations and hence by the collective discipline of architecture, at least as it defines the profession in the United States.[4] While the report centers on architectural education, it also involves discourses among all the realms of the discipline. Ernest Boyer, president of the Carnegie Foundation for the Advancement of Teaching, authored the work, along with Carnegie Senior Fellow Lee Mitgang. Among the seven interlocking recommendations, their report famously suggests "Standards without Standardization." From the viewpoint of promoting healthy subcultural fluidity, this is certainly sound advice. Unfortunately, the intentional ambiguity of the terms used has allowed for corrupt interpretation and a resulting loss of common denominator definitions. Standards, in the discourse of architecture, have somehow become focal points of resistance. "Without standardization," on the other hand, has become the lever from which much argument against empirically measurable criteria of any variety is launched. This is not at all what the Boyer Report was suggesting and a major reconsideration is in order. The study actually argues that standards without standardization should increase coherence, harmony, and integration; not the other way around. The use of "Community" in the title was meant to convey that collective spirit.

The infinite permutation of value and belief sets in subcultures is consequently both an animating force and a disruptive one. It is incumbent upon the professional association of architecture to strike the correct balance between individuality and common denominator standards. In the age of postindustrial transformation, it is also the duty of the professional domain to guard against the death of stasis and homogeneity.

On Growth and Change

"Growth, the only evidence of life."

(Thomas Scott 1779)[5]

"It is not the strongest of the species that survive, nor the most intelligent, but the one most responsive to change."

(Clarence Darrow 1925)[6]

Living things grow and growing things change. Among those living, growing, changing things we count all the pursuits of civilization we wish to nurture and sustain. In any such grand pursuit, the persistence of growth and change defines a discipline's continuing relation to society. In this case, that relation is architecture's professional domain, wherein a collective culture is maintained and disciplinary progress is promoted.

As in medicine, engineering, or any licensed profession, qualified practitioners of architecture are obligated to serve society in return for a monopoly on their exclusive title of Architect. That bargain is sealed by the life-long learning that architects invest in the mastery of a large, difficult, and evolving body of knowledge in all aspects of their field: design, technology, contracts, code, construction, materials, marketing, project management, and so forth. Mastery is coupled inextricably with a corresponding responsibility toward nurturing and growing the knowledge base through reflection and research. As a criterion for what counts as architecture then, we include works in service to society as well as work that enhances architecture's knowledge base. Individual occupation in the skilled application of that knowledge is discussed in Chapter 8, but the present topic concerns the collective domain of architecture as a professional body and institution of society.

Postindustrial Complexity

For there to be a living profession of architecture that has sufficient adaptive abilities to serve a living and growing world society, there obviously must be a process of continual growth and change in what architects do. Postindustrial complexity assures that this process is critical, and the professional domain of architecture is where such growth and change must be collectively shaped, nurtured, incentivized, and institutionalized.

Such change is never easy. Contrary to their reputation for avant-garde creativity, architects are a traditional and conservative lot who resist fundamental changes in how they should think and operate. Perhaps such change challenges too many architects' designerly self-image and their personal sensibilities about what constitutes good architecture. Perhaps the timeless accomplishments of architecture invoke a tenacious adherence to the status-quo world of how architects have always operated. Or perhaps there is just too much cognitive dissonance involved in accepting that it is, again, time for something new. At any rate, it is clear that a process of ongoing change is not accomplished by an up-swell of disciplinary innovation in the practitioner domain. It is equally clear that a collective agreement is needed to institution-alize such reforms anyway; so the infrastructure for change must be managed in the professional domain.

Worldwide, we are going to build more buildings in the next thirty years than in the last thirty thousand and there are going to be more societal, scientific, and technical upheavals in those same thirty years than in all of human history combined. The magnitude and velocity of this change cannot be overstated; its impact is likely beyond our present scope of belief even to imagine. Postindustrial evolution pushes architects through this tumult of opportunity and on into new encounters, convergences, and embraces with the complex tapestry of accelerated change. The results could be wonderful or they could be disastrous. The balance depends on the collective organization and leadership from within the professional domain of architecture. With all that is at stake, the results are not likely to be mixed.

Perhaps the role of architecture in global change is both central and marginal in the same manner as Jacques Monod, the great biologist and founder of molecular biology, once pointed out in that biology:

> the living world—being a tiny and very "special" part of the universe—is not likely to reveal general laws applicable outside the biosphere, but if the ultimate aim . . . is indeed, as I believe, to clarify man's relationship to the universe, then biology must be accorded a central position.
>
> (Jacques Monod 1971: xi)[7]

To amplify Monod's hope for what can be accomplished, even from what is arguably a tiny special position such as biology or architecture, consider the challenge presented by the linguist and activist Noam Chomsky:

> Optimism is a strategy for making a better future. Because unless you believe that the future can be better, you are unlikely to step up and take responsibility for making it so. If you assume there is no hope, you guarantee there will be no hope. . . . The choice is yours.
>
> (Chomsky, cited in Rossetto 1998: 166–167)[8]

Our most earnest hope for the profession and collective organization of architecture should be to actualize this optimism. What is design if not a "strategy for making a better future"? What is architecture if not the "responsibility for making it so"? And, even if architects are few and architecture is a tiny special concern, surely it is true that architecture is ultimately connected to clarifying our "relationship to the universe."

Chapter 8

Postindustrial Occupation in Architecture

> You never change things by fighting the existing reality. To change something, build a new model that makes the existing model obsolete.
>
> (Richard Buckminster Fuller)[1]

Our emerging neotechnic era presents a profoundly radical opportunity for individual architects. Evolutions toward social good, cybernetic exploration, ecological sustenance, evidenced validation, and global interrelatedness are not threats against good design; they are promises for it. To achieve those promises then, we must activate the eotechnic evolutions so that the measurable and the immeasurable are made whole. This is the Two Spheres model of practice in the postindustrial and postpositive era of complex and systemic consideration: we can elevate design as a third way of knowing and we can bridge "the chasm between the real and the ideal." Rampant fragmentation of underlying value structures in architecture have hindered the tapestry of World Three discourse and perpetuated World Two tangles for too long.

Some history is useful here to establish a perspective of strategy in the long view continuum of design practice (see Box 8.1 on strategic partners). For brevity this history is restricted to one vein of American architecture from about 1890 to 1970. The idea is to recast the mainstream work of notable practices to emphasize the vital importance of strategic design as embodied directly in the design team. This theme differs from the usual story line in that it attributes design success to collaborative synergy more than just to the heroic figures that are so well known for their contributions to physical design.

Box 8.1 Strategic partners

Burnham and Root, 1873–91

The firm created the modern type of highly organized architectural office suited to the planning of metropolitan buildings. Its partners were pioneers in the development of the steel-frame office building, and won international attention by their planning of the World's Columbian Exposition, Chicago, 1893. John W. Root (1850–91) spent the Civil War years in Liverpool, England, studying music and architecture. He went to New York University and graduated with a civil engineering degree in 1869. In 1872, Root moved to Chicago and secured a job as head draftsman in the firm of Carter, Drake, and Wight, where he met Daniel H. Burnham (1846–1912). In 1873 Burnham and Root established their own company. Their landmark Monadnock tower is the tallest building in the world that is supported primarily by brick load-bearing walls.

Adler and Sullivan, 1880–95

Louis Sullivan (1856–1924) studied at the Massachusetts Institute of Technology and the École des Beaux-Arts in Paris. He was employed in the Chicago office of William Le Baron Jenney, designer of the first steel-skeleton skyscraper, and later entered the office of Dankmar Adler, where he became chief draftsman, and in 1880 was made a member of the firm. Adler (1844–1900) was born in Eisenach, Germany. Moving with his family to Chicago in 1861, he was an officer in the Engineer Corps during the Civil War.

The superb acoustics of the Auditorium Building (Chicago 1889) was Adler's doing and, like the solution to the tricky problem of carrying 15,000 tons of tower on Chicago silt, was typical of his brilliant, rough mind. Adler was also the consultant on acoustics for Carnegie Hall in New York, where the fine quality of its sound repeatedly saved it from the wreckers' hammers.

McKim, Mead and White, 1879–1909

The largest architectural firm in the world in 1900, McKim, Mead and White developed a model architectural practice. Mead (1846–1928) was the in-house technologist and construction manager. He was a fellow of the American Institute of Architects and served as president of the New York chapter from 1907 to 1908. Mead was a member of the American Academy of Arts and Letters and the National Academy of Design. From 1899 to 1909 he was president of the Amherst College Alumni Association in New York. In 1909, Mead replaced his deceased partner McKim as president of the American Academy in Rome. He retained that post for eighteen years. In 1913 the American Academy of Arts and Letters conferred its first gold medal to any architect upon Mead. In 1922 he was made a knight commander of the Order of the Crown in Italy.

Frank Lloyd Wright and William Wesley Peters, 1932–59

William Wesley Peters (1912–91) attended Evansville College (1927–30), and studied engineering at Massachusetts Institute of Technology (1930–31). In 1932 he became Wright's first apprentice. Peters "provided the engineering that made many of Mr. Wright's buildings possible," says Richard Carney, CEO, Frank Lloyd Wright Foundation. Under Wright, Peters was one of the three pillars of Taliesin, including John H. Howe and Eugene Masselink. He penned more than two dozen significant professional articles and was recognized throughout the international architectural community.

Eero Saarinen and Partners, 1950–61

Eero Saarinen (1910–61) was born in Finland. He moved to the USA with his father Eliel, but studied in Paris (1929–30), Yale (1931–34), and back in Finland (1935–36). Along with Charles Eames, Eero and Eliel set out to pioneer a new approach to architecture and furniture design. Following Eero's sudden death in 1961, Roche-Dinkeloo was established as a partnership between a designer and a technologist. Roche acted as the principal designer while Dinkeloo provided expertise in construction and technology. John Dinkeloo was born in Holland, Michigan, in 1918. He studied at the University of Michigan, School of Architecture, after which he worked for Skidmore, Owings, and Merrill. He joined the firm of Eero Saarinen in 1950, making partner five years later.

Louis I. Kahn with Fred Dubin and August Komendant, 1956–74

Louis Kahn (1901–74) and fellow Estonian August Komendant's (1906–92) often stormy relationship began in 1957. Their first collaboration was Richards Medical Laboratories at the University of Pennsylvania. Komendant was famous for his expertise in concrete construction and was awarded the AIA Allied Professions Medal in 1978. Fred S. Dubin (1915–92), the prodigious mechanical engineer, was also part of the Richards Medical team.[i] After Richards, this team worked together on most, if not all, of Kahn's projects. The strategic aspects of the Salk Institute, Philips Exeter Library, First Unitarian Church, and the Kimbell Art Museum owe much to the collaborative nature of this triad.[ii] Komendant's book, *18 Years with Architect Louis Kahn*, is a revealing and intimate look at the dynamics of a world-class design team.[iii]

Notes

i   Rush, Richard (1980) "From Salk to SERI", *Progressive Architecture*, 61(4): 122–125.
ii Zimring, Craig M. and Dogan, Fehmi (2002) "Interaction of programming and design: The First Unitarian Congregation of Rochester and Louis I. Kahn", *Journal of Architectural Education*, 56(1): 47–56. doi:10.1162/104648802321019164.
iii Komendant, August E. (1975) *18 years with architect Louis I. Kahn*, Englewood Cliffs, NJ: Aloray.

Figure 8.1 contrasts a linear model of postindustrial eotechnic practice in parallel with some corresponding problems of current practice. While such phase-by-phase flowchart representations cannot capture the opportunistic and rich ambiguity of design in messy action, they can serve to distinguish conceptual differences between the two general approaches. In other words, we can study design without the threat of thereby defining design as a study; we need not confuse the subject for the topic. So this chapter sets out the Two Spheres eotechnic model by articulating successive roles of systemic complexity in each phase. Problematic representations of current practice are given here in the Kuhnian sense of growth and evolution, where erosion of the

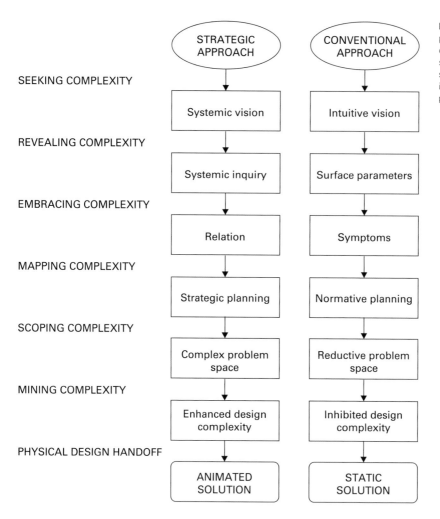

Figure 8.1 Eotechnic practice: A linear model of postindustrial era strategic practice and some parallel difficulties in current conventional practice.

SEEKING COMPLEXITY

STRATEGIC APPROACH → Systemic vision

CONVENTIONAL APPROACH → Intuitive vision

REVEALING COMPLEXITY

Systemic inquiry

Surface parameters

EMBRACING COMPLEXITY

Relation

Symptoms

MAPPING COMPLEXITY

Strategic planning

Normative planning

SCOPING COMPLEXITY

Complex problem space

Reductive problem space

MINING COMPLEXITY

Enhanced design complexity

Inhibited design complexity

PHYSICAL DESIGN HANDOFF

ANIMATED SOLUTION

STATIC SOLUTION

existing normative paradigm leads incrementally but continually toward new understanding and thus to fresh approaches to practice. Such progress is always at play and it is categorically the work of all practitioners to press that progress into action.

Seeking Complexity: Richness and Fit

> "Well, Hib, why don't you move your chair?"
> (Frank Lloyd Wright 1937)[2]

Ominous splits in the current practice paradigm reflect the ongoing fragmentation of architecture's practice and discourse. These cracks appear most distinctly along the worn joints between strategic and physical dimensions of architectural practice. The stress is prevalent enough to have effectively divided architects into two different occupations: the design architects and the project architects. Witness any project sign on a major work in the last twenty years. We need not guess which camp is more ennobled, given the design architect's primary association with the sublime immediacy of physical design consideration. The immediate and direct experience of architectural works of any scale has, in fact, become so widely valued by architects that these physical aspects have usurped the title of designer, and they have done so in almost total isolation and divorce from strategic intelligence. The designer, in turn, is usually deemed blameless for strategic failure; be it a leaky roof or any other calamity. It almost seems that reckless disregard for embodied intelligence is a heroic attribute, or perhaps the tragic flaw of a valiant storybook character— and the attribution for failure belongs to some villain counterpart. In that sorry myth, we have lost all sense of whole-minded architecture.

In the first phase of a holistic Two Spheres practice model then, architects must accept the precepts of complexity: complexity cannot be tamed; indeterminacy cannot be fixed; knowledge is never complete; and systems never rest. Denial of these basic principles is just so much spitting into the wind. Moreover, it smacks of mechanistic reductionism and oversimplification; the same complaints so often used against strategic causes of function and foresight. We must begin, therefore, not by denying complexity, but by actively seeking it out. In other disciplines this acceptance of a new complex and systemic basis of practice has been likened to the transition from bureaucracy to cyberocracy (Table 8.1).[3] The foundation of such a transition is founded in strategic feedback and robust adaptive behavior. In short, it is founded in systems thinking.

Abandoning the reductive simplifications from the old preoccupation with physical immediacy is not an easy decision. For to seek complexity, there are several crises that must be overcome and value systems that must be rethought. First, the strategic sphere must be recognized as a whole thing and not as a collection of architectural activities that are necessary but not significant. Then, the strategic sphere must be accepted as tantamount to the physical sphere. Finally, the designerly way of knowing must be elevated to that position of bridging between the strategic and physical spheres. Along the way of course, architects must realign their regard for the strategic sphere of design as a search for the unique essence of an organic whole, an animated dynamic operating in rich ambiguity. Along with the physical sphere and its epicurean motivation to form and affect, the architect must yearn in earnest for the vitality of the strategic sphere and its motivation to process, flow, and effect.

The ascendant strategic sphere does not eclipse the physical sphere; any such competitive framework only isolates them as easily identifiable parts.

Table 8.1 Comparison of bureaucracy and cyberocracy

Bureaucracy	Cyberocracy
Limits information	Thrives on information
Channels information narrowly	Disperses information broadly
Brittle practices: programs, budgets	Adaptive practices: management, cultural context
Public and private sector interests	Mixed interests

Source: After Fast (1997).

But they are not separate simply because they are identifiable; rather they are different aspects of the same whole construct that is architecture. Nonetheless, change is hard and anything other than a physical sphere centered approach to design requires much difficult change for many architects. Perhaps in crisis there is opportunity for change, but it is equally true that change imposes crises of transformation. Consider the following:

- The crisis of representation—since the Renaissance, architects have relied very heavily on image to communicate the value of their work and its comparative superiority to alternative competing solutions. While the strategic intelligence of the design may be presumed as obvious in the image, it is probably more accurate to say that strategic factors cannot be represented in presentation media that typically focus on visual simulations of the building image. Strategic aspects of design are thus often undermined by traditional lack of contribution to architectural representation,
- The crisis of authorship and identity—the collaborative and objective focus of strategically focused design is likely to blur the architect's personal signature as conventionally made by their subjective interpretation and manifested through physical immediacy in form. Although strategic elements may be used to explain and defend physical decisions, strategic insight is seldom valued for its own direct contributions. This is also an area where strategic and physical design overlap considerably and strategic decisions such as adjacency and arrangement of spaces may well be subsumed as the work of physical design,
- The crisis of design resources—compression of architectural fees has been occurring for some time, but meanwhile the expectation of architectural services and the sophistication of client projects have escalated. Further, strategic design services are usually taken for granted by the client and no special stipulations for extra layers of strategic work are made without special dispensation for "research." For these reasons, many design firms reduce strategic tasks such as programming to an informal activity that only nominally occurs on an as-needed basis. These reduced services mean that firms must rely more heavily on experience and their intuitive grasp of the project conditions. Some reflective evidence of this is found in the large number of architectural firms that specialize in one or two project types so that their knowledge base can be reused repeatedly, or in larger firms that have specialized design groups for each of the project types they generally undertake,
- The crisis of technology—the mounting impossibility of keeping up with accelerating social and technical change requires that architects develop a means of design inquiry wherein the best and most advanced ideas can be commoditized to the benefit of design. While such inquiry is now made practical by the convergence of human insight and cybernetic computation, there remains the difficulty of facilitating strategically effective means of setting criteria for selecting the best ideas and then parsing them through successive filters of

comparison, evaluation, configuration, deployment, and integration. Common sense, past experience, and intuition, which are all one and the same thing anyway, are not sufficient for these tasks,

- The crisis of integration—the comprehensive scope of architecture forbids bias and hierarchical approaches to design priorities. Compromise and predisposition are not options, because all design decisions are interwoven. Materiality, composition, cost, and performance, for example, all work as a chain of dynamic action and reaction. Modifying one factor creates a ripple of direct and indirect changes in all the others. So, rather than a parallel set of strategic and physical design operations, what is required is a continuous and sustained design logic that spans both rationales. This sustained logic introduces the need for a team approach, with different aspects of the operations being pursued by different contributors. It also serves to remember that specialization makes integration more difficult,

- The crisis of expertise—the traditions of architectural education and practice are very short on development of strategic skills. In previous times it may have been considered that strategic insight was an innate skill and a natural by-product of physical design genius. We now know that both creative and strategic skills can be effectively taught and that it is therefore the role of the profession to assure that such learning is accomplished. It remains to be seen how long it takes to catch up,

- The crisis of discourse—unlike the profession of law, whose members also prepare contracts just as architects do, designers seldom have extensive expertise in critical discourse. Like strategic skills in general, discourse is seldom formally taught in architecture schools and rarely brought to bear during internship. What passes for architectural discourse then is often likely to rely on flowery prose, clever phrasing, oversimplifications, relativism, heuristic shortcuts, or logical fallacies.[4] Architectural training simply does not equip its practitioners to do such things as recognize sophistry, or to distinguish skepticism from cynicism. Professional literature tends to perpetuate this as there are precious few scholarly reviewed journals in which these weaknesses are brought to light and the professional journals seem adverse to such internal debate. This crisis of discourse bears on the relation of physical and strategic design because its disciplinary weakness erodes the forum in which the two design aspects could be resolved into any kind of reciprocal relationship,

- The crisis of relativism—complexity, situatedness, contingency, dynamic relation, and the systemic whole must not lead to relativism or promote the position that meaning and knowledge in architecture is elusive and personal. These are a few of the problems of such relativist perspectives:[5]

  o False dilemmas—vital dialectic tandems should never get reconstructed as oppositions; in fact, these tandems are the ebb and flow of feedback forces necessary to perturb stasis and promote adaptive change, learning, and growth. We can use systems behavior and the hermeneutic model to understand these dialectics as vital,

o   The ongoing dialectic between technical progress and emancipated spontaneity of human spirit—no one can really argue that all progress is repressive or that the human spirit of each individual is the ultimate authority,

o   The dialectic of universal, or at least generalizable, truth versus contingent and personal truth—no one should argue that truth is always universal or, conversely, that all truth is always contingent on personal interpretation.

No building is due solely to a single mind, and the greater the complexity involved, the greater the reliance on collaboration and integration. The mythology of the cocktail napkin sketch, in which a single design idea is brought to light in a single moment of inspiration, is just that—mythology.

(Leslie 2006: 72–75)[6]

Revealing Complexity: Distinguishing Symptoms from Systems

A problem is half-solved if properly stated.

(John Dewey)[7]

Well begun is half done.

(Plato 360 BCE, *Laws*: 753e)[8]

When one knows what to do, there is only little time one needs for doing it. It is only when one does not know what to do that it takes so much time. And to know what to do is the secret of it all.

(Louis I. Kahn)[9]

To move from strategic vision to strategic design inquiry, we must reveal the underlying complexity embodied in the project at hand. Here is where systemic relation is discriminately set apart from symptomatic indicators. If, by way of simplistic example, you complain of a headache to your doctor and are given an aspirin, then only a superficial symptomatic approach has been taken. On the other hand, if the doctor inquires about the last time you had your vision checked, then the search for underlying relation reveals that a systemic approach is being taken toward solving the underlying complex problem. In architecture, the same distinction separates the client brief from the architectural program. The client, like the patient, can only describe symptomatically what they perceive to be their wants, needs, and resources as symptoms about their project condition. The architect's diagnosis is what forms the authentic and systemic project agenda for bringing about a vital solution. The failure to make this transformation is what Martin Pawley notes as the fallback to stenography, where the architect merely fulfills the client's demands by asking for their brief and then delivering it as the sole design outcome. Such stenography abdicates the complex and ambiguous unique essence that should drive the real design.[10]

The formulation of problem space in the process of design inquiry is thus a rigorous challenge. Separation of symptom from system requires careful insight and a questioning attitude. An open exploration is needed to diagnose the true nature of the situation and its complex relations. Confusions of bias and predisposition concerning the project mask the real situation and cloud the area of ambiguity in which design operates. Adopting a weak version of project complexity is like leaning a ladder against the wrong wall. It does not really matter how high you climb if you ultimately end up in the wrong place. Another way of saying this is that design may well be out-of-the-box and off-the-wall in a counter-intuitive and innovative way, but it is never counter-rational. Creativity and innovation always involve appropriate fit. Success in achieving this is best assured by mindfully directed intentional focus, not accidental success or serendipity.

The rigor of transformation between brief and program then, like the difference between symptomatic and systemic project indicators, lies in revealing the design parameters and knowing where they fall across the continua of design space:

- Values, goals, and needs—setting the design agenda always involves a variety of stakeholders and a range of conflicting schemes as to how the project should be defined and what the priorities should be,
- Facts, ideas, beliefs, and opinions—bias, preconception, and predisposition tend to cloud our thinking on the difference between what seems to be true and the way things really are. Hume's Law forbids the confusion of an "ought" with an "is,"
- From facts to wisdom—the range of declarative, procedural, and structural knowledge all involve different sets of information and processes for working with them. The confusion of knowledge and understanding is a typical fallacy,
- From vision to tactics—deciding on convenient tactics and comfortable strategies before establishing the project values, mission, goals, and objectives is another error of bias and preconception,
- From evidence to resolution—design proceeds through sets of interrelated decisions, and decisions always weigh alternatives and measure fitness. The warrants for these decisions should be made explicit.

Embracing Complexity: Beyond Intuition, Expertise, and Reduction

Design is not making beauty, beauty emerges from selection, affinities, integration, love.

(Louis I. Kahn)[11]

Chapter 6 enumerated four embraces of complexity as design hermeneutics, unique essence, animation, and aesthetic bridging. This present section takes a narrower view by focusing specifically on the transition from systematic inquiry in revealed complexity to the relational configuration of mapping complexity. Between revealing and mapping complexity then, the Two Spheres model of architectural design embraces complexity as a means of drawing relation and pattern out of ambiguity. Where seeking complexity began by acknowledging the indeterminate nature of wicked problems, and revealing complexity sorted symptomatic project indicators from systemic ones, embracing complexity then begins exploring and linking project elements together as a network of relations.

Bubble diagrams, for example, are familiar to us as the entity relation graphs used to capture schematic thinking about adjacency and relative size of program areas. At this level, architects try to find the inherent relations among project parameters. It is not an attempt to impose the designer's own will on the project in the realm of the physical sphere; rather the notion is to reveal and embrace the essential underlying systemic order from which the physical aspects of design can emerge. This exploration of emergent order is thus an attempt to discover form, not to invent it. All such efforts seek to gather ambiguity into the embrace of design; finding pattern, but leaving form amorphous.

Complexity extends the basic example of the bubble diagram into as many facets of the project as the designer requires. The search for rich ambiguity and the project's unique essence is not a reductive matter of deterministic thinking; it is rather the quest for vital characteristics that animates the final design. And in all such cases, the architect does not need to invent complexity; it will introduce itself.

To press this embrace a little deeper, consider just two additional dimensions of internal organizing force by zoning and the external force of shaping. This is an environmental patterning exercise beyond the venerable bubble diagram, but it is only one of many such possible explorations of complexity. The individual characteristics of these internal and external forces organize space, volume, material, and form. The overlays of combined factors reveal a rich and complex matrix of relation. But nowhere in this strategic exercise are there manifestations of the physical sphere. The sustained logic that unites the strategic and physical aspects of the design is consequently unencumbered by predisposition and bias. Therein lies the value of ambiguity.

At the internal level we find examples of revealed pattern and relation among the following organizing forces:

- Thermal zoning—orientation, exposure, scheduling, activity, unitary cooling capacity, etc.
- Luminous zoning—factors relating to visual activity, availability of natural light, acuity by color, contrast, human factors such as age and length of task, etc.
- Acoustical zoning—arrangement of noisy, quiet, silent, and buffer spaces to promote privacy, quiet, and acoustical masking; relation to outdoor noise sources, etc.

At the external level we find other examples of ordering that emerge from the discovered but ambiguously amorphous pattern and relation:

- Aerodynamic form—shaping response to winter wind and summer breeze in a predominantly static building form that accommodates seasonally differing air flow patterns, promoting natural and stack ventilation where desired, accommodating lateral loads and uplift forces, creating wind shadows of calm air, etc.
- Solar form—massing, fenestration, orientation, elongation, solar access, shading geometries, landscaping, glazing selection, passive and active solar heat gain, etc.
- Luminous form—lanterns, atriums, courtyards, depth of plan, seasonal variation, compact or splintered forms, orientation, fenestration, elongation, texture and form modeling, color rendering, contrast and glare, daylight fixtures and light shelves, toplighting, glazing selection, deciduous and evergreen landscape, view and privacy, etc.
- Acoustical form—room configuration for reverberation time, initial time delay gap, intimacy, warmth, presence, and bass ratio; prevention of echo, creep, flutter, and focusing; sound diffusion in enclosed spaces; point and linear sources of noise; barrier mass and stiffness; outdoor noise reflections and inter-reflections; noise isolation, etc.
- Hydraulic form—drainage flow, topography, roof shape, swales and berms, retention, flooding, bodies of water, etc.

In combination, these example internal and external environmental forces create complex plays of solar form overlaid on acoustical zoning, or simultaneous combinations of thermal, luminous, and acoustical zoning considered as one spatial matrix, or any other permutation of the mosaic laid out in this one extended example. The possibilities are numerous and the patterns they reveal give us an embrace on the full complexity of the project without the encumbrances of predisposition or predetermination.

Further complexity is introduced to these environmental example sets by their temporal nature. These environmental conditions are dynamic and changing, yet patterned and behaved enough to demand responsive design. Bimodal states of the building emerge as sun/shade, wind/breeze, day/night, and so forth.

As example forces then, these emergent agents of order hark back to Chapter 3 and Groák's description of buildings as organized flow, as well as to Lyle's principles of using form to manifest flow and process.[12] There is also an echo back to the Chapter 2 discussion on our phenomenological or experiential comprehension of architecture. Finally, embracing complexity in these terms illustrates the cybernetic roots of digital fabrication in the ongoing partnership of architecture and industrial design, wherein mass customization and parametric design allow for the recent advances in computer-aided design such as in the Chapter 5 story of the Sydney Opera House and Bilbao Guggenheim Museum tandem. The urge to form in all such cases involves an embrace of emergent ordering and brings us closer to the point where the algorithm of forces becomes the instruction set for fabricating the material physical form: the equation literally becomes the shape. All of this is discovered form, not invented: it is relational, not actual, and macro, not local. The physical actualization into immediate and direct experience can thus be an authentic act of bridging from the ideal to the real and back again; from the immeasurable to the measured, and back to the immeasurable.

Mapping Complexity: From Relation to Information

> Egyptian scribes sat every day in the marketplace and wrote hiero-glyphic letters, reports, memos, and proposals for their clients. At least since then, the business of assisting others to make their communications more effective has flourished. . . . Information design is the most recent manifestation of the age-old profession of communications assistance.
>
> (Robert E. Horn 1999)[13]

The wicked problems aspect of design necessitates the gathering, analysis, and interpretation of a great many interrelated parameters. Architecture is much too large and complicated a discipline to trust to unaided human intuition. In projects of any well-considered scope, there are too many user needs, priorities are too deeply interwoven, relations are complexly interrelated, and the risk of built-in-place failure is far too critical. Simple observation and well-intentioned attitudes, no matter how expert or experienced, do not suffice.

Introduction

Having sought out, revealed, and embraced complexity, this section addresses how to structure an understanding of relevant project parameters. More specifically, the term *parameter* is used here to include ideas, facts, and issues that are particular to the project situation. To avoid the confusion of different levels of data, knowledge, information, and so forth, those relevant facts, ideas, and information in this discussion are simply called parameters. *Structure* is used as a term relating to order and organization of the parameters, and how to map them into a form that transforms the raw data into usable information. Finally, the qualification of *relevant* is meant to distinguish the scope of parameters that were used to establish the project problem space.

Activities in this strategic step can be called mapping because they aim to distill a huge number of observations and parameters into coherent representations of the situation at hand. The resulting representation is a map; one that helps reduce a messy, complex situation into a comprehensible picture where patterns and relations can be identified and meaningfully grasped. Unless data are made useful in this way, they are difficult to communicate, discuss, or use as the basis of sound judgment. It should also be mentioned that mapping engages our visual thinking in direct ways that lead to better comprehension, learning, and long-term memory. As may be guessed from this description, mapping in strategic design involves the use of tables, graphs, charts, and other organizations or visualizations of the project parameters.

As an introductory case in point, consider the multitude of project parameters suggested by Peña's Problem-Seeking categories of values, goals, and needs.[14] The task of collecting all the specific facts, ideas, and issues representing these parameters covers lots of ground. It could entail interviews with the client, surveys of the users, a review of code requirements, surveys of site characteristics, discussions with builders and engineers, input from

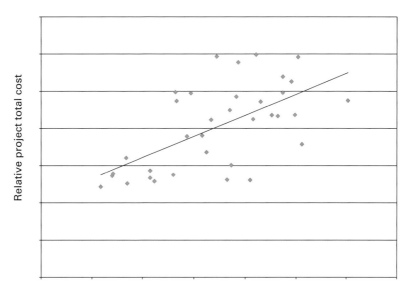

Relative project size in square feet

Figure 8.2 Scatter plot of project cost and size.

consultants, and a host of other wool-gathering ventures. Taken in isolation though, these investigations provide data that are independently meaningless and collectively overwhelming. To be useful as a basis of judgment, some process of digesting and distilling the data into information has to be undertaken. Eventually then, each of these investigations and all of the compiled data have to be usefully assimilated and recorded in a form that is informative and readily understood. An inkling of this can be gleaned from Figure 8.2 and Box 8.2.

Box 8.2 Mapping of preliminary project cost and size against that of similar buildings (after comments from Kurt Neubek)[i]

1   The x–y scatter plot in Figure 8.2 marks individual data points for the actual size and construction cost of several buildings similar to that of a new project being considered. Relation of the two factors should be visually apparent in the observed patterns of any such graph provided that a viable relation actually exists between them. If no pattern is evident, either the data are incomplete or there is probably no meaningful relation to base any decisions on. Also, tight cluster patterns of the data points indicate that factors other than size may have minimal impact on cost, whereas widely dispersed data points indicate some influence on cost by factors other than just size.[ii]

2   A linear regression line is added to show a basic relation between size and cost. Most spreadsheet software can determine and plot this line automatically. The size-to-cost relation model is also given as the equation of the line and goodness of fit is given as r^2. An r^2 of

1.0 is a perfect fit and r^2 = 0.9 or better is very good. Having more data typically increases r^2 if a real pattern exists and thus provides more confidence in the comparisons, but a visual scanning of how scattered the data will be intuitively informative as well. Close proximity of data points to the regression line identifies those precedent buildings with a normal value ratio of cost per unit of area, $/ft². Outlier points indicate higher or lower value buildings or, in extreme cases, indicate buildings that are not comparable with the others due to some unknown factor.[iii] Similarly, wide gaps between data points indicate empty realms of the relation between size and cost.

3   Next, a few existing buildings with which the client most strongly identified are marked. How these specific buildings map against and among the other building data points might help establish a design standard for expected levels of comparative quality, finish, and other fundamental parameters.

4   Time for a reality check: the client's initial criteria for size and cost are plotted and compared to both the regression line and the client's most desired precedents. The raw data now become meaningful information and good questions can be interrogated: How does the preliminary cost and size compare to a normal building of this sort? How does the client's standard of quality compare to their perceived needs and resources?

Notes

i   Neubek, K. (2010) "Requirements management in a digital age", Lecture at the University of Houston College of Architecture. Unpublished document. October 1.

ii   Note that all cost figures must be adjusted for differences in local material and labor cost factors as well as for price inflation that occurred since completion of the existing projects. Basically, all costs should be normalized to current dollar values.

iii   Note that a linear regression line is not always the best fit and other equations might better reflect the actual relation of size to cost in practice. There might, for example, be an increasing efficiency that makes economy of scale work for larger buildings; in which case a logarithmic or exponential equation might give a better fit. Further inquiry could lead to other useful maps depicting sub-questions, such as the relation of building footprint size to construction cost per square foot, storey height versus gross to net area ratios, or any imaginable number of related questions. Care should be taken, however, to match the detail level of the question to the level of decision making currently being considered at the present stage of progress.

Architects frequently use graphic tools to represent such data and then turn to abstract sketching as a means of distilling out and reasoning with application of the useful information. Bubble diagrams are useful examples here again. They generally illustrate area sizes, placements, and adjacencies as circles of proportional size drawn in some meaningful proximity to one another. The circular bubbles make the relations visual. The data are thus transformed by illustration and visualization into perceptible form. The diagram becomes operationally useful and designers gain confidence in the manipulation and evaluation of fit. How they ultimately use this information of course remains a further matter of knowledge, understanding, and wisdom.

A multitude of similar graphic transformations are used in design and in all other walks of life. Numerical data plotted on technical graphs are the most common example of illustration. When we can "see" the numbers in visual proportion we are able to intuit correlation, trends, and magnitudes much more rapidly, concisely, and deeply than by looking at the numerical table of values.

Informatics and Data Visualization

Considerable attention has been given to the development of data mapping, especially since the late 1970s as the creation of value in postindustrial society became increasingly dependent on the manipulation of complex information. Great moments in mapping are depicted in Table 8.2 to illustrate these trends.

Table 8.2 Great moments in the history of mapping and visualizing data

Date	Event	Notes
1637	Descartes: La Geometry	Cartesian coordinates
1779	Johann Heinrich Lambert: Pyrometrie	bivariate function graphs
1786	Playfair: The Commercial and Political Atlas	time series graphics, histogram, pie chart, line graph
1869	Charles Minard: Napoleon in Russia	complex information graphics
1913	H.N. Russell: Plot of the Magnitude of Stars	
1936	Otto Neurath: International Picture Language	pictographs
1949	Shannon & Weaver: The Mathematical Theory of Communication	conduit model of information theory
1954	Huff & Geis: How to Lie with Statistics	
1960	Ausubel	subsumption, importance of what user already knows
1977	John Turkey: Exploratory Data Analysis	
1977	MacDonald-Ross: How Numbers are Shown	
1980	Kosslyn: Image and Mind	
1982	Diekhoff	concept maps
1983	Jacques Bertins: Semiology of Graphics	systematic examination of visual potential
1983	Edward Tufte: The Visual Display of Quantitative Information	highlighted shortcomings of visualizations
1984	Novak, Gowin, & Johansen: The Use of Concept Mapping	concept maps

(Continued overleaf)

Table 8.2 *Continued*

Date	Event	Notes
1984	Jan White: Using Charts and Graphs	
1984	Nigel Holmes: Designer's Guide to Creating Charts and Diagrams	aggressive aesthetics to capture reader
1984	Holley & Dansereau	spatial mapping, cognitive maps
1984	Gold	concept maps
1985	William Cleveland: The Elements of Graphing Data	experimental basis of psychophysics
1989	Kosslyn: Understanding Charts and Graphs	
1989	Roger Parker: The Makeover Book	desktop publishing
1989	Cochran, Albrecht, & Green: Guidelines for Evaluating Graphical Designs	
1990	Spence: Visual Psychophysics of Simple Graphical Elements	
1990	Richard Saul Wruman: Information Anxiety	structure of information visibly explicit in design of the visualization
1990	Pinker: A Theory of Graph Comprehension	
1990	Edward Tufte: Envisioning Information	informational standards
1992	Kommers	concept maps
1992	Schiano & Tversky: Structure and Strategy in Encoding Simplified Graphics	
1993	Barton & Barton: Ideology and the Map; Modes of Power	postmodern aesthetic dimension
1993	Lohse: A Cognitive Model for Understanding Graphical Perception	
1993	Ellison: Exploratory Data Analysis and Graphic Display	
1993	DeBono	concept maps
1993	Reader & Hammond	concept maps
1994	Gaines & Shaw	concept maps
1996	Robert Harris: Information Graphics	lexicon of graph types
1996	Cheng: Diagrammatic Knowledge Acquisition. . .	
1996	Woolsey, Kim, & Curtis: VizAbility	fostering creative thought
1997	Edward Tufte: Visual Explanations	eliminate chart junk, modernist aesthetic
1997	Howard Wainer: Visual Revelations	historical perspective
1997	Bogden	concept maps
1997	Shneiderman: Designing the User Interface	data mining
1998	Monk & Howard	visualizing software development
1998	Gershon, Eick, & Card: Information Visualization	
1998	Kostelnick & Roberts: Designing Visual Language	

Events in this timeline can also be compared to the advent of cybernetics. Mapping begins with the concept of Cartesian coordinates that allow plotting of data in the x and y dimensions. Early attempts at representing data were hampered by the limitations of producing and revising such illustrations and the further problem of reproducing them for consumption (e.g. Playfair and Minard).[15] Capabilities grew though, as our cybernetic models of perception and cognition were continually refined to give insights on how the human mind interfaces with visual information (e.g. Shannon & Weaver, Cleveland, and Spence).[16] Finally, as computer graphing and visualization tools became commonplace, so did the popularity of works on how to use them effectively (e.g. Tufte, DeBono, and Harris).[17] Along the way there are some warnings about the dilution of information with mindless computer-generated decoration and the dangers of statistical deception through misrepresentation (e.g. Wainer).[18]

Today there are several fields of endeavor where the graphic digestion of data into perceptible information is of key interest. The relevant pursuits of this knowledge would necessarily include computer graphics, software design, graphic design, medical informatics, cartography, and art. Applications of this evolving knowledge are quite broad and are likely to occur in any field where data must be analyzed, drilled down, distilled, and interpreted as the basis of judgment. One extreme example might be geophysics, where decisions on expensive exploration ventures are routinely made on the basis of data maps rather than empirical observations.

Types versus Categories of Mapping

Categories of maps refer to the purpose of the mapping task, whereas type of map refers to the specific graphic technique and formatting selected to represent the map. Different map categories are used in different situations naturally, and in strategic design work there are also different authors and readers to consider. Here as well, the number of players in the design team must be considered to include everyone from owners to architects, from users to engineers, from managers to builders, from loan officers to product consultants. Mapping may be constructed by one party of the team to digest and interpret information for themselves, by one or more members of the team to communicate information to other members, or maps may even be constructed simultaneously by multiple members of the team collaborating on a shared idea. To define these maps in more definite categories, as opposed to specific map types, consider a general list:

- *Tabular representations* are simply text or numeric tables that order large amounts of data into retrievable information. Tables provide a means of using some known parameters, such as a matrix of row and column headings, to look up and determine other corresponding parameters, as found at the intersection of the appropriate row and column. Product or material catalogs usually give application data in this form,
- *Data compilation* maps are used to transform vast reams of facts and numbers into meaningful patterns of information on which priorities are established, decisions made, and results evaluated. This

sort of map ranges from simple bar charts to sophisticated three-dimensional representations, pictographic representations, and creative hybrids. The possibilities are limited only by the range of imagination given to technical communication. Annual climate data superimposed on a psychrometric chart would make one such map, representing the characteristics of 8760 hourly readings on a tool that prioritizes a building's thermal design strategies,

- *Relation* maps identify patterns of how two or more parameters interact, such as time series data,
- *Process* maps are like flowcharts,
- *Concept* maps, also called mind maps that can be used to represent complex or multidimensional relations of entities. Architects, for example, typically use abstract bubble diagrams to simultaneously map the size, adjacency, and placement of interior spaces relative to one another. Concept mapping can also be done collaboratively when several different parties need to contribute and communicate their differing perspectives, such as in focus groups or scenario planning.

Such mapping exercises are constrained by the issue of what data are meaningful as opposed to what is a distraction. Working at the right level of detail and scope of data is essential if the strategy is to stay relevant. Excessively large scope results in the paralysis of *detail-itis*; where data are collected exhaustively just for the sake of having more data. Focusing on fine detail when larger issues remain to be addressed is equally unproductive. At each point of the design process it is important to know the current scale and scope of decision making that is in progress and to match that decision making to an appropriate level of data. Consider the pine tree and the pine cone, for example: design does not begin with the selection of pencil trays for each workstation; that would be looking for the pine cone long before the pine tree was even planted.

Scoping Complexity: Toward a Clinical Practice of Architecture

Staying, for the purposes of coherent conversation, with a linear representation of the ever complex design process; the next phase is to scope out the transformation from informational map to inferential diagnosis. In more detail, this is the transitional step between the informational maps of pattern and relation, and onto a prescription for the cure. Scoping then, is one of the last strategic dimensions of design in this step wise description of the work. Medical terminology is used to capture the basis for scoping complexity because this activity is analogous to clinical practice used in the health industry. Of course clinical perspectives are used in many fields, but medicine makes for a convenient example.

Architecture is increasingly becoming a clinically based practice for precisely the same reasons that healthcare is: what doctors refer to as a targeted diagnosis leading to a plan of treatment, architects call a design intention leading to a plan of realization. Both the doctor and the architect are basing their interpretive diagnosis on an embrace of complex problem characteristics and a corresponding appreciation for the dynamic and systemic processes of the organism on which they operate.

The characteristics of clinical practice are adapted here from a description of how the clinical model is relevant in educational research (Elstein 1977).[19] These traits are useful in linking architectural design to clinical knowledge. To wit, a clinical practice is:

- Problem initiated and problem directed,
- Concerned with action directed toward a particular problem and specific case,
- Performed collaboratively,
- Involved with collecting information and drawing conclusions,
- Performed diagnostically and therapeutically to identify and resolve disorders or discordance,
- Dependent on the clinician's interpretive reading of the problem and selection of an appropriate remedy,
- Based on a comprehensive body of collected cases that comprise a clinical database for practitioners.

A medical description of clinical practice helps summarize this as a: "systematic and critical assessment, continuous experimentation, and subsequent revision of knowledge" (Malterud 2001).[20] Bearing these definitional characteristics in mind then, it is possible to appreciate how clinical databases are realized in architecture.

Chapter 3 introduced some features of architectural practice which are clinical in every sense of the definitional terms. Precedent, commissioning, post-occupancy evaluation, automation, and evidence-based design are clinical operations. Further, these pursuits are not only emblematic of the proposed Two Spheres complexity model; they are also increasingly important aspects of current professional concerns. Furthermore, each of these features is, as Elstein[21] suggests, based on a comprehensive body of collected cases that comprise a clinical database of disciplinary knowledge for architects, just as such bodies of knowledge work for other professional practitioners such as lawyers and doctors. We must conclude that the evolving postindustrial practice of architecture will increasingly rely on clinical practices to scope out and diagnose complexity.

Mining Complexity: Tools and Strategies

One level removed from the directly applied work of project complexity, it is also essential to consider how the interaction of physical and strategic sphere efforts are coordinated, how their conjoined progress matures throughout the project, and how a continuous and inclusive logic is sustained to satisfy the need for coherence. The separation from applied design work allows for an uber-plan to manage the entire process: the plan for the plan. That management and oversight are also aspects of architectural complexity, and the tools and strategies utilized to shepherd the design work along deserve their own framework of discussion.

Collecting other elements of the Two Spheres model already discussed, we can refer back to the discussions on postindustrial convergences and embraces. This yields cybernetics, hermeneutics, sustainability, and aesthetics as the working means of management, with human capital, long-term value, open ambiguity, unique essence, and animation as the driving ethical principles.

The second order result of those considerations is less abstract: computers, collaboration, rigorous discourse, investment scenarios, and multiple stakeholders. Some of these tools are already leading architects to a new generation of practice. Building Information Management (BIM), Integrated Practice (IP), and performance simulation are practically the status quo already. The landscape of architectural practice and meritorious occupation is likely to undergo increasingly rapid change in these areas.

In concluding this exploration of the occupational domain then, the strategic dimension of design is elevated to equal status with the physical dimension. Both activities involve the vital animation of architecture. In postindustrial thinking, we can now see, problem space is as sacred as the territory of solution space, and both are known as tandem aspects of design. Along the way, an appreciation for underlying inclusive complexity supplants the yearning for exclusive reduction.

Chapter 9

The Domain of Education

> Architectural theory and architectural education have been much weakened by one of the characteristic confusions of modem thought: the assumed divorce of the "rational" and the "practical" from the "aesthetic" and the "creative."
>
> (Tom Heath 1993: 83)[1]

Most critiques of architectural education agree with Heath's protest against divisive confusions. Heath's appraisal, in turn, resonates with a body of literature principally framed by C.P. Snow, E.O. Wilson, and S.J. Gould, and also with Lewis Mumford, Aldous Huxley, and Gregory Bateson who would likely be included by many readers of this genre. That collective literature is bound together by mutual resistance to the endemic rift between the scientific and the humanities and any representation of them as radically oppositional ways of knowing.

    This confused division of architectural education into two camps reflects the current chasm between physical beauty and strategic accountability so prevalent in all domains of architecture. Chapter 1 addressed this chasm as a precept of postindustrial age architecture and offered Louis Kahn's transformative measurable and immeasurable traits of great buildings as the connective bridge. The Two Spheres framework thus allies itself with the more dialectic versions of these debates, wherein confusion is avoided and useful alignment is brought about by positive interplay between the sciences and the humanities. Those two paths to knowledge must be viewed as tandem and complementary concerns. Moreover, the Two Spheres perspective holds that design is a third way of knowing that binds the other two.

    The dissonance that Snow, Wilson, and Gould observe at the scale of culture and society-at-large is clearly the same divorce that Heath, Arnheim, and others warn of in the domain of architectural education. Evidence abounds: The simultaneous conferences of the UK "Reconsideration" and US "Reaccreditation" of Architectural Education in 2008 exposed deep concern on this matter from within the realm of educational and professional domains. Furthermore, regulatory agencies that govern higher education are beginning to exert a mandatory outcome-driven accountability toward reconciliation of the whole. From a societal or administrative aspect, any stubborn antagonism between the rational and creative cultures in education is fruitless infighting. Additionally, advances in educational theory are having an impact as the scholarship of teaching and learning has led to new understandings about best and worst practices—among which architecture has some of each. The last point in this litany is that education is being transformed by digital technology and the transition from personal knowledge expertise to information age teamwork.

These external regulatory and internal evolutionary forces for educational change are increasingly close in alignment. Progress is closing in on the traditional model of architectural education and its tendency to focus more on the physical aspect of design. Resistance to this change originates in the desire to preserve studio's eroding central position as the artistic and literary humanities model of architecture. The high proportion of studio faculty votes to other faculty in most schools still serves this conservative resistance, but the walls seem to be coming down slowly. Going forward, the mission is to start with a comprehensive and operational description of where we want architectural education to go, and then to set out some alternative pedagogical scenarios for getting there successfully. A mutual destination is preferred over perpetually dividing the two cultures of architectural educators into warring camps of designosaur and erectorhead caricatures. It is far more constructive to begin with the realization that most educators ultimately share the same concern for the core values of architecture; and they probably start with a 95 percent level of agreement as to how those values are defined. It is absurdly defeatist to begin otherwise and assert that some educators want beautiful buildings that are stupid, while others strive for intelligent buildings that are aggressively ugly.

A centerist position is, however, equally useless if it assumes some complicated compromise of pieces from each of the two perspectives. That mechanistic approach will never lead to an organic whole. Instead, we must start with the holistic outcome in mind and embrace the true complexity that unity entails. To use the analogy of an ethnically diverse population: it isn't a melting pot; it's a tossed salad. And to remember the underlying systemic whole: it isn't just a mix of ingredients that matters; it's the recipe. Tangles, tandems, and tapestries are here too, because this is a complex and systemic problem.

To address this conundrum we must accept that architectural education is both a means of productive enlightenment and a measured outcome. This input–output perspective describes what, on one hand, architectural education is for and, on the other hand, how it is judged. In that context then, we can examine this teaching and learning from the inside out as a self-perpetuating or reproductive curriculum—and from the outside in as a social institution that is held accountable for its contributions.

Postindustrial Complexity in Education

Complexity from Within: Design, Built Environment, and Research

Returning again to Popper's postpositive Three World model of knowledge, the role of education is to shift students inextricably from the isolation of personal and subjective knowledge of World Two and toward participation in the shared intersubjective constructions of World Three. This is not to eliminate the personal intuition of World Two, but rather to continually balance and validate it against the confirmations of World Three, where discourse and critique operate. Popper's model is especially relevant in qualitative realms where disciplinary knowledge and occupational service are characteristically dominated by argumentative discourse more than by empirically testable evaluation. Correspondingly, personal subjective intuition and interpersonal evaluation are always the driving tandem forces that propel design. The living organism of architecture is animated in this way and architectural education must seize that animating complexity as its central mission, the strange attractor, and the unique autopoietic essence.

Interaction is required to educate students away from their isolated, personal, and subjective opinions as to what makes for good architecture. The mistaken belief that architecture is a matter of unspeakable discernment, genius inspiration, or other voodoo explanations must be dispelled. Instead, students must be compelled to share in discourse about the prize distinctions of architectural merit; and they must participate in debates on the underlying theories and principles. To interact productively in this requires polite argument within a shared body of knowledge that is both specific to the realm and embedded in larger contexts. This interactive learning component fits well with the social constructivist theories of John Dewey, Jean Piaget, Lev Vygotsky, and Jerome Bruner. As students acquire progressive layers of knowledge, their abilities to appreciate and critique are enhanced; their combined intuition, sensitivity, sensibility, and skill increases. With increasing experience there is a "scaffolding" effect of more complicated elements built on top of simple ones, and more difficult constructs compounded from basic concepts. Students can then, with increasing meaningfulness, test their own cumulative education against the ideas of others and against the scholarly literature of architecture.

Just as with the strategic and physical spheres of architecture though, it is not so much the independent or accumulated understanding of measurable and immeasurable aspects that matter; it is rather how the two spheres are made whole by meaningful interaction. It is, after all, this interactive participation in the shared discourse and scholarly literature of architecture that affects the move from World Two to World Three. To accomplish this interactive transformation, architectural educators must conduct compelling experiences in an environmental setting. That collective experience and environment should lead to a coherent set of experiences that produce capable and well-prepared graduates. With coherence then, a tapestry of knowledge and understanding is possible; without it there are only tangles. The holistic and systemic nature of this education experience cannot be overemphasized.

Adult college students in architectural education have more shared knowledge of naturally richer and broader life experience than for that of children in lower levels of development, but this only elevates the level of scaffolding and interactive participation involved. If anything, the andragogy associated with educating adult architecture students is more challenging than the corresponding pedagogy used with children. Higher levels of complexity and autonomy follow because the stakeholders in this educational domain are at a more advanced level of cognitive development. Autonomy in turn implies internal regulation, and developmental psychology confirms that learning is by and large an internally regulated process rather than an externally produced result.

Charles Sanders Peirce's distinction between the logical and psychological dimensions of this learning is important here. In Peirce's view it is mistaken to regard good cognitive reasoning simply as logical thinking.[2] In the psychological dimension, on the other hand, a proper measurement of thinking involves "the selection, organization, and transformation of information as the individual makes sense of situations." Nothing could resonate more clearly with postindustrial transformation than that psychological description of thought process. This psychological frame for thinking is clearly more complex and holistic than the simple logical definition. Making "sense of situations" in this way also corresponds directly to the hermeneutic, iterative, abductive, and feedback model of design thinking that was presented in Chapter 6 as a Two Spheres embrace of complexity.

William Perry has established nine positions of intellectual development and characterized them according to students' attitudes on knowledge (Table 9.1).[3] The four categories of these positions illustrate how architecture students can move from World Two simplistic subjectivity to World Three intersubjective complexity. From dualistic declarative knowledge, learners move on to multiplistic and relativistic procedural knowledge. Finally, with interaction and commitment, mature students become skeptical, pluralistic, structural thinkers. This is a progression of questions: from "What? Where? and When?" we move on to "How?" and finally on to "Why?"

In architecture, students progress through these levels of thinking with corresponding growth in personal development. At first they look dualistically for the right and wrong ways to make good architecture. Intermediate positions are filled with multiple, relative approaches and some resignation as to subjective opinions about correct procedural design approaches. Finally, students match the complexity of architectural challenges with various maps and navigational tools for design that they feel are convincing to themselves and worth arguing about with others in polite discourse and heated critique.

Postindustrial society further validates this concern for cohesive throughput and comprehensive output in education, and architecture schools

Table 9.1 Levels of intellectual development based on Perry's nine positions

1 Authoritarian Dualism—there are right and wrong answers that must be learned

2 Relative Dualism—some authorities are more correct than others

3 Subjective Multiplicity—right answers are a matter of opinion and argument

4 Progressive Multiplicity—right answers are a matter of right thinking

5 Procedural Relativism—responsive ways of thinking can be learned and selected from

6 Personal Relativism—individuals must argue for their own way of thinking

7 Early Commitment—individuals can select ways of thinking to fit particular conditions

8 Middle Commitment—some areas of knowledge match certain generalizable ways of thinking

9 Skeptical Commitment—confident in own thinking, accepting of others, and willing to fit new ideas into generally accepted beliefs

Source: Data compiled and interpreted from many sources.

are not exempt from such mandates. It happens however that parts of architectural education's studio tradition are part of the new paradigm. Problem-based, student-centered studio design learning with faculty providing support and guidance in the role of critic is intimately familiar to almost anyone in architecture, but the rest of the academic world is catching on too. But while the studio model is successful in its engagement and motivation of students, this success is largely dependent on the student's persistence in, and self-image as, a mythical hero designer.[4] The next step in architectural education then will be to move beyond the Beaux-Arts traditional habit of manic studio behavior and update to the postindustrial mode of measured learning outcomes.[5] Going forward into an era of collaborative and team-based architectural design will thus require a more strategically designed curriculum to complement the romantically endeared hero architect approach.

There is a remarkable and marvelous consistency that pervades architectural education and the culture of architectural students. It seems that each and every candidate architect comes to school fostering an undying belief that they personally can make the world a better place through the act of design. Educators must respect and nurture this attitude, but they must also not delude their own students. Not all policemen become Dick Tracy and not all architects win the Pritzker Prize. In 2009, for example, some 30 percent of all registered architects in the USA worked for architectural firms of over 100 employees; and while the number of major architects seems to stay quite low and steady, the number of minor architects grows constantly.[6]

Successful architectural education, as measured from the student stakeholder's well-being, needs to begin with realistic expectations. The hero genius artist renegade boutique avant-garde architect literary model is not a realistic role aspiration for the vast majority of architecture students. Encouraging that mythical expectation as students' self-image has been perpetuated as a means of motivation for too long. The time has come to realize that most architects work in teams of collective intelligence and that authorship of design is consequently a distributed attribution. Going forward now we should openly appreciate that most new architecture makes incremental contributions to the realm, just as most science, most art, and almost everything else does within their disciplinary realms. Revolutionary works are epochal, yes, but evolution is what actually keeps the ball rolling.

Thomas Kuhn's *Structure of Scientific Revolutions* sets this evolutionary principle out as a cycle of long normal progress occurring within current and useful praxis, followed by erosion of that current model as anomalies challenge current thinking's robust ability to explain events and guide practices.[7] Eventually this erosion leads to a crisis stage as too many anomalies fall outside current understandings, rival explanations are posited, and a new paradigm must be developed and tested. That new paradigm then becomes normal practice and the process repeats itself. The theories, practices, and paradigms of architecture evolve in exactly the same way; and architecture students should know where their professional and occupational place is likely to be in that procession. Despite the romantic but totally erroneous association of creativity and innovation with characteristically rogue and strong-headed hero egos, most inventive productivity is the result of "normal" progress. Most architecture and most architects will make incremental contributions, just as most scientists and most artists will push ahead from within currently prevailing ways of thinking in their own fields. Paradigm shifts do not occur every Monday morning; we must work diligently and patiently. We must refine existing practice always with an eye to the evolutionary progress from which revolutionary change will emerge.

If, on the other hand, architecture schools are dedicated to revolutionary genius works and exist largely to promote the most creatively predisposed students, then two primary failures will follow. First, such an education abdicates its obligation to transform minds, denies education to those with different native intelligences, and ends in discriminatory segregation of one class of student from the next. Education concerns the nurture part of stimulating intelligence, not the nature part recognizing inherent talents. We must therefore measure the success of every educational program not by who it enrolls or who it graduates, but rather by the difference it makes in between the two stages. Second, having such educational efforts focused on revolution over evolution would promote drama but effectively poison progress. Students cannot author change if they cannot work creatively and productively within their present context. Domain knowledge is essential to innovation. You cannot change something you do not understand; you cannot even fairly critique it.

More realistic approaches are possible, desirable, and capable of producing mastery without the tyranny of novelty or the dead-end of normative thinking. Kuhn's evolution-to-revolution model is viable in architecture because it explains progress and offers candidate architects a role as productive participants.[8] Obviously architecture students must always be challenged to think outside of simplistic directness or donkey path meandering approaches to their work. In the postindustrial Two Spheres mindset, of course, neither the simplistic normative straight line limitation nor the heroic genius meandering impossibility has much currency. Instead, the more realistic educational challenge is posed by a hermeneutic quest that starts out from architecture's native engagement of the complex whole and then marches on with a belief that the whole is something sublimely, intelligently, and complexly different from the sum of the parts.

Complexity from Without: Accountability, Assessment, and Accreditation

Viewed from outside of the academy as a social institution, education in postindustrial society is student centered, technologically enhanced, outcome driven, best-practice oriented, evidence based, and assessment validated. The study of architecture is no more of an exception than are poetry, philosophy, literature, engineering, or mathematics. The pedagogy or andragogy of architectural education must assimilate these characteristics and embrace their progressive potential. Therein lies an opportunity to become more reflective and purposeful about the mission, goals, objectives, and strategies of our architecture schools' programs.

Over the past decade, the assessment of student learning has become increasingly important and the assessment literature suggests that direct evidence of student learning is a measure of institutional excellence.[9] A list of relevant agencies in the USA is given in Table 9.2. In the UK the schools are allied with the Royal Institute of British Architects (RIBA). Starting in Europe,

Table 9.2 Agencies establishing learning standards in architectural education for the United States

---

- The Federal Commission on Colleges, COC, and its regional associations
- American Collegiate Schools of Architecture, ACSA
- National Architectural Accreditation Board, NAAB
- National Council of Architectural Registration Boards, NCARB
- American Institute of Architects, AIA
- American Institute of Architecture Students, AIAS

---

higher education also began aligning with the Bologna Process in 1999, a policy forum on "Building the Global Knowledge Society: Systemic and Institutional Change in Higher Education."[10] The Bologna Process grew to forty-seven country signatories in 2009, well beyond the boundaries of the twenty-seven members of the European Union. Their collective goals include operationally defining the learning that graduates of specific degrees can demonstrate.

In all cases, these definitions and standards of education must be understood as a common denominator basis for the fundamental aspects of learning accomplished by graduates of architecture degree programs just as for any other degree. There is no intention anywhere toward converting education to homogenized lockstep training programs; not in ACSA, not in RIBA, and not in the Bologna Process. There will always be room beyond these common denominator elements for excellence and specialization in any range of issues, topics, and ideas. All that standardization is intended to achieve is the commonalities that make interchange, communication, reciprocity, employment, and degree nomenclature meaningful contributors to the society they serve. Think of it as traffic rules and vehicle operators' licenses: no one dictates what car you drive or how you operate it; but we all have to share the road.

Pressure from accrediting agencies, government funding, employers, and the public sector will continue to encourage institutions to enhance student learning and provide empirical evidence for how that learning was accomplished. Given this mounting pressure for accountability and transparency, architecture faculty and their institutions can no longer depend on anecdotal or self-validated evidence of student learning. Assessment and accountability are here to stay.

Accountability and Evidence
A proactive perspective on accountability and assessment of student learning places the focus on program revitalization, organizational transformation, and changing accreditation processes.[11] During the 1990s, assessment and accountability were primarily defined as "the systematic collection of input, process and outcome data, as well as the use of these data to make decisions about the effectiveness of schools."[12] Today, assessment focuses on learning outcomes, direct measures, program assessment, student learning, and program responsibility rather than on institutional effectiveness.[13] Based on current literature, assessment requires:

- setting explicit and measurable expectations and making them public to all stakeholders,
- establishing appropriate criteria and standards for learning quality,
- systematic collection of empirical data as both direct and indirect evidence,
- analyzing and interpreting evidence to identify how well student performance corresponds with expectations and standards, and finally,
- using results to document, explain and improve performance, teaching, and student learning.[14]

The assessment process is an ongoing activity designed to enhance the mission of each program, discipline, and department. The process is consequently dynamic, dialectic, and long term (Figure 9.1). Recent assessment evidence emphasizes the need for identifying specific and measurable program level learning outcomes. Such measurable outcomes create opportunities to enhance program coherence and the ability to refine teaching and learning strategies. Program coherence will, in turn, help students understand what is expected of them and promote meaningful learning through self-relevance. Assessment results also contribute to future planning by promoting further examination of curricular activities and by helping to make regular periodic adjustments of the curriculum.

Measurable program learning outcomes are thus fundamental to a postindustrial curriculum. For discussion sake, learning outcomes fit in the typical planning model based on a rough hierarchy of mission, values, goals, objectives and outcomes, tactics, and strategies. At the program level a learning outcome is essentially a goal, an ultimate destination. Higher Education commissions now typically require schools to define a small number of such

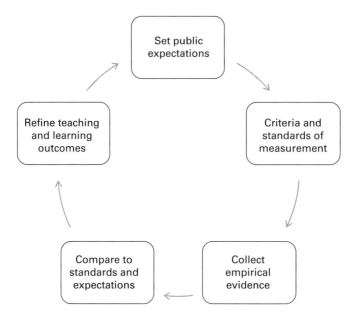

Figure 9.1 Closing the loop with assessment.

program outcomes as the end result of a graduating student's cumulative educational experience. At the level of individual courses, however, learning outcomes are more like planning model objectives. Such objectives are measurable in ways that are not open to interpretation, and are used to scale a student's success or failure and to set thresholds that operationalize any particular objective as met or unmet in defensibly empirical ways. Normally a course has many learning objectives and all student learning activities are targeted at one or more specific objectives. Program level learning outcomes are, on the other hand, more globally assessed through supporting but less scalable evidence. In the USA there are also the NAAB Student Performance Criteria (SPC) which describe course outcomes that can be identified among evidence from multiple courses. The SPC are thus larger scale than course learning objectives and smaller than program learning outcomes.

The key element is to operationalize student learning. In other words, what are architecture students ultimately expected to learn and how can that completed learning be measured in valid and reliable ways? Bresciani differentiates between program outcomes (i.e. what a graduate of an architecture program can do), learning outcomes (student learning as a result of the curriculum), and developmental outcomes (students' feelings and attitudes about their education).[15] In architecture, Watt and Cottrell define learning outcomes as a "set of competences including knowledge, understanding and skills that a learner is expected to know, understand, or demonstrate after completion of a process of learning—short or long."[16] They further discuss learning outcomes as a point of reference for curriculum design and evaluation and how such outcomes should allow flexibility and autonomy in developing curricula. Most concisely, Watt and Cottrell believe that learning outcomes provide a "common language for describing what curricula are aiming at."

The Two Spheres perspective on assessment, accountability, and accreditation in architectural education reflects the focus of postindustrial information society on the application of theory and principle as opposed to expertise, intuition, and normative practice. Purpose-driven curricula with coherent plans, operational objectives, and cybernetic feedback loops of continual refinement match the organic and systemic Two Spheres aspect of complex animation. The iterative hermeneutic cycle of observe, learn, try, and evaluate is also relevant.

Some objections might be made that the poetic qualities of architecture cannot be measured in such an empirical process, but these complaints only take us back to the divisive schisms already put to rest by the likes of Snow, White, Gould, Huxley, Mumford, and Heath. The fact is that we give grades in architectural education and to say that these grade evaluations are not empirical measures of learning is nothing less than heresy. One must not confuse the ethereal qualities and sublime experience of architecture for the measurable transitions in learning about architecture. Perhaps our students evolve through measurable and immeasurable stages of development just like great buildings do, but it is a grave error to mistake the subject for the topic, the learning for the poetry. Assessment, accountability, and accreditation are here to help us circumvent such mistakes; and they are here to stay.

Components of a Postindustrial Curriculum

History/Theory/Criticism — Undertaking the Physical Sphere of Architecture

What architectural curricula in most schools currently refer to as "History" is a collection of courses designed to introduce the canons of architectural thought and the developmental progress of that thinking through the ages. Theory and criticism are natural extensions of that chronological and thematic sequence of topics because they go beyond the narrative story to investigate what is meant by architectural progress. In the best of cases, history/theory/criticism (HTC) conveys a sensitivity and sensibility which students can absorb in an analytical critique of works within their various time frames. These cognitions should then enable students to apply the same sensitivity and sensibility to their own synthetic work in design.

In some cases, HTC gets stuck in the yoke of chronological and stylistic lists of buildings and architects arranged and covered in historical sequence. These are long lists and there is much to cover, especially in early survey courses mapping 5,000 years of architecture and culture. In this limited and more official chronicle of architecture, there is usually a good mix of art history and background social–political context, making for more and more declarative knowledge content. Hopefully in such cases these are beginning survey course experiences that are supplemented by subsequent discussion seminars with a greater focus on the theory and criticism components. In the worst scenarios, however, HTC is taught as a litany of styles and architectural events with little relation to technical, environmental, cultural, or design context. Any such reductionist approach denies the true underlying complexity inherent in the Two Spheres revelation of whole-minded architecture.

Beyond a recitation of linear chronologies, the Two Spheres model of HTC engages architectural history as a series of tangles, tandems, and tapestries. This perspective elevates HTC to a more prominent and relevant position than it currently owns.

To elaborate: any particular slice of time involves a set of wicked problems and dynamic forces of culture, society, nature, and technology. Within this tangled background, the historical continuum of architectural accomplishments and setbacks must be understood as a part of the architect's messy and complicated context. Such tangles naturally give way to discourse about the design process in its problem space, task environment, and solution space dimensions: the architect's situation, resources, and range of potential design solutions. This discourse affords the opportunity to survey both the strategic and the physical spheres of particular works and to engage their physical affect in great detail. Such attention to affect will in turn require students to investigate the sublime and transformative achievements of built and theoretical works, each within its own historical situation.

In postindustrial education then, HTC can assume much of the role currently occupied by architectural design studio. This refers specifically to the physical modes of design and their respective impacts on sublime, direct, and immediate experience of architecture. Those discourses are properly the domain of HTC because they can be conducted within the evidence and progression of great architectural achievements. In HTC these discourses can also be set within the contexts of those great seminal works so that their study conveys the construction of a design matrix: problem space, task environment, and solution space. That complex design matrix is seen in this Two Spheres approach as a whole cloth of architecture and its progression across time, culture, and place.

Taking creativity and innovation as primary outcomes of architectural education, the corollary dependence on HTC cannot be overemphasized. In a very real sense, creativity is domain-specific and thus an intimate familiarity with the great works of architecture across the ages and into the present is prerequisite to good design. This prerequisite emerges from study, practice, and discourse, not just from gifted insight. As an example, Peter Collins and William Hubbard both point out that reinterpretation of architectural precedent is more than just emulation of successful design.[17] Emulation would be the rational "right thinking" approach in the manner of dualistic right and wrong design answers. "Making sense of the situation" on the other hand requires critical thinking. Collins and Hubbard both use the analogous situation for how new law is made from precedent cases to illustrate this distinction in architecture. They also both note that such new interpretations must be accompanied by supporting warrants that anticipate and satisfy further critique. Their points can be summarized briefly to illustrate how, in the prospect of a complex design problem space, HTC would properly concern architectural precedent (see especially Hubbard).[18]

- Correction—at some point the precedent work took the wrong turn and this new interpretation corrects that,
- Extension—the new work extends beyond where the precedent work left off,
- Definition—the precedent work became diffused from its real ends and the new work provides improved concentration,
- Distillation—the new work eliminates irrelevant aspects of the precedent work and limits itself to a more prudent scope,
- Reinterpretation—the new work is truer to what the precedent work intended as its highest meaning, and
- Manifestation—the new work fully manifests what the precedent work only implied.

This proposed HTC scheme is certainly already evident in the better curricula in place today, but an explicit framework for such a body of teaching and learning is presently lacking in broad educational discourse. As complexity in the architectural design matrix is recognized, however, and as assessment policy requires, such explicit frameworks must evolve. The program learning outcomes that an architectural program graduate can demonstrate will necessarily reflect the depth suggested in this present scheme for history, theory, and criticism.

Technology—the Mantle of the Strategic Sphere

Programming, practice, structures, environments, and other analytical aspects of technology compose the strategic aspect of architecture. As proposed in Chapter 1, these design activities are all elemental to how architects embody intelligence and foresight in the built environment. In the Two Spheres educational model these topics form a distinct curriculum area as the strategic dimension of design, an area that is tantamount to and complementary with the physical dimension of history/theory/criticism. Conceptualizing the domain of architectural education in this way enhances the vitality and viability of learning because it embraces the true complexity of buildings and building design rather than attempting to tame them into simple problems that can be dispensed with without recognizing the non-local and long-term repercussions.

This Two Spheres organization of HTC and technology also reframes architectural design without diminishing its claim to aesthetic treasure. In fact, disambiguating the design dynamic in this way actually adds to its value because it makes the currency of design more accessible and convertible. Architects do not access genius inspiration to make bold formal statements out of complicated tangles; and such mythical inspiration does not translate into valuable professional services anyway. The models of art and literature are inappropriate and inadequate for full-minded architecture. Instead, architects work abductively with complex and wicked problems and they apply their mastery of a vast and difficult body of knowledge to do so. The implicit and tacit sensitivities and sensibilities that emerge in this work lead to creative and whole-minded solutions. Therein lies the value of architecture. It is not simply right thinking in the gist of correct reasoning; rather it is complex critical thinking in the manner of making sense of a situation. What architects do is special and valuable, but only in terms that can be captured as some kind of socially relevant currency.

Ultimately, the Two Spheres role of technology in architectural education is for responsive action rather than consciously contrived interventions, because while much of design is inventive, an equal share is about discovering and revealing. So the strategic part of design is exogenous to the designer and the physical part is endogenous. By revealing the natural response of design decisions through physics, chemistry, and biology, the setting of the building organism in its environment captures more of the essential complexity that animates their relations. Ignoring this complex underpinning in total favor of willful inventive intentions is more likely to lead to discord, regardless of invented appeal to immediate local perception. Cybernetic feedback in this solution space is what keeps the design organism on the adaptive edge. This is also true of the task environment where computational cybernetics allow much more sophisticated and iterative exploration than in the very recent past. And when the answers are more accessible, the questions become ever more meaningful.

Embodying human intelligence and foresight into the built environment is no small subsidiary task. But the work is not simply necessary for function; it is essential in revealing the unique essence of the design target; and vital to mining the rich ambiguity of design possibility. Technology, in this mindset, enriches design with the elegance of truth and strips away the self-conscious trappings of contrived decoration and the tyranny of novel form for its own sake. But then, the search for truth is in and of itself an aesthetic pursuit:

> Beauty is a function of truth, truth a function of beauty. They can be separated by analysis but in the lived experience of the creative

act—and of its re-creative echo in the beholder—they are as inseparable as thought is inseparable from emotion.

(Arthur Koestler 1989: 331)[19]

Or, from the education of poets:

> Beauty is truth, truth beauty,—that is all
> Ye know on earth, and all ye need to know.

(Keats, *Ode to a Grecian Urn*, 1819)[20]

Beyond the responsive and revealing formulations of the strategic dimension, there is also an Aristotelian final-cause shaping which contributes directly to authentic design creativity. Remembering that creativity requires both innovation and appropriateness, this final-cause teleological shaping is the appropriateness component. Constructability, serviceability, affordability, and all the other modes of embodied intelligence serve this strategic shaping. Learning to think a design through in the strategic dimension with full apprehension of its realized condition is a fundamental task. Without it, all design conjecture is thin air. And this strategic aspect of architectural design education is also radical, meaning that intelligent effects cannot be added on after physical affect is determined. The converse is also true. Discovery and invention must then coevolve in a continuous and sustained process; there is no hierarchy.

Finally, in the Two Spheres model, both history/theory/criticism and technology help resolve an important issue of student learning vis-à-vis the authorship of studio production. This is more of an educational infrastructure issue than a design learning issue, but it is still critically important to a cohesive framework. The current studio model leads to a confusion of authorship precisely because studio instructors work directly and individually with each studio participant. And while the instructor will have a reconstructed notion of how well the student generated the content of that conversation, it will not be a perfect or necessarily representative record. For outside critics then, how does anyone determine the extent to which the work is a product of instructor coaching versus student learning? Is it the instructor being evaluated or the student? Further, if the student is responsive to instructor mentoring over the course of the project, how can a low grade be recorded even if the evidence of learning is weak? All these difficulties are alleviated by the contribution of technical and strategic considerations because they indicate discovered responsiveness in balance with authored inventiveness. HTC contributes in a like manner by channeling the physical transformative and sublime discourse from investigations of seminal and precedent works. Together, technology and history, operating as strategic and physical aspects, can substantiate studio production and ease this dilemma of authorship.

Studio—the Aesthetic Bridge

There is no deep concern in most educational and professional circles for the quality and effort coming from student work in architectural studio learning. It is doubtful that any accreditation review has ever rebuked a school for its studio production; and a review of any school's studio projects normally exhibits heartfelt and highly motivated work. Consequently, most architecture programs pride themselves on being a "design school" without ever certifying what that label stands for or describing how its attainment is comparatively or qualitatively measured.

Current architectural studio instruction is generally committed to producing figural schemes which propose a specific solution for a given architectural problem. As ideation and development in design thinking this is a worthwhile agenda; but going forward it is clear that more ambitious learning outcomes need to be established and operationally defined. The present danger is, per Heath's critique leading off this chapter, in the mistaken idea that such work is the core element of what architects do. As architect and educator Douglas Kelbaugh has pointed out, this mistake advances several myths and misdirects what students ultimately learn and then identify as their aspirations. Some of the potential misconceptions that students might acquire are that:[21]

- design problems come preconfigured and require little analysis to arrive at a program,
- designers work alone to achieve hero celebrity status,
- originality is synonymous with creativity,
- innovation trumps context and coherence,
- budgets do not impact design,
- stakeholders have clear and consistent ideas about the project,
- there are no hidden agendas,
- engineers and consultants solve all the technical considerations without impacting design decisions,
- there is no design accountability for cost, performance, or constructability,
- there are no empirical tests of the design product,
- buildings serve the same function forever, and
- the project is over when the owner moves in.

As architectural education stands today, studio is in an impossible situation. The Beaux-Arts tradition of producing beautiful solutions with little regard for site, context, and occupancy is long over; but the hopeless task of producing a complete building proposition is equally futile. In the realm of our postindustrial complexity, it takes a team of experts many months of working together to produce holistic and synergistic solutions. One student working alone at their desk for a few weeks is clearly doing something quite different from either the Beaux-Arts production or the synergistic whole. So how should we describe the intentionally directed learning outcomes of their efforts? Studio is not truly a discourse with the occupation of architecture as it conveys little practical understanding or competency in the design matrix of problem space, task environment, or solution space. On the other hand, graduates are expected to demonstrate their practical ability to achieve comprehensive design solutions in all stages of work from programming to performance evaluation. So the studio discourse with the domain of occupation is clearly not lapsing into mere intern training, but it simultaneously falls short of the occupational preparedness mandate.

As a discourse with the profession, the role of studio in architectural education is reproductive and revolutionary, conservative and rebellious. In this conversation, studio produces the capable candidate professionals that will carry on the role of architects in service to society. Contrarily, however, studio also works to advance what architects do by subverting current thinking and developing alternative practices. It would be worthwhile to focus more on this tandem of forces; but for now this relation is a quiet one and is seldom an explicit aspect of studio learning. The other side of the conversation is equally quiet as to the architect's ethical and professional responsibility in society— professional practice conduct is usually relegated to content courses rather than bestowed studio attention.

To complete a studio map of the educational realm then, the discourse of professional ethics and societal obligation is seldom broached in studio; and the discourse of occupation is vaguely confused. That leaves the discourse of discipline and the corresponding lifetime of learning involved in mastery of the principles and theories of architecture. The domain of discipline seems fundamental to studio, but in practice there is little direct correspondence with theory, principle, and precedent in studio evaluation. The limits of this are set in the current studio emphasis on unique formal solutions and the articulation of innovative design ideas wherein imaginative authorship trumps intellectual content. Again, this ambiguous discourse with the domain of discipline is not so much an error of calculation in the conduct of studios as it is a product of outdated and conservative traditions. When physical design is taken as the big star of architecture and strategic dimensions are relegated to cameo roles as orbiting minor moons, however, we must expect that the outcome will reflect the input. That is the current state of studio education.

There are also some emerging difficulties with the present conservative studio framework that will be increasingly problematic in the future. For one, the profession of architecture has outstripped the school's engagement of task environment technology. Modeling and simulation are the key components in this, but collaborative and participative project workspace is equally significant. Building information modeling (BIM) and integrated practice (IP) are the current forerunners of this new design practice model. Energy modeling is a close companion and computational tools in general are advancing daily. Worse, while many studio faculty may be increasingly familiar with this new task environment, they are mostly digital migrants who must change the shape of their brain in order to participate. Many of them protested loudly against the advent of computer-aided drawing and design (CADD) but are now championing digital design and fabrication. This is welcome progress. Architecture students, on the other hand, are digital natives; they have never known a time when email, Internet, and computational technology were not integral to their lives. The full ramifications of this may dissipate as our students gradually become our teachers, but in the interim there is going to be some hair pulling going on.

A further new difficulty is that of best-practice teaching and learning, some of which was covered in the section above on assessment and accountability. While the studio model is admired and emulated in an increasing number of other disciplines such as business, the elements being seized on are not the ones so highly touted by architectural educators. Rather than adopting the novel outcome aspects of studio, what is being copied is its problem-based and student-centered processes. Other disciplines are seeing the value of design, but not in the context of "spark in the dark" individualist imagination and uniqueness for its own sake. As for the future of architectural studio education then, the challenge is to fortify the learning outcomes without sacrificing the learning process model. There is no empirical evidence that current studio is the best practice, precisely because there are no comparative measured outcomes to support any such claims, at least not in the realm of peer-reviewed scholarly publication where such data count as evidence. Some well-designed experiments should be undertaken.

Studio in the Two Spheres
A figural model of postindustrial era architectural studio, in the Two Spheres perspective, is much like the pot of boiling water used in Chapter 3. This refers of course to the flow of entropy through a system, wherein order emerges from flow and pattern organizes itself into a coherent whole. In this case, it is the flow of physical and strategic aspects of architecture into studio that represents the driving forces of entropy. History/theory/criticism is the physical aspect and technology/programming/practice is the strategic aspect. Too little flow results in homeostasis and disorganization. Imbalanced or excessive flow results in turbulence and chaos. Refer back to Figure 3.3 for the illustration.

Thus, the Two Spheres complexity model focuses on students' assimilation of strategic and physical dimensions of architecture, design as the complex act of bridging those dimensions, and aesthetics as the bridge's actual span. Studio is where those three elements should lead to whole and mindful architecture. Configuring studio in this way opens direct avenues to the topics of history/theory/criticism, technology, and disciplinary knowledge; wherein history provides a basis for physical immediacy and the ideal while technology is the groundwork for strategic foresight and the realization of design. This alignment also relaxes what is demanded of studio by easing its isolation from the bigger picture and alleviating its burden of unique productions that draw so heavily on constant blank page imaginative innovation. In the Two Spheres configuration, studio learning relies much more heavily on programmatic need, rich ambiguity, technical response, historical precedent, and professional service. Those elements propel the student work. Evaluation engages discourse and critique from a fuller agenda. There is more of a substantive design basis and less of a speculative and conjectural one. The aesthetic is less about inventiveness or individuality and more about connectivity and wholeness. In the place of imagination against complication there is creativity within complexity: out of the tangle and into the tapestry.

Research—the Discipline of Architecture
The definition of a professional realm necessarily includes research as its continuous pursuit of disciplinary knowledge. It follows that the educational domain of such a realm would include the recognized research paradigms that lead to new wisdom in that field. The nurturing and lifelong mastery of disciplinary knowledge is also an obligation that binds architects in service to society because architecture is given exclusive dominion to practice within that large, difficult, vital, and ever-changing body of knowledge. Figure 7.1 presented research within the disciplinary domain and its central concerns for theory, technique, and principles. Architectural education is thus responsible for

producing graduates with the ability and ethical drive to advance that knowledge; and to do so they must acquire skill and experience in the methods of architectural research.

The Two Spheres framework easily emplots architectural research within the information age, knowledge worker, and productive value constructs of postindustrial society. Research is fundamental to the strategic sphere of foresight and embodied human intelligence. Research is equally essential to the physical sphere of theory, principle, critique, and discourse. As information becomes instantly accessible and searchable, the related obligation to acquire and translate relevant data into useful design decisions is palpably unavoidable. The skill to meet that obligation involves nominal episodic research at the very least, so as to identify and meet project requirements. In this era of robust and dynamic solutions, however, research into theory and principle is also required, because procedural expertise locked into a routine task environment is doomed to failure from the start—it can repeat itself, but never advance. Further, as the wicked problems bases, unique ambiguity, complex animation, and bridging aesthetics are embraced, then the efficacy of physical sphere intuitive approaches is increasingly inadequate without enhanced strategic insight. Assuming a hermeneutic design approach to such complexity, research is vital to the abductive and dialectic thinking. "So what?" and "What if?" require methodical investigation as well as opportunistic exploration. Both are elemental to research.

But what is architectural research? Architects have little need for detailed knowledge of laboratory experiments or statistical analysis. And what is architectural knowledge? Artists make better objects; engineers make better machines; and sociologists make better environments. So what do architects know that is not adopted from higher authority? Even as to process knowledge, the wickedness of architectural design assures that operational or formulamatic design methods are impossible; so what is left to research? Is not research about arriving at new generalizable understandings based on structured evidence, while design is about new particular understandings based on general principles?

Such poorly reasoned objections ask the wrong questions by mistaking scientific method for all manner of research. As an intellectual sin, these protestations commit the straw man fallacy of arguing against only a wimpy and crippled version of the opposing view that is constructed from a non-existent model of what is being attacked. A straw man burns easily, but limited thinking like this only brings us back to Heath's critique of the artificial split in architectural education. Clearly there is more to architectural knowledge than what Paul-Alan Johnson aptly terms for some theoretical discourse as "design talk." But where is a workable framework that enfolds both the nurturing of new knowledge in architecture's service to society and the particularized knowledge of a specific design innovation?[22]

Inclusive models of architectural research are, in fact, readily available, as are a set of generalized methodologies for usefully pursuing them. In an even broader sense, design and research are philosophically more congruent than might be evident. To begin with, however, it is useful to restructure research in its epistemological purity. A sound foundational description is that research provides good answers to good questions; wherein the qualifier good denotes characteristics such as unique, new, useful, and generalizable to other situations. A basic and well-operationalized architectural definition is also Gropius's distinction between a work of architecture and a merely good building: the difference being that work which adds new wisdom to what architecture can be.[23]

Still within epistemological bases, Julia Robinson argues for a "productive relationship" in the equally valid approaches to architecture found in the tandem pair of science and myth. She offers an excellent perspective on architectural research by illuminating the sympathetic paradigms of research in anthropology (Table 9.3).[24] Robinson's cross-comparison from anthropology to architecture is also a keen but subtle warning against disciplinary chauvinism and genius-bound inspiration, as well as a clarion call for intellectual rigor. We must avoid mistaking qualitative for subjective, confusing empirical with quantitative, substituting description for analysis, and other such characteristic slips of unbridled "design talk" in its lesser forms. Such erroneous thinking links to another of Heath's writings in *What if Anything is an Architect?* (1991) and also to his fellow Australian contemporary Garry Stevens's *The Reasoning Architect* (1990). Flowery prose, sophist autocratic arguments, and relativism are high on their collective hit list.[25]

The Tandem of Design Inquiry and Research Inquiry in Architectural Knowledge
One means of orientation to architectural research inquiry is to set it in context of what students are already more acquainted with as design inquiry (Figure 9.2).[26] While student engagement in design inquiry is often more episodic or pragmatic and less theoretical than the pure research construct, design is nonetheless a reasonable way to begin considering research because the similarities and differences tend to illuminate thinking about both activities. Figure 9.2 compares the two modes of inquiry as simple linear processes for the sake of coherent conversation and clear illustration. In practice, of course,

Table 9.3 Characteristics of a research model for architecture

- Acknowledges truth embodied in the context of natural settings
- Resists existing knowledge as the foregone explanation or solution
- Allows inherent and contextual data to emerge unconstrained
- Acquires holistic understanding by observing and absorbing real situations
- Becomes embedded in complex, chaotic, contradictory situations
- Accepts paradox without requiring its resolution
- Use of dialectic conditions as a generative tension
- Uses both atomistic and holistic perspectives
- Allows both synchronic (at a time) and diachronic (across time) perspectives
- Employs both intuitive and deductive logics
- Recognizes emic (native, mythical) and etic (professional) explanations
- Uses both direct experience and modeling of reality
- Defines culture as the primary concept of interest and investigation

Source: Adapted from Robinson (1990).

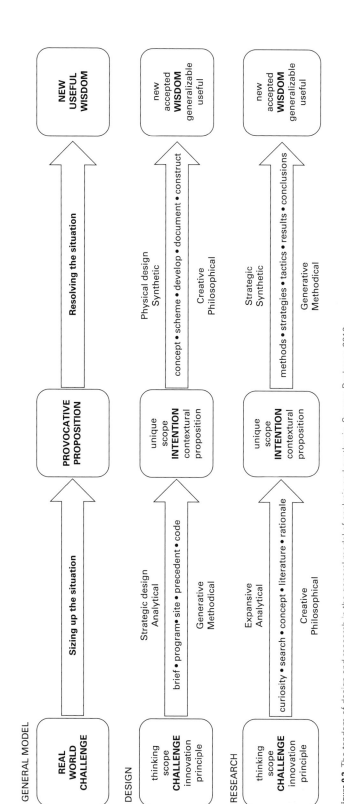

Figure 9.2 The tandem of design and research in the general model of analysis and synthesis. Source: Bachman 2010.

both activities are more opportunistic, complex, and messy; but the underlying theories concerning them both can be more readily examined if the basic relations are clearly stated as a conceptual framework.

What research and design share as modes of inquiry are three common punctuation points: beginning in problem definition, working toward a transitional midpoint proposition, and ending in new wisdom that advances the pursuit of architecture. At the beginning there are common bases in theory and quests for innovation. At the midpoint the shared emphasis is on identifying a propositional goal that is, hypothetically at least, something unique, situated, and provocative. This midpoint is critical in that it reveals the rich and complex essence of what was at first just a problem statement but becomes the "big idea" behind the entire project. In the sense of problem space, this midpoint is where the pregnant ambiguity of the situation has been identified and distilled. It is in this region of ambiguity that both design and research operate most creatively. Finally, as their common ultimate goal, both research inquiry and design inquiry strive to achieve an artifact that embodies new, useful, accepted, and generalizable wisdom—hopefully in both cases leading to validation through replication by others.

Where these two modes of inquiry differ is in the processes between those punctuations. While both can be described in the conventional problem-defining and problem-resolving sequence of analysis of the problem followed by synthesis of the solution, other aspects are actually reversed. Most fundamentally different are the roles of creative–philosophical versus generative–methodical thinking. In design inquiry, the process between beginning problem definition briefing and midpoint propositional design intention can be described as generative–methodical in terms of the analytical thinking it usually entails: programming, site analysis, precedent reviews, code analysis, and other aspects of strategic planning. Once this generative–methodical process leads to an abductive proposition midpoint, design then continues with the more creative–philosophical process of physical design from conceptual to schematic and on toward the endpoint of a realized work of novel architectural wisdom.

In broad conceptual terms, research-as-inquiry reverses those two processes. Here the initial span from beginning doubt and curiosity to the midpoint of a propositional research hypothesis is the creative–philosophical one. This is where a significant gap in existing knowledge is identified by analysis and exploration of existing knowledge. Everything after that in research is essentially methodical–generative toward the synthetic results and findings published for peer review. Now this is not to say in absolute terms that the generative–methodical modes of design programming or those of research methods do not require creativity and inspiration. Clearly the strategic planning aspect of a design challenge requires much imagination and novel thinking as does the experimental design phase of a research project. It would also be wrong to suggest that either the researcher or the designer ever works with only half of their cognitive skills activated at any one time. The main point here is that the authorship and creative credit of research lies in a reversed formulation of processes compared to that of design. It is through this sort of conceptual understanding that the common ground and varying processes of design inquiry and research inquiry can illuminate one another.

This first framework of the general argument aligning research and teaching corresponds to Walter Gropius's term "the accumulated wisdom of architecture."[27] As already noted, this is the ultimate goal of both design inquiry and research inquiry. An inquiring intention of adding to the accumulated wisdom of architecture thus serves to bond the value structure of research-as-inquiry with that of design-as-inquiry. It might be claimed, for example, that differentiation of a good but normative building from critically worthy architecture is staked on identifying what new wisdom the subject work adds to our thinking about what architecture can be and do. Vitruvian "commodity, firmness, and delight" are not, taken literally and simplistically, adequate. New and better ideas are always required to advance the cause. Research inquiry is likewise grounded in the pursuit of new knowledge, understanding, or wisdom that advances what architecture is.

Knowledge and Wisdom in the Spheres of Architectural Education
In closing, and in transition to Chapter 10's more complete treatment of research as the disciplinary domain of architecture, it is now possible to show how the Two Spheres model accommodates the different topics of architectural knowledge and folds them back into the domain of education. This accommodation of disciplinary knowledge also facilitates postindustrial society's demands for those empirically measurable results that architectural education must produce. So by defining the nature of architecture's disciplinary knowledge, we not only outline the educational system that transmits that knowledge, but also the research system that advances it.

The accompanying illustrations depict such a disciplinary knowledge base by overlaying a hierarchy of knowledge levels against Bloom's taxonomy of learning objectives. Table 9.4 and Box 9.1 on knowledge and understanding set out six fundamental levels of cognition. Figure 9.3 then illustrates Bloom's learning objectives as reconsidered by Anderson and Krathwohl (2001).[28] Combining the scales of Table 9.4 and Figure 9.3 generates thirty-six coordinates shown in Table 9.5, each coordinate forming a cognitive dimension of the disciplinary knowledge base. Finally, Table 9.6 maps these themes onto the Two Spheres framework of architectural education. Within that resulting framework we should be able to trace the foundation of the architect's discipline.

Table 9.4 Six levels of knowledge and understanding

Level	Example	Transformation	Action	Order	Context	Realm
Facts	Current Temperature	Observation	Awareness	Isolated	Explicit	Experience
Data	Average Daily Temperatures	Organization	Curiosity	Structured	Organized	
Information	Monthly Degree Days	Relation	Appreciation	Scaled	Analytical	Concepts
Knowledge	Appropriate Passive Systems	Application	Illumination	Connected	Interpretive	
Understanding	Functional Integration	Integration	Expertise	Networked	Implicit	Design
Wisdom	Systemic Integration	Theory	Virtuosity	Dynamic	Tacit, Zen	

Box 9.1 Knowledge vs. understanding: An example using climate analysis

- *Facts*

Temperature—The current temperature is just a fact. Facts exist in isolation.

- *Data*

Climate data—Data are organized collections of facts. To convert facts into data it is necessary to impose an organizational structure.

- *Information*

Degree-days—Degree-days correlate weather data to the heating and cooling requirements of buildings. Information is always useful for making decisions because it has relation. To convert data into information requires analysis or visualization to reveal patterns and relationships not discernible from raw data. This conversion is fundamentally inherent in the transformation of project information into a design agenda.

- *Knowledge*

Climate potential for passive techniques—Knowledge is the accumulation of information into consciousness. It enables conceptualization. Having a particular bit of knowledge however does not necessarily imply the ability to understand or to apply it. Operations based on knowledge alone are formulamatic, prescriptive, and inflexible to circumstances.

- *Understanding*

Integrated design solutions—Understanding is the ability to recreate information from its underlying principles and to fit it into the matrix of what we already know and understand. Understanding cannot be transmitted directly from one person to another. Strategic thinking requires understanding of relationships and principles, not just pragmatic and procedural knowledge.

- *Wisdom*

Sustainability—Wisdom arises from the accumulation of understandings. Walter Gropius declared that a work of architecture should be evaluated by its contribution to "the accumulated wisdom of architecture."

Beginning with Table 9.4 then, the levels of knowledge move up from declarative facts, data, and information to the procedural questions of knowledge and understanding. Declarative levels deal with what, when, and where; while procedural questions ask how. From there, the structural level of deep understanding and wisdom asks "why?" Using the example of climate analysis, these six levels of questioning are shown to be separated by increasingly difficult transformations, actions, ordering principles, and contexts.

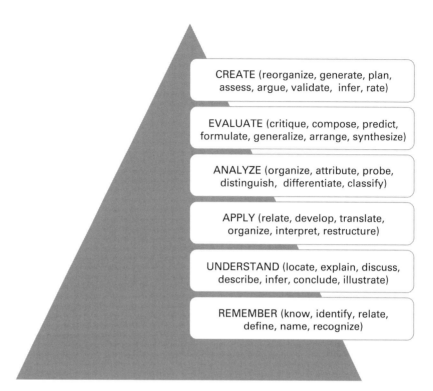

Figure 9.3 Bloom's taxonomy, after a revision by Anderson and Krathwohl (2001), adapted graphically by the author.

CREATE (reorganize, generate, plan, assess, argue, validate, infer, rate)

EVALUATE (critique, compose, predict, formulate, generalize, arrange, synthesize)

ANALYZE (organize, attribute, probe, distinguish, differentiate, classify)

APPLY (relate, develop, translate, organize, interpret, restructure)

UNDERSTAND (locate, explain, discuss, describe, infer, conclude, illustrate)

REMEMBER (know, identify, relate, define, name, recognize)

Table 9.5 Matrix of thirty-six potential coordinates

	Remember	Understand	Apply	Analyze	Evaluate	Create
Facts			Increasing complexity of knowledge aspect			
Data Information		Increasing complexity of knowledge aspect				
Knowledge						
Understanding			Multiple coordinates of learning outcomes can be targeted across both aspects			
Wisdom						

Mistaking one level of knowledge for another is thus a critical failure in framing disciplinary knowledge; and such mistakes cloud the ability to transmit such knowledge by education or to advance it by either research or design inquiry. Aldous Huxley—whose grandfather Thomas H. Huxley, coincidentally, once employed Patrick Geddes—distinguished between declarative knowledge and deep structural understanding this way:

> Correct or incorrect, relevant or meaningless, knowledge and pseudo-knowledge are as common as dirt and are therefore taken for granted. Understanding, on the contrary, is as rare, very nearly,

Table 9.6 Proposed map for frames of knowledge in architectural education

	CURRICULUM AREAS			
	Meaningful Experience	*Analytical Evaluation*	*Design Decisions*	*Architectural Ideas*
	HISTORY / THEORY / CRITICISM COURSES	*TECHNOLOGY / PROGRAMMING / PRACTICE COURSES*	*STUDIO COURSES*	*SHARED CURRICULUM*
PARALLEL CONCEPTS	Content (what)	Means (how)	Context (so that)	Ideals (why)
	Substance	Sustenance	Passion	Significance
	Inspiration	Insight	Judgment	Imagination
	Precedent	Integration	Formalization	Connection
	Vocabulary	Tools and protocols	Belief	Abduction
	Engagement	Transformation	Risk and courage	Assertion
	Domain knowledge	Procedural knowledge	Critical understandings	Structural knowledge
	Emplotment	Equilibrium and flows	Manifestation	Innovation and perturbation
	Heritage	Society	Culture	Civilization
	Knowledge	Work	Resolution	Expression
	Values	Strategy	Satisfaction	Wisdom
	Currency	Intelligence	Aesthetics	The Sublime

> as emeralds, and so is highly prized. The knowers would dearly love to be understanders.[29]

This six-level framework also clarifies the place of design at the highest levels of cognition by differentiating it from declarative information and procedural expertise. In an information society full of knowledge workers and saturated with cybernetic tools, the cognitive domains of understanding and wisdom are vitalized by the theories and principles that allow for integrative connections. No wonder then that so many professions now see design much as architects do: the ultimate means of inventing a better future through disciplinary knowledge.

Shifting from the dimension of knowledge to the dimension of human cognition, Bloom's taxonomy depicts the actions required to demonstrate upwardly difficult levels of thinking (Figure 9.3). The use of action words operationalizes each level as observable, and thus measurable, behaviors. In educational terms, this operationalizing is essential to the empirical evaluation of learning outcomes. In research, the same operational definition is essential to empirical measurement in any mode of quantitative or qualitative inquiry and is applied universally across the scales of nominal, ordinal, interval, and ratio measures. Without the empirical nature of these operations, there is no World Three territory of shared meaning; and without that shared meaning we are left in isolation with nothing more than personal World Two subjective opinions. To construct shared meaning and have useful discourse we must agree on the operationalized definitions. From operationalized definitions we can always make empirical measurements.

Table 9.5 simply illustrates that the six knowledge aspects of Table 9.4 and the six cognitive aspects of Figure 9.3 overlay to produce thirty-six possible positions. So from the simplest position of remembering facts, this matrix escalates to creative wisdom and the creation of wisdom. At the pinnacle then, we find the synthetic products of both design inquiry and research inquiry.

Finally, Table 9.6 maps a propositional framework for the Two Spheres curriculum model and reintegrates them across several parallel concepts developed from the preceding discussion. Each of the parallel concepts attempts to connect the various topic areas of the curriculum, but the continuity of each line across the table is only a loose category of knowledge and cognition interpreted from the thirty-six positions of Table 9.5 and meshed with the Two Spheres plan of topic areas in architectural education. Ultimately, this proposed model offers a transitional rearrangement of existing curriculum ideas that incorporates the physical and strategic aspects of architecture into the aesthetic embrace that celebrates them holistically. As a pattern, this model is demonstrably explicit, coherent, and practical enough to reorganize architectural curricula within. As an idea, it is arguably in agreement with the best current thinking about education; and yet it is still progressive enough to meaningfully transform architectural curricula as we know it today.

The other advantage of formalizing such an explicit and coherent model is World Three rigor. For the discipline of architecture to be advanced, we need a well-articulated map of its knowledge structures; for without such a rigorous basis it is difficult to generate and share new architectural wisdom in a mutually intelligible realm of constructed meanings, discourse, and critique. Chapter 10 carries this discussion of rigor forward in the disciplinary domain of architectural inquiry.

Chapter 10

The Domain of the Discipline

> Architectural knowledge does not flourish when skills are divorced from ideas, when practice is separated from theory but when all are brought together in the context of action. Architectural knowledge is usually challenging, sometimes uncomfortable, always open ended, inherently value laden.
>
> (Duffy and Hutton 1998:147)[1]

> We will have standing when we publish the body of knowledge upon which we base our practice.
>
> (Watson 2008)[2]

Beginning with the philosophical bases of the disciplinary domain, we first must recognize that society grants registered architects a licensed monopoly on the practice of architecture. In return, practitioners then apply their large and difficult body of disciplinary knowledge in meritorious occupation to projects that advance the interests of society.[3] Another part of this bargain is the responsibility for nurturing and growing that disciplinary knowledge through whatever means of inquiry are required to insure progress. If architects want to hold title to the application of their ideas and ideals, then they alone are positioned to advance architecture's knowledge base from within. As discussed in Chapter 9, this disciplinary knowledge is operationalized by what Walter Gropius called the "accumulated wisdom" of architecture: if it can arguably be said that some work adds new or improved wisdom to the field, then it counts as architecture.[4] Architectural inquiry is then any activity that systematically adds to the architect's store of accumulated wisdom. In research jargon, "systematically" means that this new knowledge is unique, useful, and generalizable to other situations, accepted by leaders in the specific area of knowledge, and in alignment with those current understandings that it attaches to. Anecdotal, private, or any other non-validated contributions are not systematic and therefore cannot count.

Postindustrial society embraces this inquiry as the generation of value. If, as Watson suggests, architects provide value in society, then they do so by growing, nurturing, and applying their specialized, maintained, and continually advanced body of knowledge. Service to paying clients and user-occupants of buildings is the occupational root of this work, but long-term value to society is the ultimate test of professional and disciplinary status. And then, in addition to society, owners, and users, we must add one more client group served by every project: the epicurean critics. The intersubjective basis of their high critique clearly involves Popper's World Three of the shared constructed knowledge that transcends personal and subjective experience. Critique, in turn, is especially valuable because it validates contributions to accumulated knowledge from within what Hubbard calls the "scrim" of disciplinary knowledge.[5] Outside the scrim most clients, owners, and passers-by have only normative expectations such that their own homes and the architecture around them should be pleasant, commodious, compatible, and durable; but those knowledgeable epicures inside the scrim can apply critical expectations in the full realm of existing disciplinary knowledge; they expect the architect to build on what has gone before.

Accordingly, the Two Spheres framework of postindustrial architecture maps on to the disciplinary domain as inquiry in the form of both design inquiry and research inquiry. The same focus on knowledge collection, organization, and inference as discussed in Chapter 1's definition of postindustrial society applies:

- Value is created by knowledge workers,
- Human capital and human interface are the bases of knowledge production,
- Problems and social messes are composed of interconnected factors,
- The future can be proactively invented rather than reactively encountered,
- Systemic relations among situational factors are more important than the symptoms of the problem,
- The systemic recipe for dealing with problem messes is more important than the symptomatic ingredients of the mess,
- Messy problems are wicked and complex,
- The approach to wicked messes is a hermeneutic,
- We work from complicated tangles to dynamic tandems to complex tapestries, and
- We embrace the aesthetic bridge between the real and the ideal.

Design Inquiry and Research Inquiry: How the Discipline Lives

We all understand design and research as two different modes of inquiry linked by some common characteristics and yet distinguished as alternate methodologies. To inquire is to seek the truth, and this quest always involves study, scrutiny, and exploration. Ultimately of course, such searching should produce new answers, thereby building the discipline. As we have already seen, however, getting answers in these modes of inquiry is a wicked and indeterminate problem that begins with poorly defined problems and poorly delineated techniques; both the problem space and the task environment are amorphous. Figure 10.1 distinguishes this wickedness from the more tame problems of applied thinking and mere training.

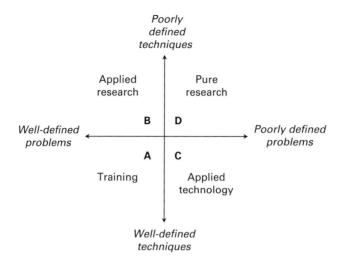

Figure 10.1 Four quadrants of inquiry.

Design Inquiry

Completed or even proposed works contribute to their disciplinary base if such works are deemed worthy by a consensus of experts, connoisseurs, or professionals. This is as true of architecture as it is for any disciplinary realm. These contributions define architectural design inquiry because built works both embody and enrich foundational architectural knowledge. Worthy buildings, components, landscapes, and townscapes all add to accumulated wisdom and therefore become part of the profession's disciplinary knowledge base; part of what practitioners are expected to spend a lifetime in learning toward mastery. This is the font of design inquiry in how architects investigate the generalized learning, principles, ethics, practices, and theories that are garnered from previous architectural accomplishments, and then apply this disciplinary knowledge to specific design challenges presented by public and private needs in the built environment. So, we must conclude that architecture's portfolio of design inquiry is consequently bound up in the higher accomplishments of our built works and visionary proposals toward built works. Furthermore, the discipline, occupation, and professional domains of the realm are all represented in the accumulation of more and more wisdom about what architecture can be and how it can serve society.

Of course design inquiry is not a purely synthetic pursuit. To arrive at a design proposition, a great deal of methodical analysis is required to first establish the particulars of what is being designed. That methodical analysis is typically considered as project programming. But to the extent that programming is mistakenly considered as just digging into the tangle of accumulated project data and converting it into useful information, this is not inquiry of any kind; it is stenographic recording and reporting. Digging and organizing are obviously essential steps in both design and research inquiry, but stopping there misses the full scope of what counts as architectural investigation. So digging and organizing are important, but they are not the full sense of what we mean by inquiry or research. Groat and Wang describe this work of digging as an "episodic" gateway for including research inquiry within the design process:

> Research of this more limited scope and duration is likely to concentrate on specific tactics by which the required information can be derived, whether from archives and documents, buildings and artifacts, or observations and conversations with people.[6]

In the end, and referring back to Table 9.4, digging and organizing are largely concerned with declarative and procedural questions at the levels of knowledge and understanding. This fails the standard of true inquiry because it falls short of the creation of new structural level understandings and wisdom. Using Figure 10.1 again, episodic digging can also be thought of as applied technology or applied research where either well-defined techniques or well-defined problems present. This helps once more to distinguish digging and reporting from higher order inquiry of pure research and design, where both the problem and the techniques are poorly defined and the work must address wicked complexity. To repeat the old saying with some added emphasis, such high order inquiry is like a blind search in a dark room for a black cat that is not there yet.

The full depth of design inquiry is vested in what happens after episodic untangling of project data and its organization into useful information. Figure 9.2 explored this depth by comparing linear representations of design and research in the general model of analysis–proposition–synthesis. Those generic formulations of design and research inquiry are reversed in the sense of where creativity is lodged. In research inquiry, the more creative and philosophical aspect is situated in the expansive analytical investigations that lead up to a unique and provocative research question. Most everything after identification of the research question is the methodical employment of measurement techniques, and those techniques are determined by the character of the research question. This leaves out the creative and innovative design of the experiment, simulation, argument, or other systematic strategy for addressing the question, but that second order creativity occurs outside of the actual value imbued in developing the primary research question to begin with.

For the core of design inquiry, on the other hand, creative and philosophical depth of meaning have conventionally been vested wholly within the physical sphere of synthetic work that comes after the midpoint of the process when a design proposition is declared, rather than in the expansive analytical phase as in research inquiry. But that old convention misses the embraces of complexity as developed in Chapter 6 as hermeneutics, unique teleological essence, animation, and aesthetic bridging. If architecture is to realize the potential of design in postindustrial complexity, these four elements of complexity must be embraced. In the fuller sense, therefore, the Two Spheres of strategic foresight and physical immediacy must both be respected as tantamount and equally significant to what properly counts as mindful architecture. In the complexity of postindustrial architecture, the conduct of design inquiry is consequently expanded to this fuller scope.

In this more complete Two Spheres scope of design inquiry, it is also useful to remember the discussion in Chapter 3 concerning the complexity of our design artifacts and the treatment in Chapter 2 of design itself as a wickedly indeterminate and richly complex activity. When buildings, components, landscapes, cityscapes, and other artifacts of design are considered complex in this way, the subject of design inquiry is invigorated by the dynamic character and animated life of its subjects.

Research Inquiry

Moving on to research inquiry in architecture, our consideration becomes one level removed from that of design inquiry. In other words, architectural research leads not to new built works of architecture, but rather to new wisdom about the activity and artifacts of design. Moving from "of" to "about" achieves one level of separation because the activity of design becomes the subject of research. Architectural research is thus a second, but not lower, order mode of architectural inquiry. Further, research inquiry also encompasses introspective components of architects looking back at architecture; and thus reflects to third order inquiry about the nature of research inquiry, fourth order inquiry that reflects back on that investigation, and so on. This separation legitimizes research inquiry as works of architecture because its introspective and reflective activities contribute directly to the accumulation of more disciplinary knowledge. The design work of formulating buildings and the research work of codifying principles and theories that guide the further work of designing are both clearly disciplinary. The two pursuits also interact in dynamic ways so that small changes in one result in corresponding shifts in the other.

So just as in design inquiry, research inquiry leads to new wisdom and must be generalizable to a range of architectural conditions beyond the one situation in which it was developed. The main difference lies in the direction of generalizing: design inquiry being those investigations leading from general principles to a specific solution, while research inquiry reverses this and leads to new wisdom in the form of generalizable theories and principles.

Validity and Reliability in Architectural Discourse

For works of inquiry in research or design to be valuable, they must be publically and empirically validated. In design inquiry and the more naturalistic branches of research inquiry such as emancipatory and logical argument, this validation has typically been established by intersubjective agreement: if enough of the recognized leaders in the topic area agree on the merits of the work then it is considered to be valid and useful. The empirical nature of the work is defined by its intersubjective agreement. We expect, for example, that independent rankings of design competition entries would have enough agreement among the expert judges to confirm the selection of the winning design. In such qualitative measurements, only strong inter-rater agreement can provide any sense of empirical validity.

Here however is where current practice begins to break down. Architects are seldom well equipped to design qualitative measurement instruments. Consequently, agreement about what is being measured in a design competition or any other aspect of architectural discourse is usually left to chance and debate. If we do not know what we mean because there is no basis of comparison, then nothing is decided either way; and neither agreement nor disagreement can have reliable consequences. In this failed situation, what passes for measurement is invalidated by its lack of reliability because we have far less confidence that another group of expert judges would arrive at similar ratings. Without that confidence, validity collapses. Likewise, whenever authoritative argument is replaced by authoritarian control or autocratic pronouncement, then discourse fails—and inquiry fails with it.

This is an unfortunate feature of architectural discipline, because the lack of understanding on qualitative measurement and how readily it is operationalized into empirical terms greatly misrepresents the true sensitivity and sensibility that many architects can contribute. In place of this understanding it seems that architects have developed a stubborn predisposition against measurement of any kind in design, mistakenly believing that measurement always connotes scientific determination in reductive terms like economy and efficiency. This mistake has crept around architectural discourse for so long that a great many important distinctions have been blurred and the validity as well as the veracity of much architectural discourse has been poisoned. Tom Heath, whose complaint against the false division of architectural qualities was quoted to open Chapter 9, complains here again about the "traps of architectural discourse":[7]

- Poetry—using fine phrases that bypass critical thought
- Objective/Subjective—evading discussion by denial of public and objective basis, substituting support for the private and subjective
- Reductionism—distilling singularity out of intolerable plurality
- Relativism and its acceptance in the case of function, or rejection in the case of aesthetics
- Humes Law—one cannot know what to do simply by observing our own feelings about right or wrong; the confusion of "is" with "ought." This is the embeddedness in our world that creates an inability to be objective. This is the dilemma of intuition, moralism, and bias.

Remediation is, however, mostly a simple matter of awareness. Architects, by and large, are not ignorant or heedless of critical distinctions; but they are caught up in a culture that has evolved a compulsive tendency to resist measurement of architectural quality. It is also true that their education generally places less value on well-reasoned argument, polite discourse, and critique than perhaps it should. Furthermore, the correction comes not from scientists, but rather from philosophers to whom the precise, and sublime, interpretation of meaning, relation, and quality is a profound search for truth and beauty. Surely architects have borrowed from philosophy long enough to appreciate and embrace the subtle character of qualitative measure. Box 10.1 on fields and fences covers several of those opportunities, many of which have already been discussed in the Two Spheres model. Like measurement standards, agreement on concepts and terminology is essential to discourse and meaning. Language is the basis of this agreement.

Box 10.1 Fields and fences: Some common conceptual mistakes of definition

Authoritative, authoritarian, autocratic

Bias, heuristic, prejudice, assumption, fallacy, relativism, Hume's Law

Causal vs. relational

Conceptual, abstract, schematic

Continuous vs. discrete variables

Correlation (strength) vs. regression (proportion)

Counterintuitive vs. irrational

Declarative, procedural, structural

Deductive, inductive, abductive

Dualistic, multiplistic, pluralistic

Evaluate, measure, scale

Experiment, simulation, qualitative, interpretive, emancipatory

Facts, data, information, knowledge, understanding, expertise, wisdom

Ideas, facts, opinion, value

Inspiration vs. counter-rational

Interpretive vs. subjective

Intersubjective vs. objective

Intuition vs. impression

Logic vs. reasoning

Model vs. miniature

Nominal, ordinal, interval, ratio

Plan, scenario, scheme, concept

Qualitative vs. subjective

Rational vs. scientific

Reliability, validity

Survey, poll, questionnaire

Talent, knowledge, expertise, genius

Values, mission, goals, strategy, objectives, tactics

Verify vs. validate

Toward a Clinical Database of Architecture

Beyond the inquiry that nurtures and grows the theories and principles of a profession, any disciplinary model of architecture also implies the development of a clinical database upon which architects rely. A description of how that database is evolving will combine, iterate, and hopefully synthesize many ideas already covered in the preceding Two Spheres perspectives.

The term clinical is defined here as the application of a body of knowledge to the diagnosis and therapeutic treatment of a specific problem case: one case based on many cases. Architect practitioners are clinicians in this sense, because they do not invent a new architecture for each and every project; and even if we attempted to do so, our intuitive sense of how to go about it is inherently based on past experience.

Law and medicine are obvious examples of professions with well-recognized and inherently essential clinical databases. Medicine has the most prolific, with epidemiology, pharmacology, toxicology, and so forth; all of which refer back to the health treatment of individual cases through principles of anatomy, biology, and chemistry; just as architecture refers back to the vitality of individual building cases through thermodynamics, statics, acoustics, and so forth. Each health case is as unique as each building case—and both medicine and architecture operate on generalizable principles. In medicine this generalizing is termed casuistry, referring to matters based collectively on the study of actual cases or case histories. An emphasis on the use of medical research in clinical practice has, for example, spawned the field of evidence-based medicine (EBM).

The clinical database of law is also nicely translated into architecture through Peter Collins's book, *Architectural Judgment* (1971).[8] Collins compares the use of precedent in law to that of precedent buildings in architecture. William Hubbard endorses Collins's take on the model of law as analogous to that of architecture: "what we want in both fields . . . is work that reflects and responds to change yet gives the impression of continuity."[9] As in medicine, each application of the law to a particular situation is simultaneously unique and generalizable—again, just as in architecture. So where medicine has its various specialized databases, law will have similar divisions of case precedents such as civil, criminal, tax, and so forth. Both legal and medical data sets provide a compendium of wisdom and history upon which new decisions can be intelligently based and without which judgment is only negligently decided.

To begin tracing the emergence of this clinical perspective in architecture, consider the words of Charles Garnier, speaking on the acoustics of his design for the 1889 Paris Opera. In the full spirit of trial and error, Garnier proclaimed a separation between the formal and performal tenets of architecture: "I must explain that I have adopted no principle, that my plan has been based on no theory, and that I leave success or failure to chance alone."[10] Today, some 120 years later, architects are gradually but decisively reversing this separation of the visibly tangible forms of their works from the invisible dynamics that buildings always manifest. There is a connecting of formal and performal thinking underway and a developing reliance on new kinds of unified insight that can inform and inspire design.

The Roots of Knowledge

Clinical knowledge of architecture and the growth of a database to capture that knowledge are both rooted in progressive historical and evolutionary forces. These forces can be enumerated as history, performance, society, planning, and nature.

History

Historically, the knowledge base of architecture has accumulated with time and with lessons learned. Initially this knowledge was knit into a contract with the cultural elite rather than with society in general. That is to say, architects worked more toward the shared cultural experiences and values of the privileged classes than toward the infrastructure and well-being of society and for the built environment at large. Architectural service directly to the general population and to civic institutions is a more recent phenomenon.

As an accumulation of knowledge and wisdom, service to culture and privilege is rooted in the epicurean pleasure principle of celebration. In that context the essential value of knowledge, function, economy, and suitability is subsumed by desire for status, glory, pomp, and monumentality. In these modern and more democratic times however architects are engaged increasingly more by the transformation of essential requirements into built forms that are meaningful, serviceable, and yet still as masterful as the monumental works dedicated to culture. It is these later works that have instigated and formalized the clinical knowledge of architecture. Along the way, several new and important societal forces also asserted themselves, such as building codes, legal liability, technical society, and licensure. Most historically important perhaps was the eventual promotion of architecture to full ranking as a profession by its taking membership in the academy (see Fisher 2008).[11]

Performance
A second root of evidence for the emergence of architecture's clinical database is found in the measured performance of buildings. It is a relatively easy point: architects design buildings to work, to do something instrumental.

So long as the historical role of architecture was one of service to cultural appetites and privileged resources, the mandate of functional performance was an assumed fait accompli and weak force. With the ascent of social and civic service, however, the practical operation and performance of a building becomes increasingly important. With the simultaneous advent of technology and the means of measuring performance, it also becomes increasingly easy to ask questions about efficiency, measure performance, and to track results over time. Finally, with the development of qualitative research methods and statistical tools, architects can empirically inquire and critique the value of more than just quantitative factors such as energy use. Qualitative issues such as human perception and environmental behavior are now also on the table. And as these answers become easier to attain, the underlying questions become much more compelling.

Society
Having invoked social transformation as a shift toward data-driven design in both a historic and a performative context, some specific influences in current events should be referenced. The characteristics of our emerging postindustrial society fulfill this need quite nicely (Bell 1973).[12]

Foremost among these influences is the transformation to a new system of value production, one that moves away from a primary basis in the value of industrial products and toward the value created by use of information. This refers not to the innate usefulness of information per se, but rather to the intelligence attained by collection, organization, and inference from data. This intelligence is what distinguishes mere data from useful information in the first place.

It is generally accepted that the leading industrialized nations had already become predominantly information and service economies by the 1950s. More recent notions of knowledge professions, service workers, information technology, learning organizations, and globalization attest to further and deepening change. Architecture as a service profession is well aligned to capitalize on the now recognizable postindustrial notion of value creation. The architect's actual ability to capitalize, however, may hinge on their willingness to point to a discrete body of captured and codified knowledge, ergo, a clinical database of architecture. Heretofore, the profession at large has been content, perhaps even secretly delighted, to maintain a kind of mystical, artistic, and cult-driven air as to architectural knowledge. While the magic of making architecture is likely to remain cloaked in professional acculturation, it is also increasingly probable that the value of what architects produce will have to become more explicit, along with the knowledge base on which their work is founded.

Planning

Another word for the operation of postindustrial intelligence is strategy, the plan of how knowledge will be collected, organized, and applied: the recipe. Expectations of postindustrial society are that a strategic meta-plan for architectural projects can be articulated at the proposal stage. This requires the architect to communicate in advance how project delivery will occur, and by what processes and sequence. All of which presupposes the existence of a specialized knowledge base (i.e. a clinical database on which to operate).

At the level where this information targets the actual design, planning is increasingly required to go beyond normative programming in the sense of creating an agenda for the client's wants and needs. The trend is for buildings to be more than static objects that house the user function. Rather, they are expected to facilitate the institution in flexible ways, and respond to continuous change and reorganization. Buildings are increasingly seen less as status objects and more as integral parts of long-range plans.

Consequently, there are new demands for information-based and evidence-driven design. Design must facilitate long-range scenario planning goals and objectives. Further, the information folded into such scenarios requires a participatory process involving not just the client owner's dictates, but rather a full spectrum of users, suppliers, consultants, and other related stakeholders.

Nature

To support the emergence of a clinical database in architecture, consider the stages of ecologically based design which architects have developed since Geddes: solar, passive, green, sustainable, and regenerative, to name a broad but probably incomplete list. While all of these relate in some way to the evidence of performance, they also involve the knowledge base of an entire ethic. More than just energy efficiency, the broader scope of designing with nature has grown to include project-specific data on indoor air quality, chemical sensitivity, eco-aesthetics, and so forth. It also involves measures at the global scale, such as carbon neutral, ecological footprint, and global warming.[13]

Keeping abreast of this rapidly escalating issue and the continuously evolving information needed for appropriate design is not possible through traditional design thinking. Postindustrial architecture requires access to a database of vetted knowledge that allows for clinical application to specific cases, again, just as in medicine and in law.

Themes of Complexity

Turning now to the sources of clinical knowledge in architecture, the four roots of evidence can be illustrated in practice. While some of these current practices are not yet recognized as clinical databases, it is increasingly clear that they will eventually be thought of in that way.

The characteristics of clinical practice are adapted here from a description of how the clinical model is relevant in educational research.[14] These traits are useful in linking architectural design to clinical knowledge. To wit, a clinical practice is:

- Problem initiated and problem directed
- Concerned with action directed toward a particular problem and specific case
- Performed collaboratively
- Involved with collecting information and drawing conclusions
- Performed diagnostically and therapeutically to identify and resolve disorders or discordance
- Dependent on the clinician's interpretive reading of the problem and selection of an appropriate remedy
- Based on a comprehensive body of collected cases that comprise a clinical database for practitioners.

To summarize, a medical description of clinical practice consists of "systematic and critical assessment, continuous experimentation, and subsequent revision of knowledge."[15] Bearing these definitional characteristics in mind, we can detail how clinical databases are realized in architecture.

Precedent
Case method has long been a recognized clinical tool of medicine and law, and although the word "case" is seldom used in architecture in the same explicitly clinical way, the use of precursor design examples is well ennobled as "precedent." The differences in architectural case work as compared with law and medicine are mostly semantic. Precedent in architecture allows access to theories about what is good design. Moreover, as Collins and Hubbard both show, precedent cases allow designers the opportunity to reread and reinterpret previous works in innovative ways that lead to authentically new designs and new design thinking.[16]

It happens then that history is a ready-made and naturally evolving clinical database of architecture. The caveat is that each precursor building case is not automatically recorded and written down in a clinical way. The designer's intention, the client's brief, the development plan, and the performance-in-use are often not made public. Frequently we are left with little more than post-hoc statements and knowledgeable but externally authored critique. Several works of architectural literature do, nonetheless, focus on the development of particular typologies or particular architectural approaches, even sometimes on particular buildings. Each of these works uses some form of case study methodology to derive generalizable knowledge, and each case thus becomes a cataloged item in a clinical database, from where present and future architects can apply the codified knowledge to appropriate new cases.

Post-Occupancy Evaluation
Post-Occupancy Evaluation (POE) is defined as the assessment of a building directly through the perceptions of the actual user-occupants. POE is a detailed

and systematic measurement performed after the occupants have had suffi-cient time to accommodate their activities to their new environment. POE provides an opportunity to identify lessons learned in the project outcomes as compared to the intended results. Studies of this sort have been undertaken since the late 1960s and are increasingly seen as an integral part of the project process.[17]

POE data are often proprietary in nature and such studies may also contain confidential information as well as potentially litigious records of warranty concerning building performance outcomes. Nonetheless, many POE reports are made public through professional and academic channels. Two models for such accessible POE data would be academic research investiga-tions and publically driven institutional inquiry. For the first model refer to the work originating with the Vital Signs Project and the case study database created at schools across the USA or the Integrated Building Technology library in Hong Kong.[18]

For the second model on publically generated institutional POE studies, refer to the example of UK Usable Building Trust publications. Most notable here are the Post-occupancy Review of Building Engineering (PROBE) Studies which tie back to the 1963 Royal Institute of British Architects (RIBA) document, *Plan of Work for Design Team Operation*, which included a section on collecting feedback from recently occupied building projects.[19] By 2002, some 500 cases later, more than twenty PROBE studies had been published in the *Building Services Journal*. Other publications from the PROBE team are now appearing in the journal *Building Research and Information*. These Usable Building Trust PROBE efforts (principally by Bill Bordass and Adrian Leaman) typically entail full disclosure releases from all parties of the building team and the opportunity for the designers to respond to the findings. As such, the collected PROBE studies form an objective and foundational literature for a clinical POE database.

Taken as a whole then, a POE database first establishes a reliable body of evidence from which the practitioner-designer can interpre-tively read new problems and then perform diagnostic and therapeutic resolution. Second, POE methodology has created new meta-knowledge on how to conduct such design studies, how to parse relevant information, and how to use such information to refine design knowledge. In either the academic case of Vital Signs or the public institutional case of PROBE, both examples point to a growing and potentially ubiquitous means of clinical archi-tectural knowledge that could arguably be seen as requisite to best practice qualification.

Continuous Commissioning
Commissioning studies and continuous commissioning investigations (Cx) are performed to confirm that the current operation and control of a building is practically aligned with the current uses of the building. These are usually engi-neering level studies as they involve detailed knowledge of building systems and building physics. It has been adequately demonstrated that commissioning is cost-effective, particularly where there is continual change in how a building is used due to organizational churn, operational changes, alterations in the insti-tutional model, or technical modifications.[20] It is not unusual for Cx to be

considered essential to the delivery of an optimal building or to be incorporated into Total Quality Management practices.

In the continuous commissioning mode, the host building and the occupant cohort are treated as two living entities. Each of the two involves complex and interactive dynamics, and they both play off one another in sometimes direct and sometimes subtle ways. Moreover, both the host and the occupant change with age, use, and modification. Optimizing the host–occupant relationship then requires annual or other periodic revisits.

The diagnostic and therapeutic role of commissioning is thus a clinical practice. As the leader of the design team, the architect must be expected to incorporate the protocols and lessons-learned knowledge issuing from the collective database of commissioning practices. With time, a database inevitably evolves case-by-case. Commissioning and the meta-knowledge attained concerning how to align the host building with occupant cohort form an evidentiary, and therefore clinical, database.

Instrumentation and Automation
Precedent, POE, and Cx demonstrate separate and distinct examples of clinical databases in architecture. Each has an underlying dimension of data acquisition, organization, and interpretation in design practice. To show how such databases evolve though, it is necessary to examine methods by which such data are acquired in the first place. This process begins with the advent of accurate and inexpensive digital instrumentation.

Digital instrumentation facilitates cybernetic feedback by enabling continual measurement and verification of how a building is being used, how controls are sensing conditions, and what the operation of the building does in response. Instrumentation furthers the feedback loop by storing these measurements digitally and making them readily available for analysis in formats as simple as a spreadsheet.

At the smallest level of instrumentation are devices that collect and log readings, and the related software that allows us to convert the raw collected data into graphic visualizations, patterns, and statistical inferences. Miniature devices capable of collecting thousands of readings across months of time divided into designated intervals between measurements are now readily available, reliable, and affordable. They are also easy to use with interface software and USB connection to a computer. With a few such devices and a good plan for how to interpret the data, it is now easy to take temperature, light level, humidity, sound, and other quantitative measurements and convert them into an accurate picture of building behavior and corresponding occupant-use patterns.

At a second level of instrumentation, the everyday digital control and operation of buildings is itself a growing source of diagnostic feedback. Direct Digital Control (DDC), for example, has been in use for more than twenty years. Systems such as these are used to automate the control logic of buildings, signal failure alarms, and to integrate the operation of several building systems such as lighting and security or energy use. Since these systems both sense building conditions and control equipment in response, they provide two-way communication between the building and the building operators. And since DDC is recordable, it creates a continuous record of events and interactions.

A third level of instrumentation takes the building to the level of artificially intelligent robot. These systems can actually learn the building's use and response patterns and decide independently how to anticipate and optimize building operation. Where features of the building are dynamic, such as operable shading devices or dimmable glazing, for example, the building-as-robot can calculate the optimum balance of daylight versus solar heat gain and adjust the building components to suit.

Finally, it is increasingly practical to allow for a building and its occupants to interact through a building-to-human interface. This might involve an animated, genie-like avatar that appears on the building computer intranet. It might also take the form of speech recognition interfaces that allow occupants to have spoken conversations with their room. This building-to-occupant interaction could easily and beneficially be used to initiate occupant control of their environment.[21] And of course the whole conversation would be a matter of record and potential diagnostics, a clinical database for better commissioning and for better design of the next building.

Impacts

In medicine, the term casuistry invokes a rich double meaning. The pejorative meaning is that of over-subtle, even dishonest or sophistic reasoning. This leads to a caveat on the proposition of clinical databases in any discipline. Medicine, for one, is having vigorous discourse on the difference between the rational scientific approach to clinical practice as contrasted to a more holistic and personalized approach. The question distinguishes expertise from wisdom very nicely.[22] It is a conversation that architects should have too.

Neither lawyers, doctors, architects, nor most other disciplines deal with simple mechanistic cause-and-effect, relationally organized challenges. Formulamatic or rule-based procedures for delimiting the problem space of complex problems, devising operations within that problem space, and even for defining a successful outcome are all to be denied. A contingent and flexible means of dealing with ambiguity is really what is needed. At the same time, the complex problem-space model also speaks strongly for the use of clinical evidence: without case histories and clinical evidence it is, after all, impossible to discriminate the immutable determinates from the irrelevant noise, and from the fertile ambiguity.

For some, the scary dark side of clinical evidence is the accountability it demands. When a bona fide database of such evidence is at hand, practitioners are professionally bound to it as a source of best practice. With such knowledge as currency, the designer can use the legal profession's model of warrants to explain how they sanction or justify their design decisions. Without such knowledge, the designer is less accountable, but also more encumbered. That encumbrance results from being continually forced to construe warrants from the ground up.

As previously discussed, design warrants in the postindustrial mindset are increasingly expected to be supported by evidence and best practice models. The mandates of precedent, POE, and Cx, along with the availability of digital measuring tools, simulation modeling, survey methods, qualitative validity, and so forth are looming close overhead. If tomorrow's designs do not embrace these clinical mandates then postindustrial society will probably force them on architecture anyway. When free market enterprise fails to meet societal needs, legal regulation always follows.

Many other impacts of clinical knowledge could be discussed here: redistribution of services, collaborative design practices, specialization, and so on. In the limited scope of this chapter, however, only one will be offered: collaborative research between academic and professional domains as a discourse in the realm.

Academia could easily be positioned as the cultivator and store-house of disciplinary knowledge. In many ways this is already the case: schools generate most architectural literature, schools store that literature in libraries, schools provide a forum for fair critique. There is however far greater opportunity. Continuing education can, for example, form a vital link between academia and practice, where occupational experience is traded for applied research, critical ideals, and updated knowledge. In the context of the profession, a new notion of internship has been proposed by Marvin Malecha as a learning organization approach to a practice academy.[23] This professional internship model would easily align with and complement the suggested continuing education link with practice.

Finally, as universities and schools of architecture continually reinvent themselves, colleges of architecture are investing in facilities such as laboratories and digital fabrication shops.[24] It is unlikely in the near term that practice firms will own such facilities or would be willing to develop expertise and protocols for the use of such resources. Instead, these new academic laboratories and shops might well be the very meeting places where continuing education and internship program activities occur.

Notes

1 Postindustrial Emergence

1. Geddes, P. (1915) *Cities in evolution: An introduction to the town planning movement and to the study of civics*, New York: H. Fertig; Mumford, L. (1934) *Technics and civilization*, New York: Harcourt Brace Jovanovich.
2. Geddes, *Cities in evolution*, cited in C. Renwick and R.C. Gunn (2008) "Demythologizing the machine: Patrick Geddes, Lewis Mumford, and classical sociological theory", *Journal of the History of the Behavioral Sciences*, 44: 67.
3. Geddes, cited in Renwick and Gunn, "Demythologizing the machine", p. 60.
4. Bell, D. (1973) *The coming of post-industrial society: A venture in social forecasting*, New York: Basic Books.
5. Novak, F.G. (1995) *Lewis Mumford and Patrick Geddes: The correspondence*, London; New York: Routledge; Lyle, J.T. (1994) *Regenerative design for sustainable development*, New York: John Wiley; Renwick and Gunn, "Demythologizing the machine", pp. 59–76.
6. Kuhn, T. (1962) *The structure of scientific revolutions*, Chicago, IL: University of Chicago Press.
7. Romer, P.M. *The concise encyclopedia of economics*. Online. Available: <http://www.econlib.org/library/Enc/EconomicGrowth.html> (accessed 11 September 2011).
8. Bronowski, J. (1965) *The identity of man*, Garden City: Natural History Press, p. 56.
9. Stevens, P.S. (1974) *Patterns in nature*, Boston, MA: Little, Brown, p. 4.
10. Snow, C.P. (1959) *The two cultures and the scientific revolution*, New York: Cambridge University Press.
11. Wilson, E.O. (1998) *Consilience: The unity of knowledge*, New York: A.A. Knopf; Gould, S.J. (2003) *The hedgehog, the fox and the magister's pox: Mending the gap between science and the humanities*, Nevada City, CA: Harmony Books.
12. Twombly, R. (ed.) (2003) *Louis Kahn: Essential texts*, New York: W.W. Norton.
13. Schopenhauer, A. (1896) *The world as will and idea*, trans. R.B. Haldane and J. Kemp, London: Kegan Paul, Trench, Trübner & Co.
14. Hubbard, W. (1982) *Complicity and conviction: Steps toward an architecture of convention*, Cambridge, MA: MIT Press.
15. Van Emden, M.H. (1971) *An analysis of complexity*, Mathematical Centre Tracts, Vol. 35, Amsterdam: Mathematisch Centrum.
16. Rand, A. (1943) *The fountainhead*, Indianapolis, IN: Bobbs-Merrill.
17. Barrow, J.D. (1995) *The artful universe*, Oxford: Clarendon Press.
18. Kelso, J.A.S. (1995) *Dynamic patterns: The self-organization of brain and behavior*, Cambridge, MA: MIT Press.
19. Sternberg, R.J. (1988) *The nature of creativity: Contemporary psychological perspectives*, Cambridge: Cambridge University Press.
20. Csikszentmihalyi, M. (1997) *Creativity: Flow and the psychology of discovery and invention*, New York: Harper Perennial.
21. Kelso, *Dynamic patterns*.
22. Duffy, F. and Hutton, L. (1998) *Architectural knowledge: The idea of a profession*, London: Spon.

Notes

2 Scoping Complexity

1. Kelso, J.A.S. (1995) *Dynamic patterns: The self-organization of brain and behavior*, Cambridge, MA: MIT Press.
2. Twombly, R. (ed.) (2003) *Louis Kahn: Essential texts*, New York: W.W. Norton.
3. Rzevski, G. (2009) "Using complexity science framework and multi-agent technology in design", in K. Alexiou, J. Johnson, and T. Zamenopoulos (eds.) *Embracing complexity in design*, London: Routledge, p. 62.
4. Senge, P.M. (1990) *The fifth discipline: The art and practice of the learning organization*, New York: Doubleday/Currency; Sterman, J.D. (2000) *Business dynamics: Systems thinking and modeling for a complex world*, New York: McGraw-Hill/Irwin.
5. Tyson, P. (2010) *Goodbye to the father of fractals*. Mandelbrot. Online. Available: <http://www.pbs.org/wgbh/nova/insidenova/2010/10/goodbye-to-the-father-of-fractals.html>
6. Rzevski, "Using complexity science framework".
7. Twombly, *Louis Kahn: Essential texts*.
8. Scruton, R. (1979) *The aesthetics of architecture*, Princeton, NJ: Princeton University Press.
9. Sullivan, L.H. (1896) "The tall office building artistically considered", *Lippincott's Magazine*, Philadelphia.
10. Gadamer, H.G. (1977) *Philosophical hermeneutics*, Berkeley: University of California Press, p. 66.
11. Bohm, D. (1980) *Wholeness and the implicate order*, London: Routledge & Kegan Paul.
12. Buckley, W. (1967) *Sociology and modern systems theory*, Englewood Cliffs, NJ: Prentice Hall; Beer, A.S. (1959) *Cybernetics and management*, London: English Universities Press; Hutchinson, G.E. (1948) "Circular causal systems in ecology", *Annals of the New York Academy of Sciences*, 50: 221–246.
13. Hawking, S.W. (1998) *A brief history of time*, New York: Bantam Books; Gibson, W. and Sterling, B. (1991) *The difference engine*, New York: Bantam Books; Gibson, W. (2003) *Burning chrome*, New York: HarperCollins.
14. Bateson, G. and Donaldson, R.E. (1991) *A sacred unity: Further steps to an ecology of mind*, New York: Cornelia & Michael Bessie Books.
15. Bateson G. (1972) *Steps to an ecology of mind*, New York: Chandler Publishing.
16. Lorenz, E.N. (1993) *The essence of chaos*, Seattle: University of Washington Press.
17. Lovelock, J. (2006) *The revenge of Gaia: Earth's climate in crisis and the fate of humanity*, New York: Basic Books.
18. Heisenberg, W. (1927) "Uncertainty principle of quantum mechanics", "Über den anschaulichen Inhalt der quantentheoretischen Kinematik und Mechanik", *Zeitschrift für Physik*, 43: 172–198.
19. Campbell, D., Crutchfield, J., Farmer, J. and Jen, E. (1985) "Experimental mathematics: The role of computation in nonlinear science", *Communications of the Association for Computing Machinery*, 28, 3: 74–84.
20. Guyer, P. and Wood, A.W. (eds.) (1999) *The critique of pure reason* (Cambridge Edition of the Works of Immanuel Kant in Translation), Cambridge: Cambridge University Press.
21. Bogdanov, A. (1922) *Tektology: Universal organization science* [Tektologiya: Vseobschaya Organizatsionnaya Nauka], 3 vols., Berlin and Petrograd-Moscow.
22. Wertheimer, M. (1925) Über Gestalttheorie [an address before the Kant Society, Berlin, 7 December 1924], Erlangen. In the translation by W.D. Ellis published in his *Source Book of Gestalt Psychology*, New York: Harcourt, Brace and Co., 1938.
23. Arnheim, R. (1969) *Visual thinking*, Berkeley: University of California Press; Arnheim, R. (1954/1974) *Art and visual perception: A psychology of the creative eye*, Berkeley: University of California Press; Arnheim, R. (1971) *Entropy and art: An essay on disorder and order*, Berkeley: University of California Press; Arnheim, R. (1977) *The dynamics of architectural form: Based on the 1975 Mary Duke Biddle lectures at the Cooper Union*, Berkeley: University of California Press.
24. Weaver, W. (2004) "Science and complexity", Classical Papers, Vol. 6, 3: 65–74; originally published in *American Scientist*, 36, 1947: 536–544.
25. Beer, *Cybernetics and management*.

26. Popper, K. (1963) *Conjectures and refutations*, London: Routledge and Keagan Paul, pp. 33–39; from T. Schick (ed.) (2000) *Readings in the philosophy of science*, Mountain View, CA: Mayfield Publishing, pp. 9–13.

27. Ascott, R. (1964) "The construction of change", in N. Wardrip-Fruin and N. Montfort (eds.) *The new media reader*, Cambridge, MA: MIT Press, 2003, pp. 128–132.

28. Buckley, *Sociology and modern systems theory*.

29. Hayek, F. (1973) "Cosmos and taxis", in *Law, legislation and liberty*, Vol. I, Chicago, IL: University of Chicago Press, pp. 35–54.

30. Bohm, *Wholeness and the implicate order*.

31. Popper, K. and Eccles, J.C. (1977) *The self and its brain: An argument for interactionism*, London: Routledge, p. 38.

32. Kant, I. (1958) *Critique of pure reason*, New York: Modern Library.

33. Bohm, *Wholeness and the implicate order*.

34. Hayek, "Cosmos and taxis".

35. Huxley, A. (1954) *The doors of perception*, London: Chatto and Windus; Simon, H. (1957) "A behavioral model of rational choice", in *Models of man, social and rational: Mathematical essays on rational human behavior in a social setting*, New York: John Wiley.

36. Hayek, "Cosmos and taxis".

37. Fitch, J.M. (1988) "Experiential context of the aesthetic process", *Journal of Architectural Education*, 41(2): 4.

38. Heidegger, M. (1962) *Being and time*, trans. J. Macquarrie and E. Robinson, London: SCM Press.

39. Read, S. (2008) "Technicity and publicness: Steps towards an urban space", *Footprint*, 3, *Architecture and Phenomenology*, p. 9.

40. Arnheim, *Entropy and art*.

41. Heidegger, *Being and time*.

42. Shelley, M. (published anonymously) (1818) *Frankenstein, or, The modern Prometheus*, 3 vols., London: Lackington, Hughes, Harding, Mavor, & Jones.

3 Buildings as Complex Systems

1. Groák, S. (1992) *The idea of building: Thought and action in the design and production of buildings*, London; New York: E & FN Spon, p. 38.

2. Vitruvius (*c.* 15 BC) *De architectura: Ten books on architecture*, trans. Sir Henry Wooton as *The elements of architecture* (1624), London: printed by Iohn Bill.

3. Groák, *The idea of building*.

4. Popper, K. (1963) *Conjectures and refutations*, London: Routledge and Keagan Paul, pp. 33–39, from T. Schick (ed.) (2000) *Readings in the philosophy of science*, Mountain View, CA: Mayfield Publishing, pp. 9–13.

5. Popper, *Conjectures and refutations*.

6. Fitch, J.M. (1988) "Experiential context of the aesthetic process", *Journal of Architectural Education*, 41(2): 4–9.

7. Groák, *The idea of building*; Norberg-Shultz, C. (1966) *Intentions in architecture*, Cambridge, MA: MIT Press.

8. Lyle, J.T. (1994) *Regenerative design for sustainable development*, New York: John Wiley, pp. 38–45.

9. Kahn, L. (1991) "Talks with students", in A. Latour (ed.) *Louis L. Kahn: Writings, lectures, interviews*, New York: Rizzoli International Publications, Lecture 6, Interviews, p. 167.

10. Mostafavi, M. and Leatherbarrow, D. (1993) *On weathering: The life of buildings in time*, Cambridge, MA: MIT Press.

11. Kant, I. (1958) *Critique of pure reason*, New York: Modern Library; Popper, K. (1963) *Conjectures and refutations*, London: Routledge and Keagan Paul, pp. 33–39, from T. Schick (ed.) (2000) *Readings in the philosophy of science*, Mountain View, CA: Mayfield Publishing, pp. 9–13.

12. Lorenz, E.N. (1963) "Deterministic nonperiodic flow", *Journal of Atmospheric Science*, 20(2): 130–141.

13. See Bachman, L.R. (2003) *Integrated buildings: The systems basis of architecture*, Hoboken, NJ: John Wiley.

14. See Bachman, *Integrated buildings*, for a case study of the project.

15. A. Bowen, 1975, personal communication.

16. Groák, *The idea of building*; Norberg-Shultz, *Intentions in architecture*; Lyle, *Regenerative design for sustainable development*, pp. 38–45.

17. Peña, W.M. (1969) *Problem seeking: New directions in architectural programming*, Houston, TX: Caudill Rowlett Scott.

18. Gabor, D. (1964) *Inventing the future*, Harmondsworth, UK: Penguin Books.

19. Gabor, *Inventing the future*.

20. Collins, P. (1971) *Architectural judgment*, Toronto: University of Toronto Press; Hubbard, W. (1982) *Complicity and conviction: Steps toward an architecture of convention*, Cambridge, MA: MIT Press.

21. Ulrich, R., Zimring, C., Zhu, X., DuBose, J., Seo, H-B., Choi, Y-S. et al. (2008) "A review of the research literature on evidence-based healthcare design", *Health Environments Research & Design Journal*, 1: 61–125.

22. Brager, G. (2008) *Occupant satisfaction and control strategies in mixed-mode buildings*, Proceedings of the 5th Windsor Conference: Airconditioning and the Low Carbon Cooling Challenge, Network for Comfort and Energy Use in Buildings, Windsor Great Park, UK.

23. Heisenberg, W. (1927) "Uncertainty principle of quantum mechanics", "Über den anschaulichen Inhalt der quantentheoretischen Kinematik und Mechanik", *Zeitschrift für Physik*, 43: 172–198.

24. Office of Naval Research, Mathematical sciences division (1958) *Digital Computer Newsletter*, 10 (n. 4). Online. Available HTTP: <www.columbia.edu/cu/computinghistory/navynewsletter1958.pdf> (accessed 19 August 2011).

25. Von Foerster, H. (1959) "On self-organizing systems and their environments", an address given at the Interdisciplinary Symposium on Self-Organizing Systems, May 5, Chicago, IL; originally published in M.C. Yovits and S. Cameron (eds.) (1960) *Self-organizing systems*, London: Pergamon Press, pp. 31–50.

26. Ashby, W.R. (1952) *Design for a brain*, London: Chapman and Hall; Ashby, W.R. (1956) *Introduction to cybernetics*, London: Chapman and Hall.

27. Ashby, W.R. (1960) *Design for a brain: The origin of adaptive behavior*, 2nd edn, New York: John Wiley.

28. Prigogine, I. and Stengers, I. (1984) *Order out of chaos*, New York: Bantam Books, cited in F. Heylighen, "The science of self-organization and adaptivity", in *The Encyclopedia of Life Support Systems*, Oxford: EOLSS Publishers, 2003.

29. Komendant, A.E. (1975) *18 years with architect Louis I. Kahn*, Englewood Cliffs, NJ: Aloray.

30. Arnheim, R. (1971) *Entropy and art: An essay on disorder and order*, Berkeley: University of California Press.

4 Encounters with Complexity

1. Peña, W.M. (1969) *Problem seeking: New directions in architectural programming*, Houston, TX: Caudill Rowlett Scott.

2. Jacobs, J. (1961) *The death and life of great American cities*, New York: Random House.

3. Simon, H.A. (1969) *The sciences of the artificial*, Cambridge, MA: MIT Press.

4. Ackoff, R.L. (1968) *Fundamentals of operations research*, New York: John Wiley; Groák, S. (1992) *The idea of building: Thought and action in the design and production of buildings*, London; New York: E & FN Spon.

5. Rittel, H. and Webber, M. (1973) "Dilemmas in a general theory of planning", *Policy Sciences*, 4: 155–169.

6. Churchman, C.W. (1967) Guest editorial: "Wicked problems", *Management Science*, 14(4): B141.

7. Alexander, C. (1964) *Notes on the synthesis of form*, Cambridge, MA: Harvard University Press, p. 1.

8. Jencks, C. (1995) *The architecture of the jumping universe*, London: Academy Editions.

9. Bell, D. (1973) *The coming of post-industrial society: A venture in social forecasting*, New York: Basic Books.

10. Simon, H.A. (1957) *Models of man: Social and rational; mathematical essays on rational human behavior in society setting*, New York: John Wiley; Simon, H.A. (1976) *Administrative behavior: A study of decision-making processes in administrative organization*, New York: Free Press.

11. Rittel and Webber, "Dilemmas in a general theory of planning".

12. Churchman, Guest editorial: "Wicked problems", B141–B142; Popper, K. (1934) *Logik der forschung*, Vienna: Verlag von Julius Springer. First published in English in 1959 by Hutchinson & Co.

13. Buchanan, R. (1995) *Discovering design: Explorations in design studies*, Chicago, IL: University of Chicago Press.

14. Ackoff, R.L. (1974) *Redesigning the future: A systems approach to societal problems*, New York: John Wiley; Horn, R.E. (2001) "Knowledge mapping for complex social messes", a presentation to the Foundations in the Knowledge Economy at the David and Lucile Packard Foundation.

15. Simon, H.A. (1956) "Rational choice and the structure of the environment", *Psychological Review*, 63(2): 129–138; Rittel and Webber, "Dilemmas in a general theory of planning".

16. Coyne, R. (2005) "Wicked problems revisited", *Design Studies*, 26(1): 5–17, p. 12.

17. Bell, *The coming of post-industrial society*.

18. Rittel and Webber, "Dilemmas in a general theory of planning"; Simon, "Rational choice and the structure of the environment".

19. Venturi, R. and Museum of Modern Art (1966) *Complexity and contradiction in architecture*, with an introduction by V. Scully, New York: Museum of Modern Art, Garden City, NY: Doubleday, pp. 22–23.

20. Jacobs, J. (1961) *The death and life of great American cities*, New York: Random House; Jacobs, J. (1969) *The economy of cities*, New York: Random House.

21. Jacobs, *The death and life of great American cities*, p. 15.

22. Jacobs, *The death and life of great American cities*, p. 376.

23. Jacobs, *The death and life of great American cities*, p. 373.

24. Laurence, P. (2006) "Contradictions and complexities", *Journal of Architectural Education*, 59(31): 49–60, p. 49.

25. Alexander, C. (1964) *Notes on the synthesis of form*, Cambridge, MA: Harvard University Press; Alexander, C. (1966) *The city as a mechanism for sustaining human contact*, Berkeley: Center for Planning and Development Research, University of California; Alexander, C.S. and Ishikawa, S. (1977) *A pattern language: Towns, buildings, construction*, New York: Oxford University Press.

26. Alexander, *Notes on the synthesis of form*, pp. 26–27.

27. Alexander, *The city as a mechanism for sustaining human contact*.

28. Venturi, *Complexity and contradiction in architecture*; Jacobs, *The death and life of great American cities*; Alexander, *Notes on the synthesis of form*.

29. Heath, T. (1984) *Method in architecture*, New York: Wiley, p. 251.

30. Sanoff, H. (1968) *Techniques of evaluation for designers*, Raleigh, Design Research Laboratory, School of Design, North Carolina State University; Peña, *Problem seeking*; Preiser, W.F.E. (1978) *Facility programming: Methods and applications*, Stroudsburg, PA: Dowden, Hutchinson & Ross.

31. Venturi, *Complexity and contradiction in architecture*, p. 19.

32. Peña, *Problem seeking*.

33. Coleridge, S.T. (1817/1989) *Biographia literaria: or Biographical sketches of my literary life and opinions*, New York: C. Wiley & Co, Chapter XIII, p. 167.

34. Sanoff, H. (1978) *Designing with community participation*, Stroudsburg, PA: Dowden, Hutchinson & Ross; Sanoff, H. (2000) *Community participation methods in design and planning*, New York: John Wiley.

35. Alexander, *Notes on the synthesis of form*, p. 1.

36. Stevens, P.S. (1974) *Patterns in nature*, Boston, MA: Little, Brown, p. 4.

37. Geddes, P. (1904) *City development, a study of parks, gardens, and culture-institutes; A report to the Carnegie Dunfermline Trust*, Edinburgh: Geddes and Co.; Geddes, P. and Thomson, J.A. (1911) *Evolution*, New York: H. Holt.

38. Mumford, L. (1922) *The story of utopias*, New York: Boni and Liveright; Mumford, L. (1924) *Sticks and stones: A study of American architecture and civilization*, New York: Boni and Liveright; Mumford, L. (1939) *Men must act*, New York: Harcourt Brace and Co.; Mumford, L. (1947) *Green memories; The story of Geddes Mumford*, New York: Harcourt, Brace; Mumford, L. (1967) *The myth of the machine: Technics and human development*, New York: Harcourt, Brace Jovanovich.

39. Geddes, *Evolution*; Mumford, *The story of utopias*.

40. Olgyay, V. (1963) *Design with climate: Bioclimatic approach to architectural regionalism*. Some chapters based on cooperative research with Aladar Olgyay. Princeton, NJ: Princeton University Press; McHarg, I. (1969) *Design with nature*, Garden City, NY: Natural History Press.

41. Carson, R. (1962) *Silent spring*, Boston, MA: Houghton Mifflin.

42. Givoni, B. (1969) *Man, climate, and architecture*, New York: Elsevier; Knowles, R. (1969) *Owens valley study: A natural ecological framework for settlement*, Los Angeles, CA: National Endowment for the Arts; Knowles, R. (1974) *Energy and form: An ecological approach to urban growth*, Cambridge, MA: MIT Press; Knowles, R. (1981) *Sun rhythm\form*, Cambridge, MA: MIT Press; Knowles, R. (2006) *Ritual house: Drawing on nature's rhythms for architecture and urban design*, Washington, DC: Island Press.

43. Mazria, E. (1979) *The passive solar energy book: A complete guide to passive solar home, greenhouse, and building design*, Emmaus, PA: Rodale Press; Mazria, E. et al. (2007) *The 2030 challenge: Environmental design in the face of climate change*, Las Vegas, NV: UNLV School of Architecture; Lyle, J.T. (1985) *Design for human ecosystems: Landscape, land use, and natural resources*, New York: Van Nostrand Reinhold; Lyle, J.T. (1994) *Regenerative design for sustainable development*, New York: John Wiley.

44. Groák, S. (1992) *The idea of building: Thought and action in the design and production of buildings*, London; New York: E & FN Spon.

45. Norberg-Schulz, C. (1966) *Intentions in architecture*, Cambridge, MA, MIT Press.

46. Lyle, *Regenerative design for sustainable development*.

47. Alexander, *Notes on the synthesis of form*.

48. Benyus, J.M. (1997) *Biomimicry: Innovation inspired by nature*, New York: Morrow.

49. Fuller, R.B. (1963) *Ideas and integrities, a spontaneous autobiographical disclosure*, Englewood Cliffs, NJ: Prentice-Hall; Fuller, R.B. (1969) *Operating manual for spaceship earth*, Carbondale: Southern Illinois University Press; Fuller, R.B. (1981) *Critical path*, New York: St. Martin's Press; Fuller, R.B. and Applewhite, E.J. (1975) *Synergetics; Explorations in the geometry of thinking*, New York: Macmillan.

50. Beer, A.S. (1994) *Beyond dispute: The invention of team syntegrity*, New York: John Wiley.

51. Bohm, D. (1980) *Wholeness and the implicate order*, London: Routledge and Kegan Paul.

52. Bateson, G. (1972) *Steps to an ecology of mind: Collected essays in anthropology, psychiatry, evolution, and epistemology*, San Francisco, CA: Chandler Publishing; Bateson, G. (1979) *Mind and nature: A necessary unity*, New York: Dutton.

53. Orr, D.W. (1979) *The global predicament: Ecological perspectives on world order*, Chapel Hill: University of North Carolina Press; Orr, D.W. (1992) *Ecological literacy: Education and the transition to a postmodern world*, Albany: State University of New York Press; Orr, D.W. (1994) *Earth in mind: On education, environment, and the human prospect*, Washington, DC: Island Press; Orr, D.W. (2002) *The nature of design: Ecology, culture, and human intention*, New York: Oxford University Press.

54. Guise, D. (1985) *Design and technology in architecture*, New York: Wiley; Rush, R.D. (ed.) (1986) *The building systems integration handbook*, New York: Wiley; Bovill, C. (1991) *Architectural design: Integration of structural and environmental systems*, New York: Van Nostrand Reinhold; Bachman, L.R. (2003) *Integrated buildings: The systems basis of architecture*, Hoboken, NJ: John Wiley.

55. Kepes, G. (1944) *Language of vision*, Chicago, IL: P. Theobald; Kepes, G. (ed.) (1965) *Structure in art and in science*, New York: G. Braziller; Kepes, G. (1966) *The man-made object*, New York: G. Braziller; Arnheim, R. (1954) *Art and visual perception; A psychology of the creative eye*,

Berkeley: University of California Press; Arnheim, R. (1969) *Visual thinking*, Berkeley: University of California Press; Arnheim, R. (1971) *Entropy and art; An essay on disorder and order*, Berkeley: University of California Press; Arnheim, R. (1977) *The dynamics of architectural form: Based on the 1975 Mary Duke Biddle Lectures at the Cooper Union*, Berkeley: University of California Press.

56. Arnheim, *Entropy and art*, p. 1
57. Bronowski, J. (1965) "The discovery of form", in G. Kepes (ed.) *Structure in art and in science*, New York: G. Braziller, p. 56.
58. Alexander, *Notes on the synthesis of form*, p. 11.

5 Converging into Complexity

1. Rivka, O. and Oxman, R. (2010) T*he new structuralism: Design, engineering and architectural technologies*, London: John Wiley.
2. Arup, O. and Zunz, G.J. (1969) "Sydney Opera House", *Structural Engineer*, 47: 3.
3. Mitchell, W.J. (1999) "Architecture and the digital revolution", *Science*, 285(5429): 839–841.
4. Simon, H.A. (1956) "Rational choice and the structure of the environment", *Psychological Review*, 63(2): 129–138; Rittel, H. and Webber, M. (1973) "Dilemmas in a general theory of planning", *Policy Sciences*, 4: 155–169.
5. Pinto, J. (2000) *Evolution of the techno human*. Online. Available: <http://www.spark-online.com/november00/esociety/pinto.html> (accessed 22 September 2011).
6. Moore, G.E. (1965) "Cramming more components onto integrated circuits", *Electronics Magazine*, 38(8): 114–117.
7. Kurzweil, R. (2005) *The singularity is near: When humans transcend biology*, New York: Viking.
8. The RIBA, CPIC, and BuildingSmart jointly proposed definition of BIM for the UK construction industry as quoted in Smith, M. (March 2011) BIM in Construction. The National Bureau of Standards. Online. Available: <http://www.thenbs.com/topics/BIM/articles/index.asp> (accessed 1 July 2011).
9. Center for the Built Environment. Occupant Indoor Environmental Quality (IEQ) Survey and Building Benchmarking. Online. Available: <http://www.cbe.berkeley.edu/research/briefs-survey.htm> (accessed 24 September 2011).
10. Usable Buildings. Online. Available: <http://www.usablebuildings.co.uk/> (accessed 24 September 2011).
11. Csikszentmihalyi, M. and Rochberg-Halton, E. (1981) *The meaning of things: Domestic symbols and the self*, New York: Cambridge University Press.
12. Bachman, L.R. (2003) *Integrated buildings: The systems basis of architecture*, Hoboken, NJ: John Wiley.
13. Friedman, T.L. (2005) *The world is flat 3.0: A brief history of the twenty-first century*, New York: Farrar, Straus and Giroux.
14. Wilde, O. (1892) *Lady Windermere's Fan*, Act III. Online. Available: <http://en.wikiquote.org/wiki/Oscar_Wilde> (accessed 22 September 2011).
15. Geddes, P. and Thomson, J.A. (1911) *Evolution*, New York: H. Holt; Mumford, L. (1924) *Sticks and stones: A study of American architecture and civilization*, New York: Boni and Liveright.
16. Bell, D. (1973) *The coming of post-industrial society: A venture in social forecasting*, New York: Basic Books.
17. Stevens, G. (1999) *The favored circle: The social foundations of architectural distinction*, Cambridge, MA: MIT Press, p. 212.
18. Stern, W.F. (1989) "Floating City—Conoco's corporate headquarters by Kevin Roche", *Cite*, 12–13.
19. Geddes, P. (1968) *Cities in evolution: An introduction to the town planning movement and to the study of civics*, New York: H. Fertig; Mumford, L. (1967) *The myth of the machine: Technics and human development*, New York: Harcourt Brace Jovanovich.
20. Bunker, J.P., Frazier, H.S., and Mosteller, F. (1994) "Improving health: Measuring effects of medical care", *Milbank Quarterly*, 72: 225–258.
21. Srinivasan, U.T., Cheung, W.L., Watson, R., and Sumaila, U.R. (2010) "Food security implications of global marine catch losses due to overfishing", *Journal of Bioeconomics*, 12: 183–200.

22. Comprehensive assessment of water management in agriculture (2007) *Water for food, water for life: A comprehensive assessment of water management in agriculture*, London: Earthscan, and Colombo: International Water Management Institute.

23. Molden, D. and de Fraiture, C. (2004) *Investing in water for food, ecosystems and livelihoods: Comprehensive assessment of water management in agriculture*. Online. Available: <http://www.infoandina.org/system/files/recursos/BluePaper.pdf>

6 Embracing Complexity

1. Thackara, J. (2005) *In the bubble: Designing in a complex world*, Cambridge, MA: MIT Press, p. 225.

2. Pérez-Gómez, A. (1999) "Hermeneutics as discourse in design", *Design Issues*, 15(2): 73.

3. Snodgrass, A. and Coyne, R. (1997) "Is designing hermeneutical? Architectural theory review", *Journal of the Department of Architecture*, 1(1): 65–97, p. 72.

4. Bloom, A.D. (1987) *The closing of the American mind*, New York: Simon and Schuster; Perry, W.G., Jr. (1988) *Intellectual and ethical development in the college years*, New York: Holt, Rinehart & Winston. (See also Chapter 14: "Models of cognitive development: Piaget and Perry", in P.C. Wankat and F.S. Oreovicz (1993) *Teaching engineering*, New York: McGraw-Hill. Online. Available: <https://engineering.purdue.edu/ChE/News_and_Events/Publications/teaching_engineering/chapter14.pdf> (accessed 5 April 2007).)

5. Kuhn, T. (1962) *The structure of scientific revolutions*, Chicago, IL: University of Chicago Press; Rittel, H. and Webber, M. (1973) "Dilemmas in a general theory of planning", *Policy Sciences*, 4:155–169.

6. Pawley, M. (1990) *Theory and design in the second machine age*, Cambridge, MA: Blackwell.

7. Kelso, J.A.S. (1995) *Dynamic patterns: The self-organization of brain and behavior*, Cambridge, MA: MIT Press.

8. Shelley, M. (published anonymously) (1818) *Frankenstein, or, The modern Prometheus*, 3 vols., London: Lackington, Hughes, Harding, Mavor, & Jones; Kelso, *Dynamic patterns*.

9. Mostafavi, M. and Leatherbarrow, D. (1993) *On weathering: The life of buildings in time*, Cambridge, MA: MIT Press.

10. Scruton, R. (1979) *The aesthetics of architecture*, Princeton, NJ: Princeton University Press.

11. Gadamer, H.G. (1986) *The relevance of the beautiful and other essays*, Cambridge, MA: Cambridge University Press, p. 67. Online. Available: <http://alex.golub.name/gadamer> (accessed 24 September 2011).

12. Snow, C.P. (1959) *The two cultures and the scientific revolution*, The Rede Lecture, Cambridge: Cambridge University Press.

13. Pérez Gómez, A. (1983) *Architecture and the crisis of modern science*, Cambridge, MA: MIT Press.

14. Glazebrook, T. (2003) "Art or nature?", *Ethics & the Environment*, 8(1): 22.

15. Peat, F.D. (1988) "Non-locality in Nature and Cognition", in M.E. Carvallo (ed.) *Nature, cognition, and system: Current systems-scientific research on natural and cognitive systems*, Dordrecht: Kluwer, p. 304.

16. Scruton, *The aesthetics of architecture*; Gadamer, H.G. (1975) *Truth and method*, trans. from German and edited by G. Barden and J. Cumming, London: Sheed & Ward.

17. Kahn, L. (1960) "Form and design", in A. Latour (ed.) (1991) *Louis I. Kahn: Writings, lectures, interviews*, New York: Rizzoli International Publications, p. 116.

18. Carlson, A. (2001) "On aesthetically appreciating human environments", *Philosophy & Geography*, 4(1): 9–24.

19. Prigogine, I. (1997) *The end of certainty:Time, chaos, and the new laws of nature*, New York: Free Press, p. 7.

7 Mapping Complexity onto the Profession

1. Piotrowski, A. and Robinson, J.W. (2000) *The discipline of architecture*, Minneapolis: University of Minnesota Press.

2. See also Bachman, L. (2010) "The teaching of research and the research on teaching: Two frameworks and their overlay in architectural education", *Proceedings of the 2010 ARCC/EAAE*

International Conference on Architectural Research, Washington, DC. Online. Available: <http://info.aia.org/arcc/program/program.html> (accessed 22 September 2011).

3. Piotrowski and Robinson, *The discipline of architecture*.
4. Boyer, E.L. and Mitgang, L.D. (1996) *Building community: A new future for architecture education and practice*, Princeton, NJ: The Carnegie Foundation for the Advancement of Teaching.
5. Scott, T. (1779) *The force of truth*, London: Keith; quoted in Cardinal J.H. Newman, *Apologia pro vita sua*, Chapter 1, "History of my religious opinions to the year 1833" (1864).
6. Darrow, C. (1925) (commonly misattributed to Charles Darwin). Published in *Improving the quality of life for the black elderly: Challenges and opportunities*, Hearing before the Select Committee on Aging, House of Representatives, One Hundredth Congress, first session, September 25, 1987 (1988).
7. Monod, J. (1971) *Chance and necessity*, New York: Alfred A. Knopf, p. xi.
8. Chomsky, N., cited in Rossetto, L. (1998) "Change is good", *Wired Magazine*, 6(1): 163–207, pp. 166–167.

8 Postindustrial Occupation in Architecture

1. Fuller, R.B. (n.d.) FinestQuotes.com. Online. Available: <http://www.finestquotes.com/author_quotes-author-R. Buckminster Fuller-page-0.htm> (accessed 6 September 2011).
2. Wright, F.L., replying to his client for the 1937 Wingspread residence, the industrialist Hibbard Johnson, as recounted in a television interview by the late Mr. Johnson's son, regarding the famous story about his father sitting with distinguished guests, being dripped on by a rain roof leak, and phoning Wright to complain. Online. Available: <http://www.galenfrysinger.com/racine_wingspread.htm>
3. Fast, W.R. (1997) "Knowledge strategies: Balancing ends, ways, and means in the information age", in R.E. Neilson (ed.) *Sun Tzu and information warfare, A collection of winning papers from the Sun Tzu Art of War in information warfare competition*, Washington, DC: National Defense University Press.
4. Heath, T. (1991) *What, if anything, is an architect?*, Melbourne: Architecture Media Australia; Stevens, G. (1990) *The reasoning architect: Mathematics and science in design*, New York: McGraw-Hill.
5. Van Laar, J.A. (2003) *The dialectic of ambiguity: A contribution to the study of argumentation*. Online. Available: <http://dissertations.ub.rug.nl/faculties/fil/2003/j.a.van.laar/?FullItemRecord=ON> (accessed 24 September 2011).
6. Leslie, T. (2006) "Unavoidable nuisances: August Komendant, Louis I. Kahn, and the difficult relationship between architecture and engineering", *MAJA Estonian Architectural Review*, 4(50): 72–75. Online. Available: <http://www.solness.ee/maja/?mid=136&id=334&p=1> (accessed 24 September 2011).
7. Dewey, J. Online. Available: <http://www.goodreads.com/author/quotes/42738.John_Dewey> (accessed 25 September 2011).
8. Plato, cited in Edinton, R.V. (1974) "The ancient idea of founding and the contemporary study of political change", *Polity*, 7(2): 163–179.
9. Ronner, H. and Jhaveri, S. (1987) *Louis I. Kahn: Complete works 1935–1974*, Basel: Birkhauser, p. 158.
10. Pawley, M. (1990) *Theory and design in the second machine age*, Cambridge, MA: Wiley-Blackwell.
11. Kahn quoted in Conrads, U. (1975) *Programs and manifestos on 20th-century architecture*, Cambridge: MA: MIT Press, p. 170.
12. Groák, S. (1992) *The idea of building: Thought and action in the design and production of buildings*, London: E & FN Spon; Lyle, J.T. (1994) *Regenerative design for sustainable development*, New York: John Wiley.
13. Horn, R.E. (1999) "Information design: The emergence of a new profession", in R. Jacobson (ed.) *Information Design*, Cambridge, MA: MIT Press.
14. Peña, W.M. (1969) *Problem seeking: New directions in architectural programming*, Houston, TX: Caudill Rowlett Scott.

15. Playfair, W. (1786) *The commercial and political atlas, Representing, by Means of Stained Copper-Plate Charts, the Exports, Imports, and General Trade of England, at a Single View. To Which are Added, Charts of the Revenue and Debts of Ireland, Done in the Same Manner by James Corry*, London: Debrett; Robinson; and Sewell; Minard, C.J. (1869) Carte figurative des pertes successives en hommes de l'armée qu'Annibal conduisit d'Espagne en Italie en traversant les Gaules (selon Polybe). Carte figurative des pertes successives en hommes de l'armée française dans la campagne de Russie, 1812–1813. lith. (624 × 207, 624 × 245), 20 November 1869. ENPC: Fol 10975, 10974/C612. [Annibal Napoléon Espagne Italie Russie armée flow-map comparison.]

16. Shannon, C.E. and Weaver, W. (1949) *The mathematical theory of communication*, Urbana: University of Illinois Press; Cleveland, W. (1985) *The elements of graphing data*, Monterey, CA: Wadsworth; Spence, I. (1990) "Visual psychophysics of simple graphical elements", *Journal of Experimental Psychology: Human Perception and Performance*, 16(4): 683–692.

17. Tufte, E. (1983) *The visual display of quantitative information*, Cheshire, CT: Graphics Press; Bono, E. de (1993) *Serious creativity: Using the power of lateral thinking to create new ideas*, New York: Harperbusiness; Harris, R.L. (1996) *Information graphics: A comprehensive illustrated reference*, Oxford: Oxford University Press.

18. Wainer, H. (1997) *Visual revelations: Graphical tales of fate and deception from Napoleon Bonaparte to Ross Perot*, New York: Springer-Verlag.

19. Elstein, A. (1977) "Characteristics of the clinical problem solving model and its relevance to educational research", Annual Meeting of the American Educational Research Association, New York.

20. Malterud, K. (2001) "The art and science of clinical knowledge: Evidence beyond measures and numbers", *Lancet*, 358(9279): 397.

21. Elstein, "Characteristics of the clinical problem solving model".

9 The Domain of Education

1. Heath, T. (1993) "The architectural theory of Rudolf Arnheim and its implications for teaching", *Journal of Aesthetic Education*, 27(4): 83–95, p. 83.

2. Peirce, C.S. (1956) "The criterion of validity of reasoning", in J. Buchler (ed.) *The philosophy of Peirce: Selected writings*, London: Routledge & Kegan Paul (reprinted from *Lectures on pragmatism*, Harvard University, 1903).

3. Perry, W.G., Jr. (1970) *Forms of intellectual and ethical development in the college years: A scheme*, New York: Holt, Rinehart, and Winston; Perry, W.G., Jr. (1981) "Cognitive and ethical growth: The making of meaning", in A.W. Chickering and Associates, *The Modern American College*, San Francisco, CA: Jossey-Bass, pp 76–116.

4. Bachman, L. and Bachman, C. (2009) "Designing student learning outcomes in undergraduate architecture education: Frameworks for assessment", *ARCC Journal*, 6(1): 49–67.

5. Bachman, L. and Bachman, C. (2009) "Editorial: Affecting change in architectural education", *ARCC Journal*, 6(1): 4–5.

6. American Institute of Architects (2009) "Overview of the 2009 AIA firm survey", *AIArchitect*, 16. Online. Available: <http://info.aia.org/aiarchitect/thisweek09/1009/1009b_firmsurvey.cfm> (accessed 24 September 2011); Stevens, G. (2002) *The favored circle: The social foundations of architectural distinction*, Cambridge, MA: MIT Press.

7. Kuhn, T.S. (1970) *The structure of scientific revolutions*, Chicago, IL: University of Chicago Press.

8. Kuhn, *The structure of scientific revolutions*.

9. Bresciani, M.J., Zelna, C.L., and Anderson, J.A. (2004). *Assessing student learning and development: A handbook for practitioners*, Washington, DC: NASPA.

10. *Building the global knowledge society: Systemic and institutional change in higher education*. Online. Available: <http://www.ond.vlaanderen.be/hogeronderwijs/bologna/> (accessed 24 September 2011).

11. Ratcliff, J.L., Lubinescu, E., and Gaffney, M.A. (2001) *How accreditation influences assessment: New directions for higher education*, No. 113, New York: Jossey-Bass, p. 5.

12. Education Commission of the States (1988) *Designing and implementing standards-based accountability systems*. ECS Distribution Center, Denver, CO, p. v.

13. Rogers, G. (2009) *Using assessment to drive improvement without driving faculty crazy*, Texas A&M Assessment Conference. Online. Available: <http://assessment.tamu.edu/resources/conf_2009/Rogers_Plenary_Assessment4Improvement.pdf>(accessed 24 September 2011).

14. Angelo, T.D. (1995) "Reassessing (and defining) assessment", *AAHE Bulletin*, 48(2): 7–9.

15. Bresciani, M.J. (2001) Writing measurable and meaningful outcomes. Online. Available: <http://www.uwlax.edu/learningoutcomes/edreading/WritingOutcomesBrescianiArticle.pdf> (accessed 24 September 2011).

16. Watt, K. and Cottrell, D. (2006) "Grounding the curriculum: Learning from live projects in architectural education", *International Journal of Learning*, 13(8): 97–104.

17. Collins, P. (1971) *Architectural judgment*, London: Faber; Hubbard, W. (1982) *Complicity and conviction: Steps toward an architecture of convention*, Cambridge, MA: MIT Press.

18. Hubbard, *Complicity and conviction*, pp. 120–126.

19. Koestler, A. (1989) *The act of creation*, London: Arkana, p. 331.

20. Keats, *Ode to a Grecian Urn*, 1819. Original text: Annals of the Fine Arts, 15 (December 1819). Reprinted with minor changes in John Keats, *Lamia, Isabella, The Eve of St. Agnes, and Other Poems* (1820). Facs. edn.: Scolar Press, 1970. PR 4830 E20AB Fisher Rare Book Library (Toronto).

21. Kelbaugh, D. (2004) "Seven fallacies in architectural culture", *Journal of Architectural Education*, 58(1): 66–68.

22. Johnson, P.A. (1994) *The theory of architecture: Concepts, themes and practices*, New York: Van Nostrand Reinhold.

23. Gropius, W. (1956) *Scope of total architecture*, New York: Allen & Unwin, p. 8.

24. Robinson, J. (1990) "Architectural research: Incorporating myth and science", *Journal of Architectural Education*, 44(1): 20–32.

25. Heath, T. (1991) *What, if anything, is an architect?*, Melbourne: Architecture Media Australia; Stevens, G. (1990) *The reasoning architect: Mathematics and science in design*, New York: McGraw-Hill.

26. Bachman, L. (2010) *The teaching of research and the research on teaching: Two frameworks and their overlay in architectural education*, ARCC/EAAE International Conference on Architectural Research, Washington, DC. Online. Available: <http://info.aia.org/arcc/program/program.html> (accessed 24 September 2011).

27. Gropius, *Scope of total architecture*, p. 8.

28. Anderson, L.W. and Krathwohl, D.R. (2001) *A taxonomy for learning, teaching and assessing: A revision of Bloom's Taxonomy of Educational Objectives*, New York: Longman.

29. Huxley, A. (1956) "On knowledge and understanding", *Vedanta and the West*, Los Angeles, CA: Vedanta Society of Los Angeles.

10 The Domain of the Discipline

1. Duffy, F. and Hutton, L. (1998) *Architectural knowledge: The idea of a profession*, London: Taylor & Francis, p. 147.

2. Watson, D. (2008) *"Defining sustainability"*, Address to the Society of Building Science Educators Annual Retreat on "Resetting the Agenda", The New Forest, UK: Wessex Institute of Technology. Online. Available: <http://www.architecture.uwaterloo.ca/faculty_projects/terri/sbse/2008/> (accessed 24 September 2011).

3. Duffy and Hutton, *Architectural knowledge*, p. 147.

4. Gropius, W. (1956) *Scope of total architecture*, New York: Allen & Unwin, p. 8.

5. Hubbard, W. (1982) *Complicity and conviction: Steps toward an architecture of convention*, Cambridge, MA: MIT Press.

6. Groat, L. and Wang, D. (2003) *Architectural research methods*, New York: Wiley, p. 13.

7. Heath, T. (1993) "The architectural theory of Rudolf Arnheim and its implications for teaching", *Journal of Aesthetic Education*, 27(4): 83–95.

8. Collins, P. (1971) *Architectural judgment*, Toronto: University of Toronto Press.

9. Hubbard, W. (1982) *Complicity and conviction: Steps toward an architecture of convention*, Cambridge, MA: MIT Press, p. 91.

10. Garnier quoted in Athanasopulos, C.G. (1983) *Contemporary theater: Evolution and design*, New York: John Wiley, p. 26.

11. Fisher, T. (2008) "Design thinking in the university", talk given at the ACSA Administrators Conference, November 7, Savannah, GA.

12. Bell, D. (1973) *The coming of post-industrial society; A venture in social forecasting*, New York: Basic Books.

13. McHarg, I.L. (1969) *Design with nature*, Garden City, NY: Natural History Press.

14. Elstein, A.S. (1977) "Characteristics of the clinical problem solving model and its relevance to educational research", Annual Meeting of the American Educational Research Association, New York.

15. Malterud, K. (2001) "The art and science of clinical knowledge: Evidence beyond measures and numbers", *Lancet*, 358(9279): 397.

16. Collins, *Architectural judgment*; Hubbard, *Complicity and conviction*.

17. Preiser, W.F.E. (1999) "Post-occupancy evaluation: Conceptual basis, benefits and uses", in J.M. Stein and K.F. Spreckelmeyer (eds.) *Classical readings in architecture*, New York: McGraw-Hill.

18. University of California, Berkeley. Vital Signs curriculum materials project. Online. Available: <http://arch.ced.berkeley.edu/vitalsigns/> (accessed 24 September 2011); University of Hong Kong (2008) Integrated Building Technology library in Hong Kong, University of Hong Kong. Online. Available: <http://www.arch.hku.hk/teaching/learn.htm> (accessed 24 September 2011).

19. Bordass, W. and Leaman, A. (2005) Usable Buildings. Online. Available: <http://www.usable-buildings.co.uk/> (accessed 24 September 2011).

20. Portland Energy Conservation, Inc. (2002) "The top 10 commissioning issues and how to deal with them, module 10-filtration issues". Online. Available: <http://www.peci.org/documents/PECI_Top10CxIssues1_1002.pdf> (accessed 24 September 2011).

21. Brager, G. and Baker, L. (2008) *Occupant satisfaction in mixed-mode buildings*, University of California, Berkeley: Center for the Built Environment. Online. Available: <http://escholarship.org/uc/item/40k1s1vd> (accessed 24 September 2011).

22. Malterud, "The art and science of clinical knowledge".

23. Malecha, M. (2005) *The learning organization and evolution of practice academy concepts*, Raleigh: North Carolina State University College of Design.

24. Fisher, "Design thinking in the university".

Bibliography

Ackoff, R.L. (1968) *Fundamentals of operations research*, New York: John Wiley.

Ackoff, R.L. (1974) *Redesigning the future: A systems approach to societal problems*, New York: John Wiley.

Alexander, C. (1964) *Notes on the synthesis of form*, Cambridge, MA: Harvard University Press, p. 1.

Alexander, C. (1966) *The city as a mechanism for sustaining human contact*, Berkeley: Center for Planning and Development Research, University of California.

Alexander, C.S. and Ishikawa, S. (1977) *A pattern language: Towns, buildings, construction*, New York: Oxford University Press.

American Institute of Architects (2009) 'Overview of the 2009 AIA firm survey', *AIArchitect*, 16. Online. Available: <http://info.aia.org/aiarchitect/thisweek09/1009/1009b_firmsurvey.cfm> (accessed 24 September 2011).

Anderson, L.W. and Krathwohl, D.R. (2001) *A taxonomy for learning, teaching and assessing: A revision of Bloom's Taxonomy of Educational Objectives*, New York: Longman.

Angelo, T.D. (1995) 'Reassessing (and defining) assessment', *AAHE Bulletin*, 48(2): 7–9.

Arnheim, R. (1954/1974) *Art and visual perception: A psychology of the creative eye*, Berkeley: University of California Press.

Arnheim, R. (1969) *Visual thinking*, Berkeley: University of California Press.

Arnheim, R. (1971) *Entropy and art: An essay on disorder and order*, Berkeley: University of California Press.

Arnheim, R. (1977) *The dynamics of architectural form: Based on the 1975 Mary Duke Biddle Lectures at the Cooper Union*, Berkeley: University of California Press.

Arup, O. and Zunz, G.J. (1969) 'Sydney Opera House', *Structural Engineer*, 47: 3.

Ascott, R. (1964) 'The construction of change', in N. Wardrip-Fruin and N. Montfort (eds.) *The new media reader*, Cambridge, MA: MIT Press, 2003, pp. 128–132.

Ashby, W.R. (1952) *Design for a brain*, London: Chapman and Hall.

Ashby, W.R. (1956) *Introduction to cybernetics*, London: Chapman and Hall.

Ashby, W.R. (1960) *Design for a brain: The origin of adaptive behavior*, 2nd edn, New York: John Wiley.

Athanasopulos, C.G. (1983) *Contemporary theater: Evolution and design*, New York: John Wiley.

Bachman, L.R. (2003) *Integrated buildings: The systems basis of architecture*, Hoboken, NJ: John Wiley.

Bachman, L.R. (2010) 'The teaching of research and the research on teaching: Two frameworks and their overlay in architectural education', *Proceedings of the 2010 ARCC/EAAE International Conference on Architectural Research*, Washington, DC. Online. Available: <http://info.aia.org/arcc/program/program.html> (accessed 22 September 2011).

Bachman, L.R. and Bachman, C. (2009) 'Designing student learning outcomes in undergraduate architecture education: Frameworks for assessment', *ARCC Journal*, 6(1): 49–67.

Bachman, L.R. and Bachman, C. (2009) 'Editorial: Affecting change in architectural education', *ARCC Journal*, 6(1): 4–5.

Barrow, J.D. (1995) *The artful universe*, Oxford: Clarendon Press.

Bateson, G. (1972) *Steps to an ecology of mind: Collected essays in anthropology, psychiatry, evolution, and epistemology*, San Francisco, CA: Chandler Publishing.

Bibliography

Bateson, G. (1979) *Mind and nature: A necessary unity*, New York: Dutton.

Bateson, G. and Donaldson, R.E. (1991) *A sacred unity: Further steps to an ecology of mind*, New York: Cornelia & Michael Bessie Books.

Beer, A.S. (1959) *Cybernetics and management*, London: English Universities Press.

Beer, A.S. (1994) *Beyond dispute: The invention of team syntegrity,* New York: John Wiley.

Bell, D. (1973) *The coming of post-industrial society: A venture in social forecasting*, New York: Basic Books.

Benyus, J.M. (1997) *Biomimicry: Innovation inspired by nature*, New York: Morrow.

Bloom, A.D. (1987) *The closing of the American mind*, New York: Simon and Schuster.

Bogdanov, A. (1922) *Tektology: Universal organization science* [Tektologiya: Vseobschaya Organizatsionnaya Nauka], 3 vols., Berlin and Petrograd-Moscow.

Bohm, D. (1980) *Wholeness and the implicate order*, London: Routledge & Kegan Paul.

Bono, E. de (1993) *Serious creativity: Using the power of lateral thinking to create new ideas*, New York: Harperbusiness.

Bordass, W. and Leaman, A. (2005) Usable Buildings. Online. Available: <http://www.usablebuildings. co.uk/> (accessed 24 September 2011).

Bovill, C. (1991) *Architectural design: Integration of structural and environmental systems*, New York: Van Nostrand Reinhold.

Boyer, E.L. and Mitgang, L.D. (1996) *Building community: A new future for architecture education and practice*, Princeton, NJ: The Carnegie Foundation for the Advancement of Teaching.

Brager, G. (2008) *Occupant satisfaction and control strategies in mixed-mode buildings*, Proceedings of the 5th Windsor Conference: Airconditioning and the Low Carbon Cooling Challenge, Network for Comfort and Energy Use in Buildings, Windsor Great Park, UK.

Brager, G. and Baker, L. (2008) *Occupant satisfaction in mixed-mode buildings*, University of California, Berkeley: Center for the Built Environment. Online. Available: <http://escholarship.org/ uc/item/40k1s1vd> (accessed 24 September 2011).

Bresciani, M.J. (2001) Writing measurable and meaningful outcomes. Online. Available: <http:// www.uwlax.edu/learningoutcomes/edreading/WritingOutcomesBrescianiArticle.pdf> (accessed 24 September 2011).

Bresciani, M.J., Zelna, C.L., and Anderson, J.A. (2004). *Assessing student learning and development: A handbook for practitioners*, Washington, DC: NASPA.

Bronowski, J. (1965) 'The discovery of form', in G. Kepes (ed.) *Structure in art and in science*, New York: G. Braziller.

Bronowski, J. (1965) *The identity of man*, Garden City, NY: Natural History Press.

Buchanan, R. (1995) *Discovering design: Explorations in design studies*, Chicago, IL: University of Chicago Press.

Buckley, W. (1967) *Sociology and modern systems theory*, Englewood Cliffs, NJ: Prentice Hall.

Bunker, J.P., Frazier, H.S., and Mosteller, F. (1994) 'Improving health: Measuring effects of medical care', *Milbank Quarterly*, 72: 225–258.

Campbell, D., Crutchfield, J., Farmer, J., and Jen, E. (1985) 'Experimental mathematics: The role of computation in nonlinear science', *Communications of the Association for Computing Machinery*, 28, 3: 74–84.

Carlson, A. (2001) 'On aesthetically appreciating human environments', *Philosophy & Geography*, 4(1): 9–24.

Carson, R. (1962) *Silent spring*, Boston, MA: Houghton Mifflin.

Center for the Built Environment. Occupant Indoor Environmental Quality (IEQ) Survey and Building Benchmarking. Online. Available: <http://www.cbe.berkeley.edu/research/briefs-survey.htm> (accessed 24 September 2011).

Churchman, C.W. (1967) Guest editorial: 'Wicked problems', *Management Science*, 14(4): B141–142.

Churchman, C.W. (1968) *The systems approach*, New York: Dell.

Cleveland, W. (1985) *The elements of graphing data*, Monterey, CA: Wadsworth.

Coleridge, S.T. (1817/1989) *Biographia literaria: or Biographical sketches of my literary life and opinions*, New York: C. Wiley & Co.

Collins, P. (1971) *Architectural judgment*, London: Faber; Toronto: University of Toronto Press

Conrads, U. (1975) *Programs and manifestoes on 20th-century architecture*, Cambridge: MA: MIT Press.

Coyne, R. (2005) 'Wicked problems revisited', *Design Studies*, 26(1): 5–17.

Csikszentmihalyi, M. (1997) *Creativity: Flow and the psychology of discovery and invention*, New York: Harper Perennial.

Csikszentmihalyi, M. and Rochberg-Halton, E. (1981) *The meaning of things: Domestic symbols and the self*, New York: Cambridge University Press.

Duffy, F. and Hutton, L. (1998) *Architectural knowledge: The idea of a profession*, London: Spon.

Edinton, R.V. (1974) 'The ancient idea of founding and the contemporary study of political change', *Polity*, 7(2): 163–179.

Education Commission of the States (1988) *Designing and implementing standards-based accountability systems*, Denver, CO: ECS Distribution Center.

Elstein, A.S. (1977) 'Characteristics of the clinical problem solving model and its relevance to educational research', Annual Meeting of the American Educational Research Association, New York.

Fast, W.R. (1997) 'Knowledge strategies: Balancing ends, ways, and means in the information age', in R.E. Neilson (ed.) *Sun Tzu and information warfare, A collection of winning papers from the Sun Tzu Art of War in information warfare competition*, Washington, DC: National Defense University Press.

Fisher, T. (2008) 'Design thinking in the university', talk given at the ACSA Administrators Conference, November 7, Savannah, GA.

Fitch, J.M. (1988) 'Experiential context of the aesthetic process', *Journal of Architectural Education*, 41(2): 4–9.

Friedman, T.L. (2005) *The world is flat 3.0: A brief history of the twenty-first century*, New York: Farrar, Straus and Giroux.

Fuller, R.B. (1963) *Ideas and integrities, A spontaneous autobiographical disclosure*, Englewood Cliffs, NJ: Prentice-Hall.

Fuller, R.B. (1969) *Operating manual for spaceship earth*, Carbondale: Southern Illinois University Press.

Fuller, R.B. (1981) *Critical path*, New York: St. Martin's Press.

Fuller, R.B. and Applewhite, E.J. (1975) *Synergetics; Explorations in the geometry of thinking*, New York: Macmillan.

Gabor, D. (1964) *Inventing the future*, Harmondsworth, UK: Penguin Books.

Gadamer, H.G. (1975) *Truth and method*, trans. from German and edited by G. Barden and J. Cumming, London: Sheed & Ward.

Gadamer, H.G. (1977) *Philosophical hermeneutics*, Berkeley: University of California Press.

Gadamer, H.G. (1986) *The relevance of the beautiful and other essays*, Cambridge, MA: Cambridge University Press.

Geddes, P. (1904) *City development, a study of parks, gardens, and culture-institutes; A report to the Carnegie Dunfermline Trust*, Edinburgh: Geddes and Co.

Geddes, P. (1915/1968) *Cities in evolution: An introduction to the town planning movement and to the study of civics*, New York: H. Fertig.

Geddes, P. and Thomson, J.A. (1911) *Evolution*, New York: H. Holt.

Gibson, W. (2003) *Burning chrome*, New York: HarperCollins.

Gibson, W. and Sterling, B. (1991) *The difference engine*, New York: Bantam Books.

Givoni, B. (1969) *Man, climate, and architecture*, New York: Elsevier.

Glazebrook, T. (2003) 'Art or nature?', *Ethics & the Environment*, 8(1): 22.

Gould, S.J. (2003) *The hedgehog, the fox and the magister's pox: Mending the gap between science and the humanities*, Nevada City, CA: Harmony Books.

Groák, S. (1992) *The idea of building: Thought and action in the design and production of buildings*, London; New York: E & FN Spon.

Groat, L. and Wang, D. (2003) *Architectural research methods*, New York: Wiley.

Bibliography

Gropius, W. (1956) *Scope of total architecture*, New York: Allen & Unwin.

Guise, D. (1985) *Design and technology in architecture*, New York: Wiley.

Guyer, P. and Wood, A.W. (eds.) (1999) *The critique of pure reason* (Cambridge Edition of the Works of Immanuel Kant in Translation), Cambridge: Cambridge University Press.

Harris, R.L. (1996) *Information graphics: A comprehensive illustrated reference*, Oxford: Oxford University Press.

Hawking, S.W. (1998) *A brief history of time*, New York: Bantam Books.

Hayek, F. (1973) 'Cosmos and taxis', in *Law, legislation and liberty*, Vol. I. Chicago, IL: University of Chicago Press.

Heath, T. (1984) *Method in architecture*, New York: Wiley.

Heath, T. (1991) *What, if anything, is an architect?* Melbourne: Architecture Media Australia.

Heath, T. (1993) 'The architectural theory of Rudolf Arnheim and its implications for teaching', *Journal of Aesthetic Education*, 27(4): 83–95.

Heidegger, M. (1962) *Being and time*, trans. J. Macquarrie and E. Robinson, London: SCM Press.

Heisenberg, W. (1927) 'Uncertainty principle of quantum mechanics,' 'Über den anschaulichen Inhalt der quantentheoretischen Kinematik und Mechanik', *Zeitschrift für Physik*, 43: 172–198.

Heylighen, F. (2003) 'The science of self-organization and adaptivity', in *The Encyclopedia of Life Support Systems*, Oxford: EOLSS Publishers.

Horn, R.E. (1999) 'Information design: The emergence of a new profession', in R. Jacobson (ed.) *Information Design*, Cambridge, MA: MIT Press.

Horn, R.E. (2001) 'Knowledge mapping for complex social messes', a presentation to the Foundations in the Knowledge Economy at the David and Lucile Packard Foundation.

Hubbard, W. (1982) *Complicity and conviction: Steps toward an architecture of convention*, Cambridge, MA: MIT Press.

Hutchinson, G.E. (1948) 'Circular causal systems in ecology', *Annals of the New York Academy of Sciences*, 50: 221–246.

Huxley, A. (1954) *The doors of perception*, London: Chatto and Windus.

Huxley, A. (1956) 'On knowledge and understanding', *Vedanta and the West*, Los Angeles, CA: Vedanta Society of Los Angeles.

Jacobs, J. (1961) *The death and life of great American cities*, New York: Random House.

Jacobs, J. (1969) *The economy of cities*, New York: Random House.

Jencks, C. (1995) *The architecture of the jumping universe*, London: Academy Editions.

Johnson, P.A. (1994) *The theory of architecture: Concepts, themes and practices*, New York: Van Nostrand Reinhold.

Kahn, L. (1960) 'Form and design', in A. Latour (ed.) (1991) *Louis I. Kahn: Writings, lectures, interviews*, New York: Rizzoli International Publications.

Kahn, L. (1991) 'Talks with students', in A. Latour (ed.) (1991) *Louis L. Kahn: Writings, lectures, interviews*, New York: Rizzoli International Publications.

Kant, I. (1958) *Critique of pure reason*, New York: Modern Library.

Keats, *Ode to a Grecian Urn*, 1819. Original text: Annals of the Fine Arts, 15 (December 1819). Reprinted with minor changes in John Keats, *Lamia, Isabella, The Eve of St. Agnes, and Other Poems* (1820). Facs. edn.: Scolar Press, 1970. PR 4830 E20AB Fisher Rare Book Library (Toronto).

Kelbaugh, D. (2004) 'Seven fallacies in architectural culture', *Journal of Architectural Education*, 58(1): 66–68.

Kelso, J.A.S. (1995) *Dynamic patterns: The self-organization of brain and behavior*, Cambridge, MA: MIT Press.

Kepes, G. (1944) *Language of vision*, Chicago, IL: P. Theobald.

Kepes, G. (ed.) (1965) *Structure in art and in science*, New York: G. Braziller.

Kepes, G. (1966) *The man-made object*, New York: G. Braziller.

Knowles, R. (1969) *Owens Valley study: A natural ecological framework for settlement*, Los Angeles, CA: National Endowment for the Arts.

Knowles, R. (1974) *Energy and form: An ecological approach to urban growth*, Cambridge, MA: MIT Press.

Knowles, R. (1981) *Sun rhythm#lBform*, Cambridge, MA: MIT Press.

Knowles, R. (2006) *Ritual house: Drawing on nature's rhythms for architecture and urban design*, Washington, DC: Island Press.

Koestler, A. (1989) *The act of creation*, London: Arkana.

Komendant, A.E. (1975) *18 years with architect Louis I. Kahn*, Englewood Cliffs, NJ: Aloray.

Kuhn, T. (1962/1970) *The structure of scientific revolutions*, Chicago, IL: University of Chicago Press.

Kurzweil, R. (2005) *The singularity is near: When humans transcend biology*, New York: Viking.

Laurence, P. (2006) 'Contradictions and complexities', *Journal of Architectural Education*, 59(31): 49–60.

Leslie, T. (2006) 'Unavoidable nuisances: August Komendant, Louis I. Kahn, and the difficult relationship between architecture and engineering', *MAJA Estonian Architectural Review*, 4(50): 72–75.

Lorenz, E.N. (1963) 'Deterministic nonperiodic flow', *Journal of Atmospheric Science*, 20(2): 130–141.

Lorenz, E.N. (1993) *The essence of chaos*, Seattle: University of Washington Press.

Lovelock, J. (2006) *The revenge of Gaia: Earth's climate in crisis and the fate of humanity*, New York: Basic Books.

Lyle, J.T. (1985) *Design for human ecosystems: Landscape, land use, and natural resources*, New York: Van Nostrand Reinhold.

Lyle, J.T. (1994) *Regenerative design for sustainable development*, New York: John Wiley.

Malecha, M. (2005) *The learning organization and evolution of practice academy concepts*, Raleigh: North Carolina State University College of Design.

Malterud, K. (2001) 'The art and science of clinical knowledge: Evidence beyond measures and numbers', *Lancet*, 358(9279): 397.

Mazria, E. (1979) *The passive solar energy book: A complete guide to passive solar home, greenhouse, and building design*, Emmaus, PA: Rodale Press.

Mazria, E. et al. (2007) *The 2030 challenge: Environmental design in the face of climate change*, Las Vegas, NV: UNLV School of Architecture.

McHarg, I. (1969) *Design with nature*, Garden City, NY: Natural History Press.

Minard, C.J. (1869) Carte figurative des pertes successives en hommes de l'armée qu'Annibal conduisit d'Espagne en Italie en traversant les Gaules (selon Polybe). Carte figurative des pertes successives en hommes de l'armée française dans la campagne de Russie, 1812–1813, 20 November. ENPC: Fol 10975, 10974/C612. [Annibal Napoléon Espagne Italie Russie armée flow-map comparison.]

Mitchell, W.J. (1999) 'Architecture and the digital revolution', *Science*, 285(5429): 839–841.

Molden, D. and de Fraiture, C. (2004) *Investing in water for food, ecosystems and livelihoods: Comprehensive assessment of water management in agriculture*. Online. Available: <http://www.infoandina.org/system/files/recursos/BluePaper.pdf>

Monod, J. (1971) *Chance and necessity*, New York: Alfred A. Knopf.

Moore, G.E. (1965) 'Cramming more components onto integrated circuits', *Electronics Magazine*, 38(8): 114–117.

Mostafavi, M. and Leatherbarrow, D. (1993) *On weathering: The life of buildings in time*, Cambridge, MA: MIT Press.

Mumford, L. (1922) *The story of utopias*, New York: Boni and Liveright.

Mumford, L. (1924) *Sticks and stones: A study of American architecture and civilization*, New York: Boni and Liveright.

Mumford, L. (1934) *Technics and civilization*, New York: Harcourt Brace Jovanovich.

Mumford, L. (1939) *Men must act*, New York: Harcourt Brace and Co.

Mumford, L. (1947) *Green memories; The story of Geddes Mumford*, New York: Harcourt, Brace.

Mumford, L. (1967) *The myth of the machine: Technics and human development*, New York: Harcourt, Brace Jovanovich.

Bibliography

Neubek, K. (2010) 'Requirements management in a digital age', Lecture at the University of Houston College of Architecture. Unpublished document. October 1.

Norberg-Schulz, C. (1966) *Intentions in architecture*, Cambridge, MA: MIT Press.

Novak, F.G. (1995) *Lewis Mumford and Patrick Geddes: The correspondence*, New York: Routledge.

Office of Naval Research, Mathematical sciences division (1958) *Digital Computer Newsletter*, v. 10, n. 4. Online. Available HTTP: <www.columbia.edu/cu/computinghistory/navynewsletter1958.pdf> (accessed 19 August 2011).

Olgyay, V. (1963) *Design with climate: Bioclimatic approach to architectural regionalism*. Some chapters based on cooperative research with Aladar Olgyay. Princeton, NJ: Princeton University Press.

Orr, D.W. (1979) *The global predicament: Ecological perspectives on world order*, Chapel Hill: University of North Carolina Press.

Orr, D.W. (1992) *Ecological literacy: Education and the transition to a postmodern world*, Albany: State University of New York Press.

Orr, D.W. (1994) *Earth in mind: On education, environment, and the human prospect*, Washington, DC: Island Press.

Orr, D.W. (2002) *The nature of design: Ecology, culture, and human intention*, New York: Oxford University Press.

Pawley, M. (1990) *Theory and design in the second machine age*, Cambridge, MA: Wiley-Blackwell.

Peat, F.D. (1988) 'Non-locality in nature and cognition', in M.E. Carvallo (ed.) *Nature, cognition, and system: Current systems-scientific research on natural and cognitive systems*, Dordrecht: Kluwer.

Peirce, C.S. (1956) 'The criterion of validity of reasoning', in J. Buchler (ed.) *The philosophy of Peirce: Selected writings*, London: Routledge & Kegan Paul (reprinted from *Lectures on Pragmatism*, Harvard University, 1903).

Peña, W.M. (1969) *Problem seeking: New directions in architectural programming*, Houston, TX: Caudill Rowlett Scott.

Pérez Gómez, A. (1983) *Architecture and the crisis of modern science*, Cambridge, MA: MIT Press.

Pérez-Gómez, A. (1999) 'Hermeneutics as discourse in design', *Design Issues*, 15(2): 73.

Perry, W.G., Jr. (1970) *Forms of intellectual and ethical development in the college years: A scheme*, New York: Holt, Rinehart & Winston.

Perry, W.G., Jr. (1981) 'Cognitive and ethical growth: The making of meaning', in Arthur W. Chickering and Associates, *The Modern American College*, San Francisco, CA: Jossey-Bass.

Perry, W.G., Jr. (1988) *Intellectual and ethical development in the college years*, New York: Holt, Rinehart & Winston.

Pinto, J. (2000) *Evolution of the techno human*. Online. Available: <http://www.spark-online.com/november00/esociety/pinto.html> (accessed 22 September 2011).

Piotrowski, A. and Robinson, J.W. (2000) *The discipline of architecture*, Minneapolis: University of Minnesota Press.

Playfair, W. (1786) *The commercial and political atlas, Representing, by Means of Stained Copper-Plate Charts, the Exports, Imports, and General Trade of England, at a Single View. To Which are Added, Charts of the Revenue and Debts of Ireland, Done in the Same Manner by James Corry*, London: Debrett; Robinson; and Sewell.

Popper, K. (1934) *Logik der forschung*, Vienna: Verlag von Julius Springer. First published in English in 1959 by Hutchinson & Co.

Popper, K. (1963) *Conjectures and refutations*, London: Routledge & Kegan Paul (reprinted in T. Schick (ed.) (2000) *Readings in the Philosophy of Science*, Mountain View, CA: Mayfield Publishing).

Popper, K. and Eccles, J.C. (1977) *The self and its brain: An argument for interactionism*, London: Routledge.

Portland Energy Conservation, Inc. (2002) 'The top 10 commissioning issues and how to deal with them, module 10-filtration issues'. Online. Available: <http://www.peci.org/documents/PECI_Top10CxIssues1_1002.pdf> (accessed 24 September 2011).

Preiser, W.F.E. (1978) *Facility programming: Methods and applications*, Stroudsburg, PA: Dowden, Hutchinson & Ross.

Preiser, W.F.E. (1999) 'Post-occupancy evaluation: Conceptual basis, benefits and uses', in J.M. Stein and K.F. Spreckelmeyer (eds.) *Classical readings in architecture*, New York: McGraw-Hill.

Prigogine, I. (1997) *The end of certainty: Time, chaos, and the new laws of nature*, New York: Free Press.

Prigogine, I. and Stengers, I. (1984) *Order out of chaos*, New York: Bantam Books.

Rand, A. (1943) *The fountainhead*, Indianapolis, IN: Bobbs-Merrill.

Ratcliff, J.L., Lubinescu, E., and Gaffney, M.A. (2001) *How accreditation influences assessment: New directions for higher education*, No. 113, New York: Jossey-Bass.

Read, S. (2008) 'Technicity and publicness: Steps towards an urban space', *Footprint* v. 3, *Architecture and Phenomenology*.

Renwick, C. and Gunn, R.C. (2008) 'Demythologizing the machine: Patrick Geddes, Lewis Mumford, and classical sociological theory', *Journal of the History of the Behavioral Sciences*, 44: 67.

Rittel, H. and Webber, M. (1973) 'Dilemmas in a general theory of planning', *Policy Sciences*, 4: 155–169.

Rivka, O. and Oxman, R. (2010) *The new structuralism: Design, engineering and architectural technologies*, London: John Wiley.

Robinson, J. (1990) 'Architectural research: Incorporating myth and science', *Journal of Architectural Education*, 44(1): 20–32.

Rogers, G. (2009) *Using assessment to drive improvement without driving faculty crazy*, Texas A&M Assessment Conference. Online. Available: <http://assessment.tamu.edu/resources/conf_2009/Rogers_Plenary_Assessment4Improvement.pdf> http://assessment.tamu.edu/conference/hand-outs_2009/Rogers_Plenary_Assessment4Improvement.pdf (accessed 24 September 2011).

Ronner, H. and Jhaveri, S. (1987) *Louis I. Kahn: Complete works 1935–1974*, Basel: Birkhauser.

Rossetto, L. (1998) 'Change is good', *Wired Magazine*, 6(1): 163–207.

Rush, R.D. (ed.) (1986) *The building systems integration handbook*, New York: Wiley.

Rzevski, G. (2009) 'Using complexity science framework and multi-agent technology in design', in K. Alexiou, J. Johnson, and T. Zamenopoulos (eds.) *Embracing complexity in design*, London: Routledge.

Sanoff, H. (1968) *Techniques of evaluation for designers*, Raleigh, Design Research Laboratory, School of Design, North Carolina State University.

Sanoff, H. (1978) *Designing with community participation*, Stroudsburg, PA: Dowden, Hutchinson & Ross.

Sanoff, H. (2000) *Community participation methods in design and planning*, New York: John Wiley.

Schopenhauer, A. (1896) *The world as will and idea*, trans. R.B. Haldane and J. Kemp, London: Kegan Paul, Trench, Trübner & Co.

Scott, T. (1779) *The Force of Truth*, London: Keith; quoted in Cardinal J.H. Newman, *Apologia pro vita sua*, Chapter 1, 'History of my religious opinions to the year 1833,' (1864).

Scruton, R. (1979) *The aesthetics of architecture*, Princeton, NJ: Princeton University Press.

Senge, P.M. (1990) *The fifth discipline: The art and practice of the learning organization*, New York: Doubleday/Currency.

Shannon, C.E. and Weaver, W. (1949) *The mathematical theory of communication*, Urbana: University of Illinois Press.

Shelley, M. (published anonymously) (1818) *Frankenstein, or, The modern Prometheus*, 3 vols., London: Lackington, Hughes, Harding, Mavor, & Jones.

Simon, H.A. (1956) 'Rational choice and the structure of the environment', *Psychological Review*, 63(2): 129–138.

Simon, H.A. (1957) 'A behavioral model of rational choice', in *Models of man, social and rational; mathematical essays on rational human behavior in a social setting*, New York: John Wiley.

Simon, H.A. (1957) *Models of man: Social and rational; mathematical essays on rational human behavior in society setting*, New York: John Wiley.

Simon, H.A. (1969) *The sciences of the artificial*, Cambridge, MA: MIT Press.

Simon, H.A. (1976) *Administrative behavior: A study of decision-making processes in administrative organization*, New York: Free Press.

Smith, M. (2011) BIM in Construction. The National Bureau of Standards. March. Online. Available: <http://www.thenbs.com/topics/BIM/articles/index.asp> (accessed 1 July 2011).

Snodgrass, A. and Coyne, R. (1997) 'Is designing hermeneutical? Architectural theory review', *Journal of the Department of Architecture*, 1(1): 65–97.

Snow, C.P. (1959) *The two cultures and the scientific revolution*, The Rede Lecture, Cambridge: Cambridge University Press.

Spence, I. (1990) 'Visual psychophysics of simple graphical elements', *Journal of Experimental Psychology: Human Perception and Performance*, 16(4): 683–692.

Srinivasan, U.T., Cheung, W.L., Watson, R., and Sumaila, U.R. (2010) 'Food security implications of global marine catch losses due to overfishing', *Journal of Bioeconomics*, 12: 183–200.

Sterman, J.D. (2000) *Business dynamics: Systems thinking and modeling for a complex world*, New York: McGraw-Hill/Irwin.

Stern, W.F. (1989) 'Floating City—Conoco's corporate headquarters by Kevin Roche', *Cite*, 12–13.

Sternberg, R.J. (1988) *The nature of creativity: Contemporary psychological perspectives*, Cambridge: Cambridge University Press.

Stevens, G. (1990) *The reasoning architect: Mathematics and science in design*, New York: McGraw-Hill.

Stevens, G. (1999/2002) *The favored circle: The social foundations of architectural distinction*, Cambridge, MA: MIT Press.

Stevens, P.S. (1974) *Patterns in nature*, Boston, MA: Little, Brown.

Sullivan, L.H. (1896) 'The tall office building artistically considered', *Lippincott's Magazine*, Philadelphia.

Thackara, J. (2005) *In the bubble: Designing in a complex world*, Cambridge, MA: MIT Press.

Tufte, E. (1983) *The visual display of quantitative information*, Cheshire, CT: Graphics Press.

Twombly, R. (ed.) (2003) *Louis Kahn: Essential texts*, New York: W.W. Norton.

Tyson, P. (2010) *Goodbye to the father of fractals*. Mandelbrot. Online. Available: <http://www.pbs.org/wgbh/nova/insidenova/2010/10/goodbye-to-the-father-of-fractals.html>

Ulrich, R., Zimring, C., Zhu, X., DuBose, J., Seo, H-B., Choi, Y-S. et al. (2008) 'A review of the research literature on evidence-based healthcare design', *Health Environments Research & Design Journal*, 1: 61–125.

United States Department of Labor, Bureau of Labor Statistics (2008) Online. Available: <http://www.bls.gov/spotlight/2008/around_the_world/data.htm> (accessed 18 September 2011).

University of Hong Kong (2008) Integrated Building Technology library in Hong Kong, University of Hong Kong. Online. Available: <http://www.arch.hku.hk/teaching/learn.htm> (accessed 24 September 2011).

Van Emden, M.H. (1971) *An analysis of complexity*, Mathematical Centre Tracts, Vol. 35, Amsterdam: Mathematisch Centrum.

Van Laar, J.A. (2003) *The dialectic of ambiguity: A contribution to the study of argumentation*. Online. Available: <http://dissertations.ub.rug.nl/faculties/fil/2003/j.a.van.laar/?FullItemRecord=ON> (accessed 24 September 2011).

Venturi, R. and Museum of Modern Art (1966) *Complexity and contradiction in architecture*, with an introduction by Vincent Scully, New York: Museum of Modern Art, Garden City, NY: Doubleday.

Vitruvius (*c.* 15 BC) *De architectura: Ten books on architecture*, trans. Sir Henry Wooton as *The elements of architecture* (1624), London: printed by Iohn Bill.

Von Foerster, H. (1959) 'On self-organizing systems and their environments', an address given at the Interdisciplinary Symposium on Self-Organizing Systems, May 5, Chicago, IL; originally published in M.C. Yovits and S. Cameron (eds.) (1960) *Self-organizing systems*, London: Pergamon Press.

Wainer, H. (1997) *Visual revelations: Graphical tales of fate and deception from Napoleon Bonaparte to Ross Perot*, New York: Springer-Verlag.

Wankat, P.C. and Oreovicz, F.S. (1993) 'Models of cognitive development: Piaget and Perry', in P.C. Wankat and F.S. Oreovicz, *Teaching engineering*, New York: McGraw-Hill.

Watson, D. (2008) '*Defining sustainability*', Address to the Society of Building Science Educators Annual Retreat on 'Resetting the Agenda', New Forest, UK: Wessex Institute of Technology. Online.

Available: <http://www.architecture.uwaterloo.ca/faculty_projects/terri/sbse/2008/> (accessed 24 September 2011).

Watt, K. and Cottrell, D. (2006) 'Grounding the curriculum: Learning from live projects in architectural education', *International Journal of Learning*, 13(8): 97–104.

Weaver, W. (2004) 'Science and complexity', Classical Papers, Vol. 6, 3: 65–74; originally published in *American Scientist*, 36, 1947: 536–544.

Wertheimer, M. (1925) Über Gestalttheorie [an address before the Kant Society, Berlin, December 7, 1924], Erlangen. In the translation by W. D. Ellis published in his *Source Book of Gestalt Psychology*, New York: Harcourt, Brace and Co., 1938.

Wilson, E.O. (1998) *Consilience: The unity of knowledge*, New York: A.A. Knopf.

Index

Numbers in **bold** type indicate figures, tables and boxes